Engadin Art Talks

AF473689

Cristina Bechtler, Hans Ulrich Obrist,
Beatrix Ruf (eds.)

TABLE OF CONTENTS

II MAPPING THE ALPS

III VISIONS FOR THE ALPS

Foreword
Cristina Bechtler

Located in the Swiss Alps, Engadin is renowned for its magnificent scenery, winter sports and the glamour of the jet set gathering yearly in St. Moritz. Yet amidst all this allure and decadence, it is also a place that has inspired artists and thinkers, nurturing an environment of creativity.

Notable figures connected with the region include academics Theodor Adorno, Ernst Bloch and Albert Einstein; writers Marcel Proust, Paul Celan, Thomas Mann, Hermann Hesse, Rainer Maria Rilke, Jean Cocteau and Thomas Bernhard; and film-makers Claude Chabrol and Luchino Visconti. The German philosopher Friedrich Nietzsche lived in the Sils-Maria area, the Italian painter Giovanni Segantini in Maloja, and the Giacometti family from the neighbouring Val Bregaglia always kept close ties with the Engadin.

With the aim of creating a temporary venue for a dialogue on the arts and paying homage to the history of Engadin as a location for focused thinking and conversation, I initiated the Engadin Art Talks/E.A.T, a symposium on art and architecture. As artistic director I succeeded in winning the support of the renowned curators Hans Ulrich Obrist and Beatrix Ruf, as well as the art historian Philip Ursprung.

Since its inception in 2010, E.A.T has featured an illustrious circle of participants: artists and architects who have allowed themselves to be inspired by the prospect of travelling to the Engadin for a weekend and discussing their work from different perspectives. Previous talks have included Doug Aitken and Nina von Albertini on "The Glass Chain"; Nairy Baghramian, Hamish Fulton, Sarah Morris and Lawrence Weiner on "Mapping the Alps"; and Vito Acconci, Ron Arad and Jefferson Hack on "Visions". Quite a complex compendium, each on its own, but altogether intertwined.

Introduction

Cristina Bechtler, Hans Ulrich Obrist and Beatrix Ruf

in Conversation

Cristina Bechtler The idea of the Engadin Art Talks (E.A.T.) came up in 2003. In conjunction with Art 34 Basel, I was organizing a podium discussion entitled "Kunst und Architektur: Das Museum der Zukunft" (Art and architecture: the museum of the future). This was long before the *Conversations* of Art Basel started. The podium discussion brought together leading artists, curators, art historians and architects. I remember well that John Armleder was there speaking about a One-Man Museum of the explorer Scott of the South Pole. Jacques Herzog and Didier Fiuza Faustino participated, too; Rem Koolhaas was due to take part by Skype from China, but this did not work for technical reasons. Also taking part were Philip Ursprung, professor of art history at the ETH, the Swiss Federal Institute of Technology, Zurich, Hans Ulrich and Beatrix – and Hans Ulrich, you moderated the round-table discussion. More than 200 people attended – mainly students – and the discussion was very intense and lasted for two and a half hours. So far, it has not been published, partly because I had not yet started my book series on art and architecture.

Hans Ulrich Obrist Back then you already had the intention to do something with discussions that could lead to books. And you were thinking about doing something that was related to the Engadin. One day, Beatrix and I got your call inviting us to think about the Engadin region, about an area that has attracted many people, from Friedrich Nietzsche to Gerhard Richter. I had worked in the Engadin previously when I worked with Gerhard Richter on the show for the Nietzsche Haus. The reconnection to the Engadin was exciting. We decided to do E.A.T, this ongoing project, as a kind of triumvirate of the three of us.

CB That's right. We wanted to do something that was related to the Engadin – a region that has, as you say, attracted many creative people. One could even state that the Engadin, and the mountains in general, have always been an important place of inspiration, a haven and a place of the sublime, as well as an uncanny place rich in myth. Of course, the transalpine link between north and south has been extremely important for prosperous development since the Middle Ages. This is why we have such incredible architectural structures in the Engadin, despite the fact that Switzerland was poor for centuries.

Beatrix Ruf I remember our first discussion very well, when we reflected upon the best time of the year for our E.A.T. We spoke extensively about walking in the mountains, about the Philosopher's Walk, and decided not to organize it in winter. We decided that there should be another aspect to the talks: how we think about art, architecture and mountains. Robert Walser was important, but also Heidegger, even Heidegger's Walk. In general, philosophy was an important starting point, also with regard to art and architecture.

CB And of course Friedrich Nietzsche was also relevant. He stayed in the Engadin several times in the 1880s and walked regularly from Sils to the nearby Chastè peninsula.

HUO In this context, I would also like to mention Lucius Burckhardt and his idea of a "Spaziergangwissenschaft" (the science of taking a walk in the urban landscape). He founded his "Promenadologie" with his recently deceased wife, Ann-Marie Burckhardt, at the Gesamthochschule Kassel in 1997. His intention was to bring sociology and urbanism together with landscape planning and art. He said that taking a walk was comparable to a conference, that a walk was also a trigger for conversations. But at the same time, we were interested in the idea of sustainability. What has developed since then is indeed a real industry of conferences all over the world, with more and more conferences and symposia taking place, in the same way that there is an exhibition industry. Neither is particularly interesting if the events are held as a matter of routine. From the start, our idea was to do something that would last for ten or 20 years, and to learn from it during this period of time. One year would lead to the next, like in a feedback loop.

The Engadin region has always attracted scientists, philosophers, painters, writers and film-makers. You may think of Marcel Proust and Thomas Mann, of Ernst Bloch and Albert Einstein or of Claude Chabrol and Luchino Visconti, to name but a few, so our idea was to bring different disciplines together. The name "Engadin Art Talks" is loosely related to the historical phenomenon of "Experiments in Art and Technology", where art and engineering come together. Our talks are about creating new things, not only bringing different disciplines together, but really about different practitioners who collaborate and network.

BR It is true that through history the Engadin has attracted many people, but it is also very important to us to prolong this ongoing discussion up to the present day and to include people who live or are active in the Engadin now, people who are currently engaged with mountains and with specific approaches to mountainous areas.

CB For each E.A.T. – which take place within the framework of the St. Moritz Art Masters – we have chosen a main topic. In 2010, it was *The Crystal Chain (Die Gläserne Kette)*. This topic refers to a utopian written exchange between artists and architects that took place in 1919–20, initiated by the German architect Bruno Taut. In 2011, it was *Mapping the Alps,* where we took up historico-cultural topics and thought about what it meant to be in a mountainous region and what the notion of seclusion was. And in 2012, our theme was *Visions for the Alps,* focusing on ideas, projects and sketches that were visionary – even utopian.

BR And it was striking that each main topic developed from discussions we had had the year before, so you could call it a kind of progression from one year to the other. We did not plan the topics for the whole series at the beginning, but it has somehow grown organically.

THE CRYSTAL CHAIN

CB As mentioned before, *The Crystal Chain* was a written exchange that took place in the late 1910s. It was initiated by Bruno Taut at a time when his engagement for social housing came to a near standstill because of World War I. Taut turned to a more theoretical approach and initiated the Crystal Chain Letters just after the war. The members of his circle sketched out their utopian ideas and thoughts in letters, which they forwarded to each other. So the letters were a place of retreat, a place of reflection and vision in an unstable and desperate political situation.

HUO This was a very interesting written exchange. The members were mostly architects, as for example Bruno and Max Taut, Walter Gropius, Hans and Wassili Luckhardt, and Hans Scharoun, but there were also a few artists, such as Wenzel Hablik. They were not interested in writing a manifesto, but instead in exchanging their ideas in correspondences, in a chain letter. Since we also wanted to begin with this idea of an exchange, of bringing different people together, we thought that *The Crystal Chain* was a good starting point, especially because the mountains were constantly present in those letters. Besides, many contemporary artists have been inspired by the texts and sketches contained in the *The Crystal Chain.*

BR One artist we invited was in fact directly relating to *The Crystal Chain.* It was Josiah McElheny, who had just curated the exhibition *Crystalline Architecture* at the Andrea Rosen Gallery, New York, where he included different disciplines and approaches. He brought together the historical *Crystal Chain* with Robert Smithson and the contemporary artist Heather Rowe. Besides McElheny, there were other interesting artists such as Doug Aitken, who spoke about a notion of landscape that was more of a psychological space than a physical topography. Cerith Wyn Evans established an autobiographic link to the Engadin, and the dancer Simone Forti contributed a performing lecture.

CB Then there were the architects: Philippe Rahm spoke about his innovative approach of replacing rooms separated by walls and floors with spaces created by gradation and about his involvement in creating park landscapes. Camilo Restrepo presented his new projects, with which he seeks a performative rather than a representative architecture that always takes into account the mountainous region of Medellín. Mumbai-based architect Bijoy Jain focused on the cultural value of gesture, emphasizing that most of his work is produced through gestures, whereas Hans-Jörg Ruch spoke about the challenge of building in a remote mountainous area and about his unique minimalist restorations of Engadin farmhouses. And finally, it was also interesting to hear how Nina von Albertini, who is originally from the Engadin, engages with the sensitive soil and environment of the valley in her ecological and pedological construction supervision.

MAPPING THE ALPS

CB In our second year, we turned to the geology of the Alps, to the natural forces, to climate change, to the view from above and finally, to the mapping of the mountains. How have the Alps shaped our view and how have they inspired art and architecture? Two hundred years ago, the mountains were perceived as hostile and inaccessible, but with the scientific exploration and the rise of tourism – initiated and advanced in the Engadin by the British – the Alps were discovered more and more.

BR Exactly, and we intended not only to show what models of mapping there are, but also to speak about fictional elements. For example in the artistic approaches of Nairy Baghramian or Walid Raad, who emphasized the fictionality of the mountains, and who juxtaposed science, fiction and ideas. But the approaches taken by Sarah Morris, Ritu Sarin and Tenzing Sonam, Kai Schlenter and Lawrence Weiner to the notion of landscape were also very inspiring.

HUO The talks showed that the notion of complete objectivity in cartography is an illusion. There is always a subjective element in it. Maps and cartography inspired many artists – from Alighiero Boetti to conceptual artists and to contemporary artists. Simultaneously, cartography and its possibilities have become especially relevant in our digital era. Digital technologies have triggered a major shift and reconfigured the mapping experience, as Bruno Latour wrote in his 2010 essay *Entering a Risky Territory: Space in the Age of Digital Navigation* (with Valérie November and Eduardo Camacho-Hübner). According to Latour, one should not mistake a digital map with a representation of topography, and geography should be freed from the notion of a base map on which different secondary layers will be inscribed. Instead, he argues for maps that are used navigationally, especially since we are not looking at a map anymore, but are logging in to a media platform, where the difference between "physical" and "human" geography – that is to say, between an "outside material world" and "a subjective symbolic world" of human beings – has become obsolete. Digital cartography is understood as dashboards of a calculation interface. People can pinpoint signposts and thus move through the world. So the relation between what lasts, what is reiterativ and what is ephemeral is questioned. This led to new platforms and new forms of cartography.

CB Therefore it was inspiring to listen to Jan von Brevern, who looked back on Viollet-le-Duc's excursion to Mont Blanc and his analogy of the mountain with a ruin, trying to reconstruct the supposed original outlines on his drawings, which is – again – a different form of a map, far away from a digitalized one. Hamish Fulton embodies the idea of mapping with his Art Walks directly: walking becomes a form of appropriation and contemplation of landscape. For Gianni Pettena, mountains are a kind of abstract architecture and it was only because of our E.A.T. that he started to think about his own work as being a reaction to the power of those mountains. Finally, Andrea Deplazes presented the New Monte Rosa Hut he was able to build in an absolutely remote area, and Annalisa and Peter Zumthor dreamt about their vision of a hotel in the Alps. Nikolaus Hirsch found a way to commemorate a counter-history with his Hinzert Document Centre. With this project, it became obvious that mapping can also be understood as a geographical research going back in time: mapping the layers of history, so to speak.

VISIONS FOR THE ALPS

CB At our 2012 E.A.T., we discussed ideas, sketches and projects that were exceptional, uncommon, and sometimes even utopian. A visionary is – in the very sense of the French word "visionnaire" – a pioneer who develops innovative, groundbreaking and sometimes uncomfortable ideas and questions established traditions. Within this visionary approach, we especially wanted to discuss projects that were related to the Alps.

HUO Yes, and it was exciting to hear not only of extraordinary artistic approaches, but also of some utopian buildings designed for mountainous regions. It became obvious that mountains can be as immense and sometimes impenetrable as a jungle. If you speak or think about mountains, it always includes the question of scale. Their size prompts huge projects and, at the same time, there is this restriction or barrier due to a tough climatic situation or a topography that is difficult to access. Many projects do remain unrealized, as, for example, those of Vito Acconci; since he started to work as an architect, only a few of his designs have been built. And some of the participants also drew attention to historical projects that have never been realized or have ceased to exist. I would just like to mention Tobias Rehberger's artistic preoccupation with a project by Giò Ponti for the Dolomites, where 18 hotels should have been built and linked with a 160-kilometre-long network of cable railways, Mai-Thu Perret with her fictional narrations about utopian groups, or Paulo Sergio Niemeyer: they were important inputs. And I remember well how the Torre David project of Urban-Think Tank took up the idea of a new utopian city.

BR In this conference, it was impressive to see the relation between the monumentality and the intervention with concrete models. There is a kind of intermediate zone, which can be fictional, or mythological and narrative. And this zone is exactly what we want to aim at this year. But speaking about the last E.A.T., there were these wonderful approaches by Vito Acconci or François Roche – both breaking with the idea of monumentality. In conjunction with mythology and narrative, the poetic talk by the members of Raqs Media Collective was very inspiring: what they thought about yakshas, mountain spirits who also appear by rivers, and how they were thinking about a way to return the sea to the mountains.

CB Right, and then again those wonderful visionary projects for the Alps, as, for example, Ron Arad's unrealized project for Les Diablerets, or Arthur Loretz's equally unrealized idea for Porta Alpina – an underground station in the middle of the Gotthard Base Tunnel. Also present were Hans Danuser, presenting his artistic occupation with slate and erosion, Rolf Sachs showing his photographic project that formed a kind of timeline, or Helen Marten, who talked about her Corian heads turning into the outlines of mountains. Jefferson Hack took us on a wonderful trip on the traces of Robert Walser, and Dominique Gonzalez-Foerster showed us her project for Inhotim. Christophe Girot shared with us the latest technology in topology, which leads to a conceptual revolution in the way we look at the Alps.

HUO All these projects revealed that we did not want to be the people who decided what utopia was. Instead, it is very important to speak about projects that have not yet been realized, but could be. We hope to create a reservoir and a set of new ideas. And we hope that such projects will be sources of inspiration for others. The visions presented during the E.A.T. might perhaps even trigger new forms of interesting architecture for alpine regions.

BR In the Engadin, there are many strict rules about what architects are allowed to build. But I think that with the three topics – *Visions, Mapping* and *The Crystal Chain* – we have also demonstrated that many established roles and especially clichés, even self-awareness, have started to change: new approaches have become possible, whereby it is also important to look at other mountainous regions and to learn about what this type of landscape stands for in other cultural areas.

HUO Coming back to the conference as such, I would like to emphasize that this is so far the first phase, the beginning of this series of E.A.T. It is important to establish a global dialogue, because there are mountains in India, Lebanon and many other places, so our intention is to create a global mountain dialogue that is – at the same time – rooted in the local area of the Engadin. In this regard, Peter Zumthor is a good example. He worked at the Department for the Preservation of Monuments in the canton of Graubünden for ten years, and this local knowledge formed the basis for his later work. But we also invited many other locally rooted people, such as Andrea Deplazes and Nina von Albertini.

We are happy to be preparing this book with extracts from most of the speeches. It will be completed at the next meeting, which will cover the topic *The Alps: Ghosts and the Uncanny.*

BR Interestingly, at the last E.A.T., there were many talks about the fictional and the role of landscape within nature, but also the role of myths and legends. If you think of Michael Steiner's and This Brunner's conversation about Steiner's movie *Sennentuntschi,* where alpine myths are crucial, it becomes obvious how one topic – the topic of *Visions for the Alps* in this case – can lead to the next, where ghosts and the uncanny will be the focus. Steiner has even offered to organize a walk in the mountains, a kind of filmic experience. But in general, one thing is joined to the next – like in a chain – and it has thus been like a projection in the future to use *The Crystal Chain* as the main topic of our first E.A.T. With this written exchange, we have been able to express metaphorically not only the conjunction of different topics and disciplines, but also the encounters and collaboration of various avant-garde artists and architects who are relevant today.

CB We have started on a small scale, growing organically over the years. I would like to thank you, Beatrix and Hans Ulrich, for your ongoing commitment and inspiring ideas and discussions. Let's hope that the E.A.T. continue to develop so prosperously and that they will become an international cultural exchange.

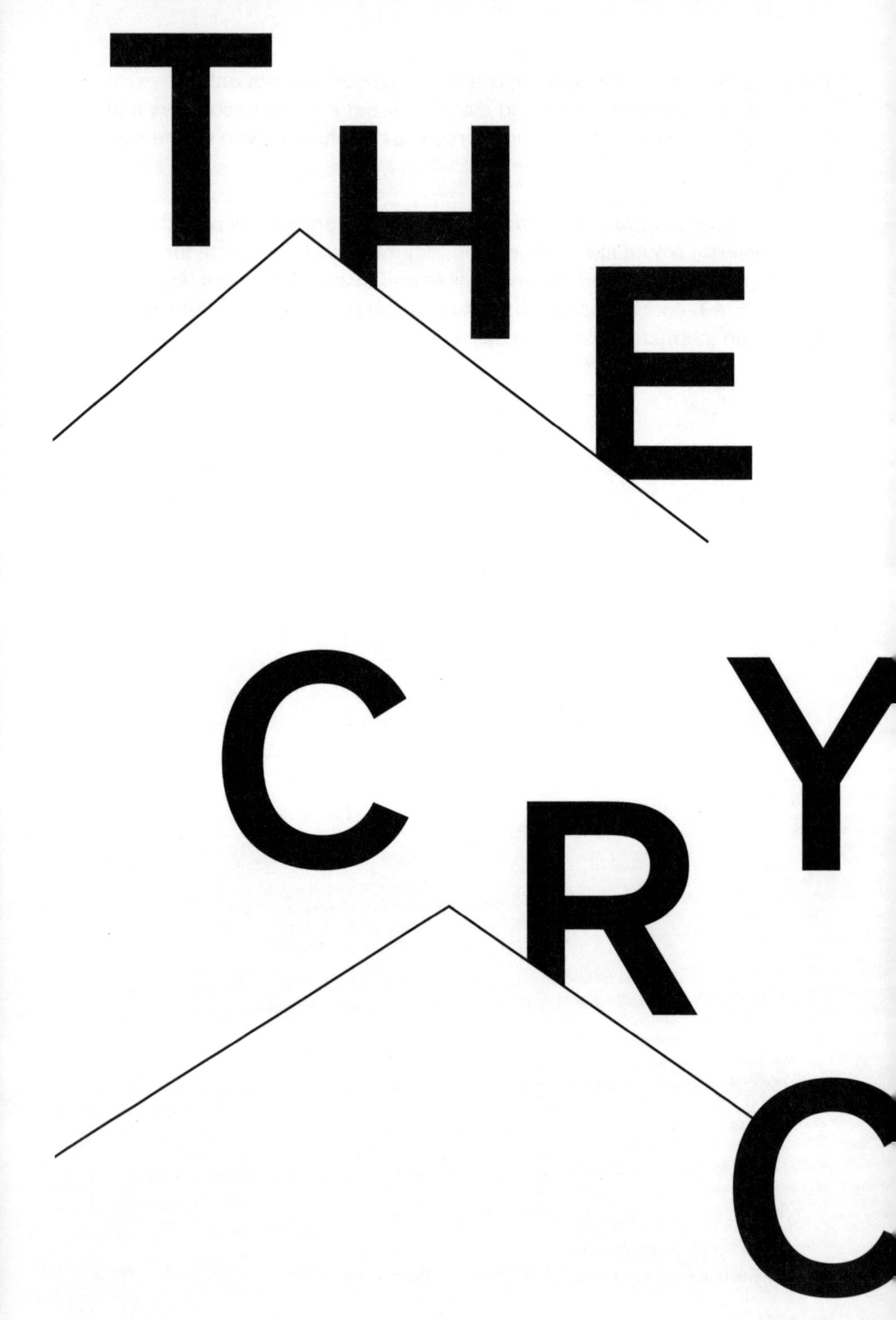
THE
CRY

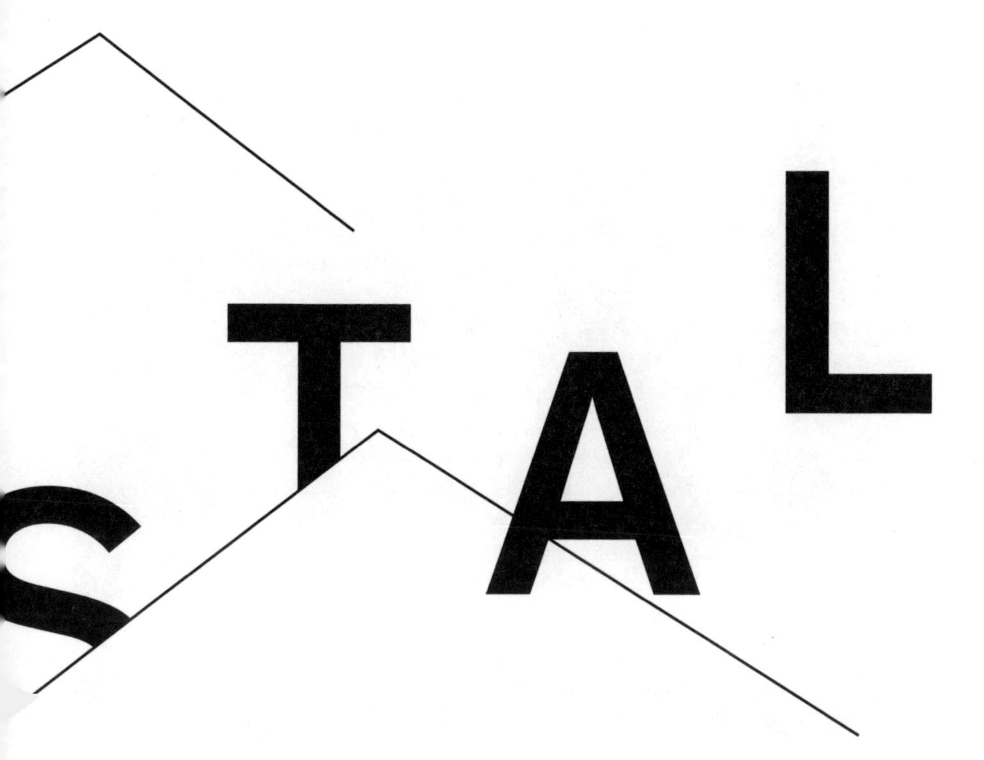

H A I N

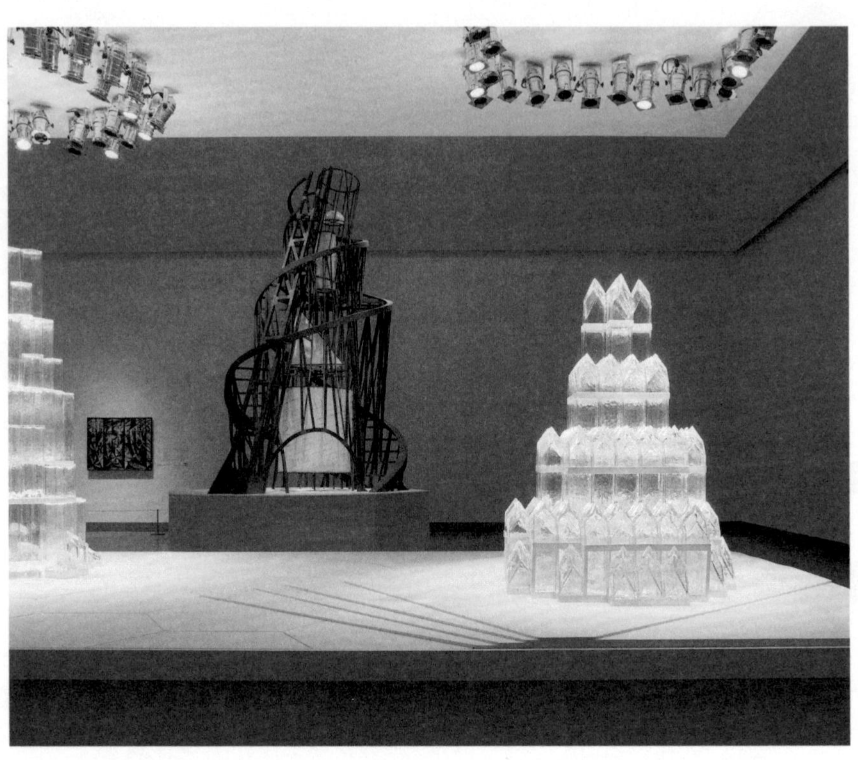

Josiah McElheny, *The Alpine Cathedral and the City-Crown* (2007)
Installation view: Moderna Museet, Stockholm

Josiah McElheny

On Bruno Taut and Paul Scheerbart in the Mountains*

I am an artist who works in a project kind of way, in which I explore one set of histories or ideas for a number of years and then move on to another. Right now I am very focused on the history of architecture and it is particularly exciting today – and synchronous – that the subject of my recent work has focused on the modernist developments and often Alpine proposals of Bruno Taut and others in his circle. To introduce my work, I would like to start with my recent exhibition, *Crystalline Architecture* at Andrea Rosen Gallery in New York. An essay for this show begins as follows: "This exhibition began with a question: Is it possible for a particular aesthetic form or structure to express both abstract concepts and political ideals?" I guess that question is, in a way, what a lot of my work is about: looking for a way to read aesthetics as having a kind of political history, possibly. We think of modernism traditionally as being something that developed around the concept of efficiency and in terms of the aesthetic of the grid. So I've been very interested to learn more about a relatively forgotten moment, pre-1923 more or less, in which a modernism developed that was based not on the grid and not on efficiency but was instead very much connected to socialist ideals. It did not become the historically accepted or dominant modernism – and in 1923 was even renounced by some of the very people who began it – but it has been rediscovered by many people around the world in the past 15 years. In this exhibition, I tried to relate something of this rediscovery, but also to say that this idea continued from the post-World War I period to the 1960s and all the way to the present day.

You could, for example, compare some woodcuts composed out of crystalline elements by Lyonel Feininger from before 1920 with sculptures made of mirrors and crystal forms by Robert Smithson in 1964. You could further make a comparison with a contemporary crystalline mirror sculpture by the New York artist Heather Rowe. There are also watercolours by Wenzel Hablik – who was an architect but also a quite interesting painter – that depict crystalline architectures, which here form the interior of a crystalline, almost temple-like space. And one can see in Hablik's drawings how his ideas have been taken up by a number of artists and architects in the past ten to fifteen years. We can think of any number of buildings by Norman Foster that echo Hablik's vision, whether consciously or unconsciously. But Hablik's watercolours can also be compared with Feininger's *Cathedral of Socialism*, which was used for the cover of the Bauhaus Manifesto, published at the opening of the Bauhaus in Weimar in 1919, and also with Gropius's own essay printed in the manifesto that was most certainly very much influenced by Taut and Paul Scheerbart. Finally, you could also compare Gropius's *Monument to the March Dead* of 1922 with my work *Crystal Mirror.* My piece is a crystalline-shaped object made of a mirror that is 100 mm thick and which has a very strong optical effect when you look inside it. Gropius's *Monument* – an abstract "lightning bolt" made of concrete – was dedicated to the people who protested against the coup that was attempted against the central socialist government in 1919. Erected in 1922 and later destroyed by the Nazis, the monument has recently been rebuilt. It was this kind of crystalline structure that Gropius renounced – a year after he built it – along with all of its related ideals and ethics. He followed this with a general renunciation of the Bauhaus's previous efforts by saying that the school should now be a school of technology, that is to say, a school about efficiency.

But most importantly, I would like to speak about Bruno Taut's *Alpine Architecture* (first published in German in 1918), which triggered the experiment with which I tried to trace the ideas about a crystalline structure. What did it mean conceptually, and what could it have meant politically or ethically? Is it an idea that could continue, and is it something that keeps returning, even if it was suppressed in the past? I would like to turn to some more examples from my work that explore the same sort of ideas about questioning whether aesthetics and politics can be expressed through abstraction. This type of thinking about an abstract aesthetic can be found in my work *Extended Landscape Model for Total Reflective Abstraction* of 2004, which refers to a 1929 conversation between the architect Buckminster Fuller and the sculptor Isamu Noguchi. They had speculated about an environment without shadow and postulated that the only way to achieve this would be to situate a totally reflective object within a totally reflective space. They never completely realized their idea, so I tried to imagine what it would have looked like. Inspired by Noguchi's models for landscapes, I tried to create an architectural scale model of what a totally reflective landscape and a totally reflective architecture would look like. It is a very seductive thing to do but it is probably one of the most terrifying ideas one can have, because it would be a world in which surveillance was constant, in which surveillance of surveillance was constant, and in which one was constantly confronted with one's own and sometimes distorted reflections. In some sense, this purely aesthetic decision could at the same time represent a horrific set of political ideals.

A couple of my projects are specifically related to Taut. *The Alpine Cathedral and The City-Crown* (2007), for example, is again of an architectural model, although it is presented in a theatrical form. It is lit in a shifting array of coloured theatre lights that are constantly changing colour, and it consists of a kind of abstracted landscape made of crystalline glass, metal, and painted wood based on the idea of an octagonal grid and of mountain peak topography. It refers to Taut's *Die Stadtkrone* (The City Crown; an illustrated book first published in 1919). He was pursuing the idea that we should reform society by erecting a building, i.e. a tower, in the centre of the city that was neither a city hall nor a cathedral, but a secular, spiritual and political hall to inspire the worker. Furthermore, everybody should have access to nature, understand his place on earth and go up to the mountain top – to the so-called *Alpine Cathedral* – where he or she could commune with the sky. It shouldn't be an efficient structure, but should be based on natural crystalline forms. It should also not be transparent, but translucent. It would hide and obfuscate, since it is not about exposing the body to every other body. It is actually a place where light can be in relationship to the body even though it is not about exposure or reflection per se. The light was meant to change constantly: to turn red, green, yellow or blue.

This sculptural installation I made was first shown at the Museum of Modern Art in New York in 2007. I was able to display it at the Moderna Museet in Stockholm in 2007/08, an installation where we took away its collection of early modernism. Instead, we tried to retell this history of modernism from a different point of view, through the installation of different works such as Vladimir Tatlin's Tower – which was also a utopian architectural vision of a better world to be constructed on the basis of Communist ideas – and works by Hilma af Klint, the very first abstract artist, even before Kandinsky. She considered herself to be divinely or spiritually inspired, so her work might represent a strange coming together of a kind of socialist politics and spirituality. Something similar might be said about Kasimir Malevich, who also had both political and spiritual motivations. Since around 1912, Taut was very much following the direction or inspiration of the writer Scheerbart, who I have become quite fascinated with. I have become obsessed with one of his most obscure stories, *Der Lichtclub von Batavia. Eine Damennovelette* (The Light Club of Batavia: a Ladies' Novelette), first published in German in 1912. It is the story of an architect and a group of socialites who meet in Jakarta and form a club to build a spa for bathing – not in water, but in light – at the bottom of an abandoned mine shaft. It is really a utopian story, one in which utopia fails, mostly because they forget how people will interact with it. I read about this story in a footnote – I often find my way forward from footnotes – and actually it took a very long time to find it, I believe there are only five copies of the original story in libraries around the world. I look for things in footnotes in part because it seems that if things haven't been spoken about too much, then it is easier to start again from that point of view. It is much more difficult to convince people to think about something in a new way, in a revisionist way, if the issue is already too familiar. So, at some level, it seems that if something is very obscure, it is easier to access. But at the same time, it has been a kind of accidental adventure and a lot of my work is like this. I don't speak German, so I didn't know what the story was truly about until we had finished the translation. When I understood it better, I understood how significant this history might be. In 2008, I made a model of an imaginary film set of what this fictional underground city could look like *(Model for a Film Set (The Light Spa at the Bottom of a Mine)*. Then I tried to turn the story into a play – into a performance – which I did in Berlin and then in New York with artists and art historians reading the various parts of this strange story. And then I made a kind of structuralist film in which you hear a long voice-over about the history of this bizarre idea of a buried light spa.

The last project I would like to present is also specifically related to Taut. He and Mies van der Rohe were great rivals. Taut won the argument until 1923. However, after 1923, Mies was triumphant and excluded Taut from all the major architectural exhibitions. But before that, in 1922, Mies made a maquette for a glass skyscraper that Taut published in his magazine. I reprised his first model and altered it in a way I imagined Taut would have if he had dared to. The work is called *Bruno Taut's Monument to Socialist Spirituality (after Mies van der Rohe)* (2009). It is a multicoloured tower that is not transparent but translucent, that has rough, obfuscating surfaces and is not a restrained form, but is transformed into a crystalline shape. In a related work, *Bruno Taut on Mies van der Rohe* (1922), I took some of the photographs Mies had made of his maquette and drew on them, again as if Taut had been roughly correcting them – Taut literally "on" Mies. This project is multicoloured as well and hopes to offer an alternative history and idea of society based on socialist ideals and colour itself. In the original black-and-white versions of the photographs, Mies van der Rohe wanted to dominate history, wanted to dominate the past. The buildings around the tower are very likely based on the horror movie *Nosferatu* (1922) and are supposed to look like a decrepit, decaying Berlin. Mies wanted his new architecture to dominate it and in some sense to decimate it, whereas Taut wanted to incorporate the past into a new future.

Thinking about Bruno Taut's *Crystal Chain* group, I would like to add that when I came to Switzerland for the first time a couple of months ago, being in the mountains here, I understood the *Crystal Chain* in a new way, especially the work of Wenzel Hablik. Besides his drawings of buildings, he also did paintings of crystalline architectural structures, which are clearly based on the forms of the mountains – of the mountains in Switzerland, I think. And obviously, Taut's book *Alpine Architecture* is very much connected to the mountains here, too. Perhaps the constantly changing weather here in the valley and the way light can change so dramatically, especially up high in the mountains, was a part of their inspiration. The idea that light is not constant, that it can change, is really important. It is very unusual for architectural plans to take constantly changing light into account; usually they are based on one set of light conditions. Even in New York you see these absurd plans for skyscrapers that are depicted in a single light condition and then the built structure almost never looks like that because the light is actually very different at different times. In Scheerbart's story *The Light Club,* the club is obsessed with the idea of a constant, perfect illumination, and this idea that one would never be deprived of what one wants, of light, is an important and disturbing thought. What does it mean to accept that things change? I am fascinated by the fact that in terms of the history of architecture, there is such an intense focus on the notion of transparency. And obviously, there is a connection between transparency and light. I guess the question is: Does light have to be constant?

*at Hall at Plazzet in Zuoz on Saturday, August 28, 2010

The artist Josiah McElheny (b. 1966 in Boston, Massachusetts) is known especially for his work with glass and other materials – work that addresses history, modernism, cosmology, reflection, infinity, purity and utopia. He has exhibited at the Museum of Modern Art and the Andrea Rosen Gallery in New York, the Donald Young Gallery in Chicago, the Institut im Glaspavillon in Berlin, the Moderna Museet in Stockholm, the White Cube in London, and the Museo Nacional Centro de Arte Reina Sofía in Madrid. He lives and works in New York.

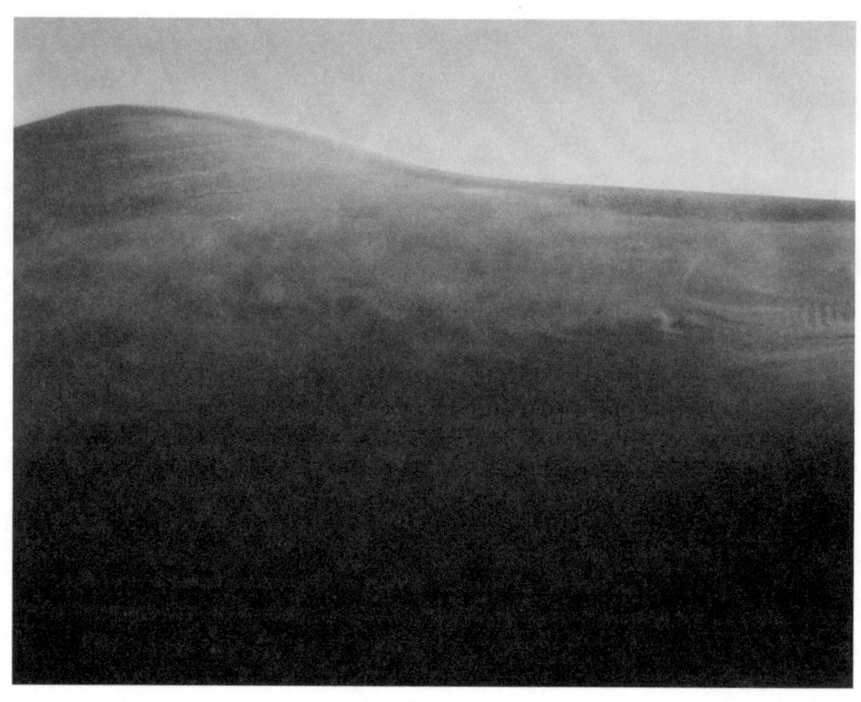

Doug Aitken, *Diamond Sea* (1997)
3-channel video installation on DVD with 3 projections, 1 monitor, and Duratran lightbox; room dimensions vary (approx. 18 × 8 m); 11:26-minute cycle

Doug Aitken

On Diamond Sea

The notion of landscape, and the idea of landscape have always been profound during my earlier visits to the Engadin. However, one of the things that I find when I visit the region is the idea of a landscape that is not so much a physical topography but more of a psychological space. I for myself have been very curious in exploring psychological spaces in different ways and over different projects – for example in *Diamond Sea,* an older work, which was filmed in Namibia in the diamond mines. It was an area that was approximately 75,000 square kilometres in size, a region that has been closed off to the outside world since 1908. We stayed within the zone for about a month, and it was really almost like an exorcism of landscape. I didn't want to make a documentary, nor did I want to make something that was a fiction or superimpose my own stories on this landscape. Instead, I just wanted to bring it to a standstill and let it move only through the lens of the camera. Around this time, I think it was the mid-nineties, I found myself increasingly frustrated with cinema, with the rigidity of the viewer watching a screen until the reel of film had ended. I wanted to find a way to kind of shatter the screen and make something that was more immersive or more architectural or flowing, and I think that series of projects happened around that time. They were exploring that tendency.

Born in Redondo Beach, California, in 1968, Doug Aitken studied in his home state at the Art Center College of Design, BFA, Pasadena, and Marymount College, Palos Verdes. His main focus is on time, space and memory as fluid concepts, and he is particularly interested in the relation between the topography of the landscape and the electronic flows of the media. Known for his mural-size video installations, Aitken also works with photography, sculpture, sound, and architectural interventions. In 2009, his Sonic Pavilion opened to the public in the forested hills of Brazil at the Inhotim cultural foundation. He lives and works in Los Angeles and New York.

Electrical Substation Albanatscha

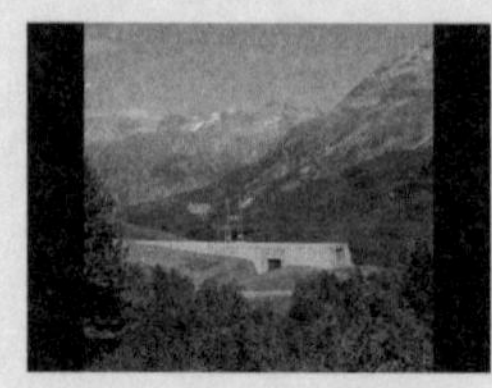

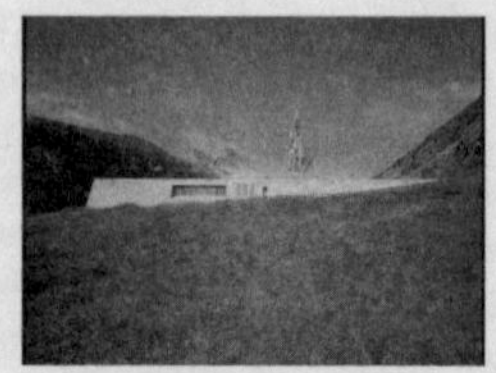

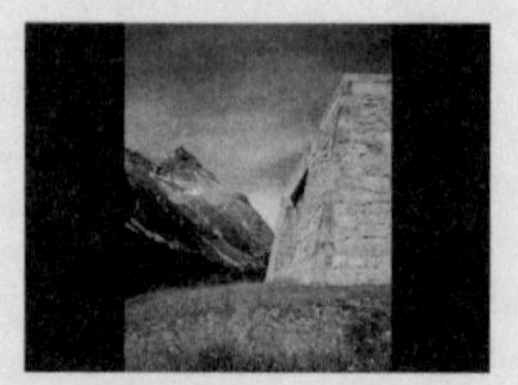

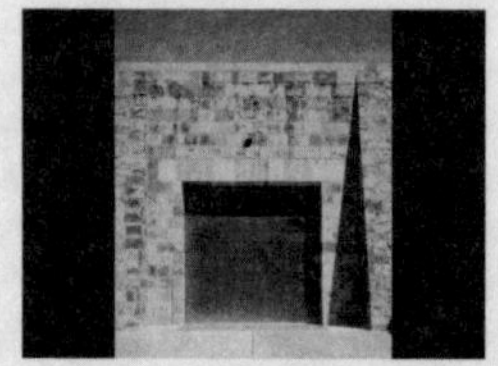

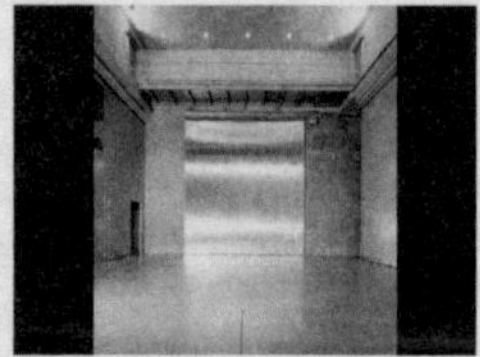

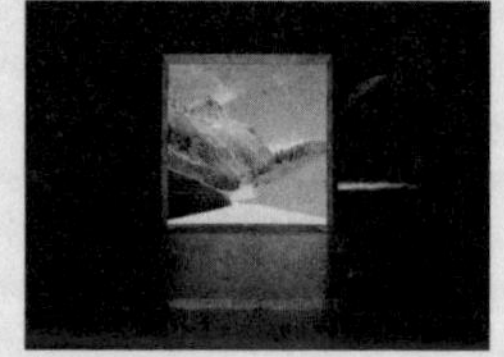

Chesa Andrea Madulain

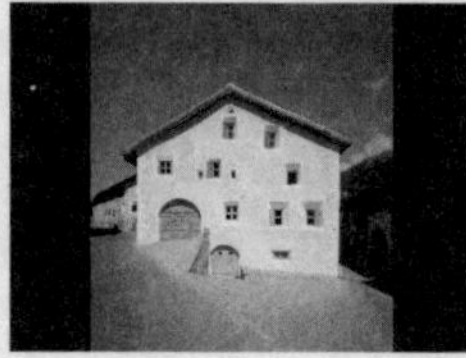

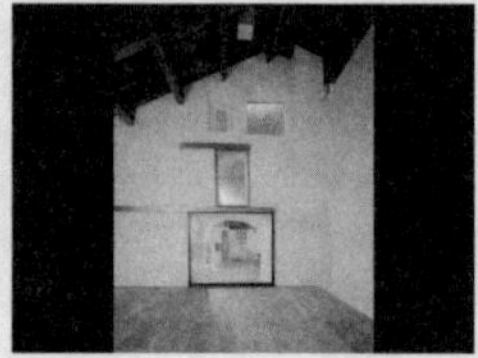

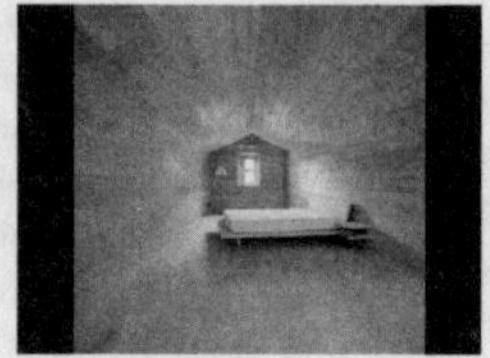

Chesa Madalena Zuoz

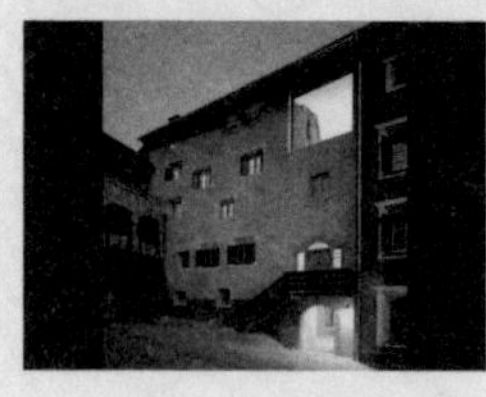

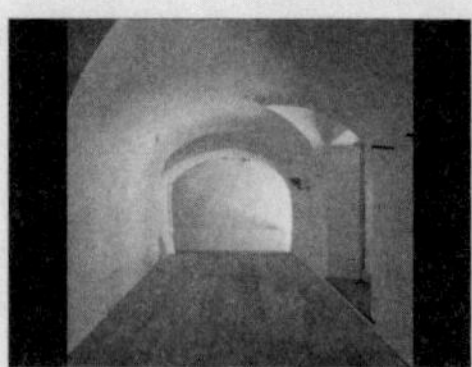

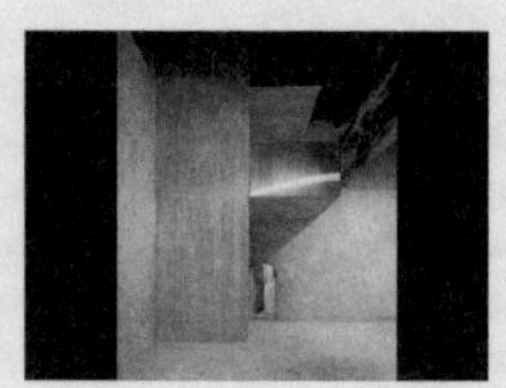

Hans-Jörg Ruch

Building in the Engadin – a Critical Approach to Landscape and Building Tradition

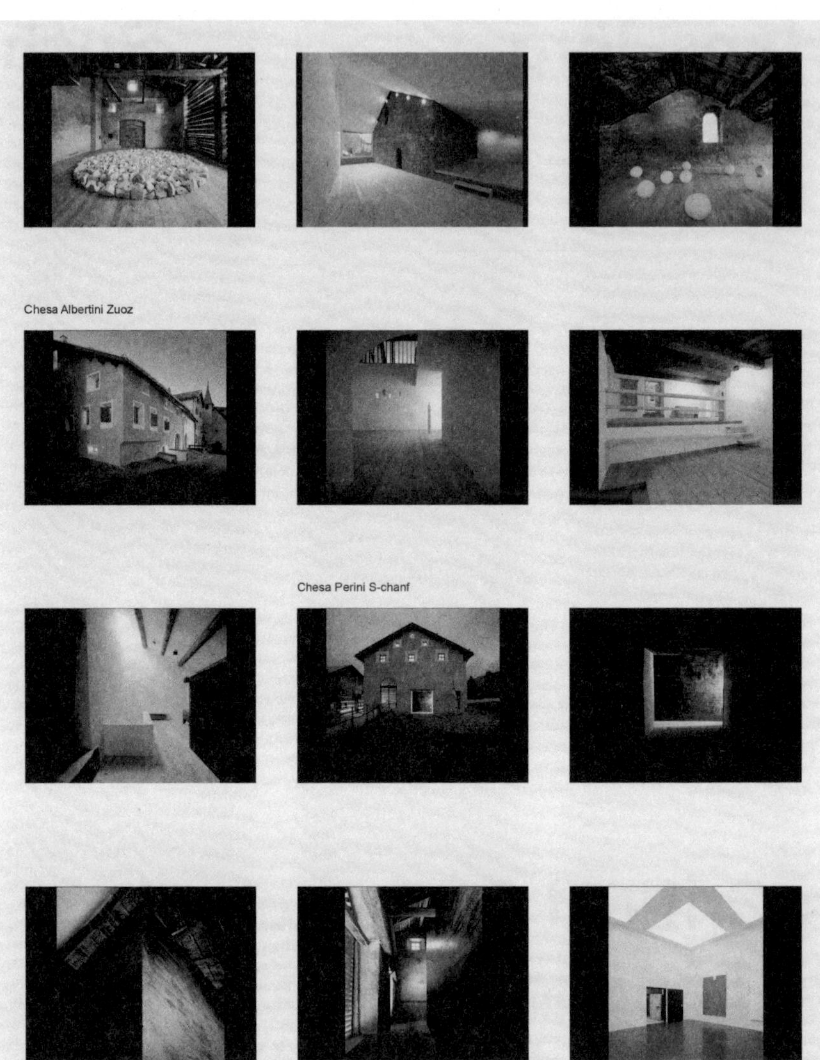

Chesa Albertini Zuoz

Chesa Perini S-chanf

The Engadin is probably one of the most beautiful valleys one can find in the world. Its lakes, and mountains, the changing light and the different weather conditions make it unique. The energy of all the interesting people who have ever visited the area – the painters and the philosophers – is still in this valley. But, as a local architect, I have to say that the Engadin is also a valley full of contradictions where architecture is concerned. We basically have two problems up here: a problem of quantity and a problem of quality. The quantity problem is that too many people want to come to this beautiful valley and, obviously, it is difficult to cope with the number of visitors with different expectations. But there is also a quality problem I would like to talk about, namely the increase in "Transplant Architecture": building types that are transplanted from the city to the mountains and vice versa. Apart from this, people in our region have found a very easy solution to the quality problem: according to them, everything just has to look like an old farmhouse. No matter if it is a hotel, a bank, or an apartment, just take the rural elements and mix them. You take the volume of the historic Engadin farmhouse, for example, blow it up, enlarge it, and there you have the solution. And if an architect does not agree with this approach, he may well find it hard to work in this valley.

One of the biggest challenges for us architects is to build outside the "building zones", high up in the mountains, for instance. I think any architect who gets the chance to construct buildings in such an incredible environment takes on a great responsibility. In this context, I would like to talk about the Albanatscha electrical substation, which we built on the Julier Pass route in 1997. Imagine if we had put up a huge farmhouse just because obviously everything can be packed into a farmhouse. Our project – placing an electricity pylon directly on the roof of the substation – virtually pops out of the earth. The energy flows into the earth and virtually lifts the ground. It's more a land art approach to developing the project. The core of the construction is a concrete building. We excavated the earth, put it aside, blasted the rocks and put a concrete box into the hole. The excavation material was used to build a kind of a coat around the concrete box. So for the coating, no material had to be transported to the site or away from it.

There is a huge entrance that allows lorries to bring in or take out the heavy transformers. In this electrical substation, the energy is transformed from 150 kilovolts down to 50 kilovolts and then distributed throughout the valley. The door – a sliding door – measures 7 × 7 metres and is made out of brass. On the outside, it already taken on a patina, but on the inside, where it is protected from the elements, it is still golden and illuminated from the window across the hall. There are no ordinary windows with frames. The windows are composed of glass bricks. When the door opens, a framed landscape appears. I used to say: We architects, we have to design the buildings in such a way that the mountains will not laugh at our work.

Let's change to the other topic, also one of my favorites, which is the restoration, renovation and conversion of old Engadin farmhouses. A very typical project is Chesa Andrea in Madulain (1999). As is common for this typology, the house has two main entrances. The larger of the two is where the hay wagons were moved into the hay barn, and the smaller one is where the cattle went in and out in the basement. I tend to refer to the hay barns as the cathedrals of the Engadin. These are fantastic spaces! You could easily build five or six apartments into such a huge structure, but this is exactly what I try to avoid. In this case, we left the hay barn as a cold space. Our intervention comprised two sliding doors and a window in the upper part, but apart from this, we kept the large space as it was. A new space completely done in massive wood was built in under the roof, reaching from the front façade to the hay barn.

The art gallery projects I was able to realize helped me a great deal when it came to carrying out such unconventional conversions, to preserve the large spaces. One example is the Tschudi Gallery, located in Chesa Madalena in Zuoz (2002). It is one of the most interesting works we have been able to do so far, because of the presence in the building of a medieval tower 16 metres high, and 10 × 10 metres large. In medieval times, there were about 25 to 30 such towers in Zuoz. The village looked very much like San Gimignano: a little smaller, but with more towers. Anyone who came to the valley and saw all those towers popping out of the landscape must have been very impressed by the sight. There was an entrance in the upper part of the tower that was used in times of war. People would seal the entrance at the bottom to keep out the enemy and then climb up using rope ladders. Inside the hay barn, we installed a lift. The shell is made of concrete and the railings of the platforms are of massive iron, forming a sharp contrast to the older parts of the house. I always try to make my interventions visible in this context. Therefore, I never work with old wood, but use new wood from the valley. In this case, the timber had been cut about one kilometre away from the house. The tower is now used as an art space and many beautiful exhibitions have been held there. Besides this project, I have made other interventions in houses that became art galleries, for example at the Gallery Monica De Cardenas in Chesa Albertini in Zuoz (2006), or at the Gallery von Bartha, located in the Chesa Perini in S-chanf. The latter is an example of how houses in the region have changed over the centuries: from a medieval tower house in the 14th century to a farmhouse in the 16th century, and to a patrician house in the 17th or 18th century. I could talk a lot about the discoveries we made; how the windows from the farmhouse had been altered. They were arranged more symmetrically, making them more representative of a patrician's house. When we did the renovation of the main house almost 20 years ago, and I was asked by the owner to also build apartments into the hay barn, I said: Well, I will do the renovation, but please do not insert apartments into this beautiful space. I think it was a wise decision, because almost 20 years later we were able to build an art gallery into this hay barn. I decided to insert a black cube, 7 × 7 × 7 metres into the barn. It is a wooden construction that marks a strong contrast to the old part of the house, especially since we had the outside walls of the box covered with tar. When people enter the barn, they just walk towards this black wall, which reminds them of the black painting by Kasimir Malevich, and they have to look for the entrance, which is somehow hidden: they have to walk around until they find the door to go in.

In general, I am very much interested in restoring, renovating and restructuring old Engadin farmhouses, but the most important thing is that the old and the new parts remain distinguishable for a visitor. In most of the cases in the Engadin valley, however, this is not happening. Another problem is that there are so many new buildings designed to resemble old houses. This is misleading and tourists admire these seemingly beautiful old buildings without knowing that they are fakes. Whenever I build new houses I try to find a way not to make them look like old Engadin farmhouses. I think that it is important to understand the old constructions: they have these characteristic small windows because people wanted to be protected when they came back home after a hard day's work outside. The glass technology was not as sophisticated as it is now and small windows were needed in order to keep the warmth inside the house. Today there are other parameters: we want to have a nice view, huge windows, and to let the sunshine in to heat the house. So why do we take the old Engadin farmhouse as a model for new houses? I have learned a lot about how people worked with materials like stone and wood for hundreds and hundreds of years, and I am well aware of this building tradition. But this in no way means that I have to copy it.

Hans-Jörg Ruch (b. 1946 in Bellach/Switzerland) studied architecture at the Swiss Federal Institute of Technology (ETH), Zurich, and at the Rensselaer Polytechnic Institute, Troy, New York (master's degree 1973; visiting professor 1990). He worked in the architectural offices of Obrist & Partners in St. Moritz (1974–77) and with Urs Hüsler in St. Moritz (1977–88). In 1989, he set up his own practice in St. Moritz. Besides architectural work in farmhouses and patrician houses in the Engadin, his main projects have included the extension of Hotel Saratz, Pontresina, and the renovation of the Segantini Museum in St. Moritz.

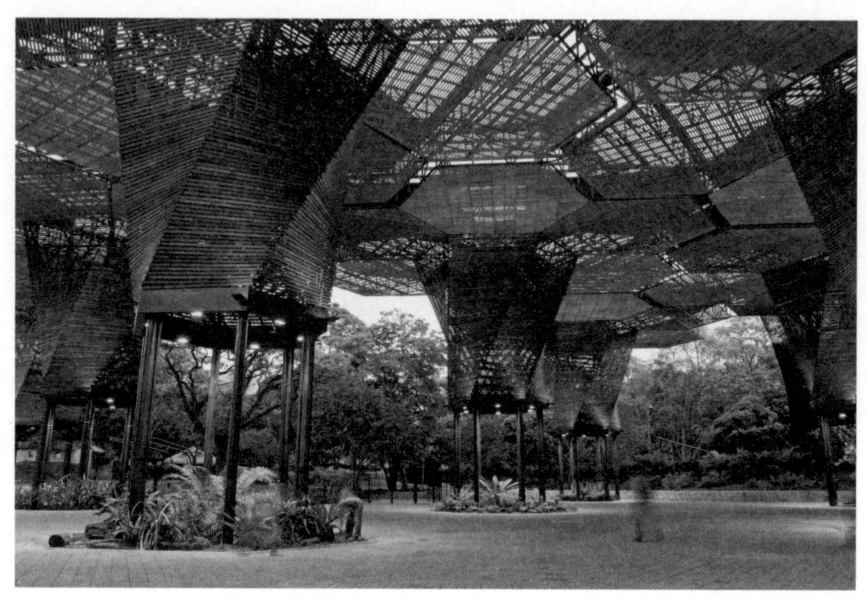

J. Paul Restrepo, Camilo Restrepo & plan: b,
Orquideorama (2005–06)

Camilo Restrepo Ochoa

Performing Architecture: Managing the Production and Administration of Space

It may sound strange but we are very interested in monsters and fossils. You know that fossils are stones that used to be animals that used to be plants. So if you want to trace the history of the world, take a look at a fossil and you will see a history that has been carved naturally in stone through a series of processes. Fossils have the particularity of being able to talk us through history while at the same time tracing their own genealogies and developments. Monsters don't do that. Monsters don't show us history, they tell stories. And we are more interested in monsters than in fossils, because they can be extremely ugly, because they have capacities, much like our mobile phones, because they breathe fire, and because they can fly. Sometimes they are creative, and some of them even drink blood, but most of all they are almost mythical. You never know who created them or where they are, and you never really know the reason for their existence. They are just there. We like to think of ourselves as being on the monsters' side. Mythical they might be, but there is also something beautiful and historical in the way they enable us to recreate culture. Sometimes they are a combination of all kinds of animals and figures, of nature, humans and even vegetable life.

We perform architecture as a thoughtful action for managing the production and administration of space. To illustrate this, I would like to take the housing project *Edificio 5G* (2004) as an example. It was conducted in association with my father, J. Paul Restrepo, who is also an architect, and our intention was to create a building that offered different options. Comparable to the menus at McDonald's, our clients were able choose from three variations. Menu number one was an empty unit, where the clients could hire their own architect to design the apartment to fit their needs. In menu number two, we offered our clients different types of kitchens, wardrobes, closets and bathrooms, which they could then order and assemble according to their needs. For menu number three, we designed apartments of different sizes – 80, 90, 100 or 110 square metres – with the result that there were 48 units of different-sized apartments and 34 architects working on the building site at the same time. In trying to organize the information needed for everyone, we were acting more like an agency than a traditional architectural office. The façade assumed shape in a somewhat spontaneous way since people were able not only to choose the window's width (1.5, 2.6, 3 or 6 m), and just one height of 2.6 m, but also had a choice of various types of balconies to be placed wherever they wished. Inside the house, there is an architectural office on the 6th floor, another one on the 3rd floor and a photographic studio on the 2nd floor, while one of the apartments is home to a 60-year-old. In brief: such a structure creates diversity.

If you look at a society, it is obvious that things change over the years, and we also realized that there were things that do not stay the same. Medellín, for example, with its three million inhabitants is located in the middle of Colombia, and on a map the landscape seems to be entirely flat. This impression is deceptive, for the city is actually situated in the Aburrá Valley, 600 metres above sea level. It is only 300 kilometres from Medellín to Bogotà, but it takes us eight hours by car because of the specific topography. People in Bogotá refer to us contemptuously as mountaineers. Yes, we live in the mountains and we try to transform the mountains and turn them into a place where we can live together. This has been hard in the past owing to all those drug-related conflicts and politics and everything else you see in the news. There is a river flowing through the city, and 20 years ago, neighbourhoods located on either side of it were enemies. There was a lot of conflict and violence in these neighbourhoods. For instance, people living on one side of the river belonged to guerilla groups and people on the other side to paramilitary groups. They created their own borders and if you crossed the line you ran the risk of being killed. Things have changed, and today there is a metro cable system, which is part of the public transportation linking different city districts with each other. But the use of land has also changed. For example, a rubbish dump was transformed into a park under the last administration. This required moving all the local inhabitants to another neighbourhood. The area will be closed for the next 15 years until all the organic waste is deemed safe enough for people to return. Within this development, we architects see ourselves as intermediaries who create symmetrical links between humans and their surroundings. It is very important to us to act as an agent of change. We like projects that facilitate the work and establish relations with others. We intermediate by delegating certain activities and making connections with other people.

Let me illustrate this with our project *Interphasephyta Multicapacitaceae* (2008–10), which is a machine made in Italy that purifies the air of a city. The machine is placed within a tree-like structure and works, technically, like a thunderstorm. Inside this structure, it creates a sort of thunder, which dissolves all the molecules and, as a consequence, all the microparticles of dust come down in a kind of rain within the structure. Briefly speaking, the air is absorbed by the machine and comes out purified. Before delivery, the importers called us and asked if we wanted to sell advertising space on the machine in the form of stickers. We thought that it was a waste to have such a nice machine just to have stickers on it. So we developed a software interface and, by using recycled PVC tubes, we created branches with an LED system at their ends. As a result, you can now connect with the machine via your mobile phone to check for traffic information, for example, and at the same time post some messages to your girlfriend, if you want, or to your football team, or send the message "red" to number 234 and the machine will turn red immediately. Moreover, a number of water pumps have been installed at the ends of the branches to create a sort of mist in the middle of the night or whenever you want. With this project, we wanted to create an associative link – we can say an affective link – with which people can relate to all these machines, because in Medellín, and in Colombia in general, it is very important to establish a link with things so that people will take care of them. Since a machine like this, or a park or a building is such a big investment to make, it is always crucial to generate affection for it so that people will feel that it belongs to them. In two months, the first machine will be finished and we are planning to have 50 in the city within the next two years. At the moment, we are drawing sketches of the machine because we are even thinking about generating a kind of new species, like in biology. That is why we called it *Interphasephyta Multicapacitaceae,* which means: a tree you can interact with.

We like to place ourselves in a third order, understood as an open gate, which avoids the division between subject and object. This means that our approach is one of practical theory and theoretical practice at the same time. Theoreticians in Colombia think that we are not theoretical enough when we write and other architects think that we are too theoretical. We actually like the situation of being in the middle without alliances or without any obligations towards any of these groups. That leaves us free to do and to organize everything the way we want, for example, to understand a book also as a project, as a way to construct ideas, to put them forward, to discuss them, to be open. So in a way, this is how we develop our theoretical approach as well. Furthermore, we believe that each project has its own sense of rules. We are therefore developing and operating a graphic system specific to each case: to draw means to think. Each project has to be accomplished in a way that makes what we are doing comprehensible.

We are currently carrying out a project in the mountains called *Casa DG* (2010), and it is related to the problems of optics. In order to avoid a conflict with the neighbours, the house cannot be built too high, and because the building site is on a slope, there is also the question of how to preserve the view of the beautiful landscape. That is why we are developing a kind of periscope – like those used in submarines – with some very big mirrors. We have decided to sink the construction partly into the soil and to resolve the problem of the hidden view by means of an optical technique used mainly in the 18th and 19th centuries. In this way, we are able to bring the landscape into the house. At the same time, we have been developing a kind of drawing technique, such as scanning images from colour transparancies from the 1960s and 1970s so as to create all kinds of landscapes. It is an investigation of how colour is made in film and the different surfaces that we use to represent our thoughts.

We believe that architecture is neither about the beautiful game of volumes nor about giving shape to the void. We are seeking a performative architecture rather than one that is merely representative. We think that there is more to architecture than building things; it is also about creating transparency and about creating links between things that we are doing and things that have an effect somewhere else, as for example in the small installation *Balanzas de Agua* (2009), which we made for a fair. We designed several pairs of balances using differently shaped bottles filled with natural water from a creek and different weights on top. We wanted to show the relation between different actions and their consequences by creating a chain reaction. When people took water from one scale, another bottle was lifted so high that it was no longer available to anyone else. Our installation was placed at the entrance to the fair. A couple of hours after the fair opened, the bottles within reach were nearly empty and it was not easy for people to get at the rest of the water. This was our way of trying to raise awareness about our resources. No matter where we get the water from and where we install our scales, there is always someone else who loses out. Architecture here also means creating consciousness about if and how easily resources are accessible. This project shows that we intend to develop specific architecture, for specific situations, for specific societies with local and global values at the same time.

We like to situate our actions within a paradigm shift – a shift from the mechanical to the ecological, as for example in *Orquideorama* (2005–06), which was designed in association with plan:b arquitectos, and with my father. We wanted to create a big structure, a canopy that will resemble, transfer and translate the structure of nature. Our intention was to create a forest with the possibilities and the ability of a garden: when you plant flowers in a garden, you can plant some here, some there and organize and arrange the space as you wish. We were trying to do the same. We developed steel structures covered with pinewood and called them "flower-trees" because their shapes resembled flowers, and because their sizes and proportions were comparable to those of a tree. In our project, which won the public competition, we planned to display fourteen of them, but budget problems allowed us to build only ten of them. *Orquideorama* is located in the botanical garden in the northern part of the city, where temperatures range between 14 and 28 degrees Celsius all year long – a climate to be out in all the time. In order to have the same temperature inside and outside our structure, what we created was simply a kind of semi-permeable roof, and the way the structure changes with the light during the day and at night is a beautiful sight. In the space underneath the roof there all kinds of activities going on: yoga in the morning and elderly people playing bingo at midday and in the afternoon, while at night there is usually a music festival, fashion show or similar event. Its use is always changing. The gardens we planted at the bottom of some "flower-trees" are very big now. In general, we like situations that cannot be categorized easily, like not knowing whether something is a zebra or a donkey. And we want to have as many tools as possible to create and produce whatever is needed at a specific moment.

I have to say that we are not only interested in a site or landscape for its own sake, but especially in the relation we can form with it, such as the library we built (*Biblioteca San Cristóbal,* 2009). It is located in a town that is almost linked with Medellín. Sixty per cent of the vegetables and the fruits that the city consumes are produced in San Cristóbal. So when we took part in a competition for the library, we of course wanted to build it, but at the same time we thought that it should also be a social intervention. Since many of the inhabitants of this peasant town are illiterate, it would have been ignorant just to put a library there. The people have a great cultural knowledge, especially about planting. So we decided to use the building as a border to define an area, a green area with a creek. Then we ploughed and planted the site. We thought that the whole site should become an open school for kids. Therefore we wanted all these children to learn not only the tradition of planting, but also to get involved in new technologies. After using the library for, say, ten years, they will have learned the traditions of planting and, at the same time, will be able to work on a computer, write a blog, and handle devices that allow them to connect to the world and exchange experiences with other people around the globe.

We also conceived the "Agrotag" in response to the big problem over landownership in Colombia, where just a few families own huge areas of land. They do not usually cultivate their land, or sometimes just let their cattle graze there. However, cattle pose a severe problem for the soil in of Colombia: either fertile ground, which should be used for plantation, is reserved for them, or rainforest areas are cut and turned into pasture. Intact rainforests have a very particular and sensitive biological structure, emitting and absorbing vast quantities of carbon dioxide. But despite the growth of a great variety of vegetation, soil quality is very poor and therefore not suitable for cattle grazing. We thought we could link land-holding versus planting situation to a democratic issue, which was to make public what was being planted in a specific area. We chose a public site, owned by the municipality, which we could turn into a kind of "green market": children are now able to study how to plant and how to produce agricultural products. People passing on the nearby highway can see how the land is used and have the opportunity to stop and buy produce, such as onions and carrots. We collect all the rainwater in tanks at the bottom of the very steep building area so as to water the entire system. Moreover, we try to collect all the organic waste in the small town, the aim being to feed it through a specially designed machine, a kind of digester, to produce the energy for the whole library. At the same time, the waste, being organic, also works as a fertilizer. So what we have created is a loop, a closed circuit involving all the different actors and elements in and around the library. Ever since we put screens up on the façade, the peasants passing by on their way to sell their goods at the market have been able to check the prices of different agricultural products. Comparable to the New York Stock Exchange, this system connects all the markets in the city. It serves as a reference point for the peasants. They know the seasonal and even daily or hourly value of their goods, which enables them to ask good money for their products and not to be exploited. Another feature of the project is that people can adopt a coffee plant. Colombian coffee is very well received and here, too, our idea is to create an affective link with the plant. People not only adopt a coffee plant, but also monitor it by means of a camera via the Internet: they water it, and see how it grows. This adoption is thought of as a kind of a scholarship for students. After a number of years – when the plant begins to produce coffee – they will get their own coffee as a reward for their help.

The impulse for what we do can best be described as coming from the uncertainty of life in Colombia – no matter where you come from or how wealthy your family is. We were raised according to what one can call the reality of everyday life, not in Michel de Certeau's meaning, but in the way that each day could be your last. When you were young in the 1980s or 1990s, you could never be certain that your father or mother would still be alive when you got home, because it was a time of war between the Medellín cartels and the national state. As a consequence, you began to develop something that resembled a shield of immunity. So if a terrible thing happened, it no longer astonished you. Simultaneously, each time something dreadful occured, you knew that whatever you did, apart from it representing someone or something, it also had to be a powerful action – it had to transform something or someone. So in a way, we were raised in the consciousness that every project is a possibility, and an opportunity for change.

Camilo Restrepo Ochoa (b. 1974 in Medellín) studied architecture at the Universidad Pontificia Bolivariana, Medellín, and has a master in urbanism, urban culture and architecture from the Universidad Politècnica de Catalunya, Barcelona. He lives and works in Medellín. He has his own architectural studio, now under the name of AGENDA (Agencia de Arquitectura). Restrepo is concerned with an architecture that responds to specific social and political conditions. His projects involve curating, public competitions, private commissions and research into territorial and urban issues.

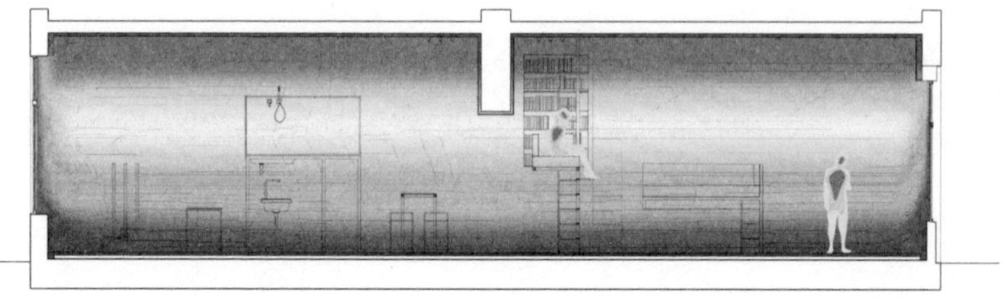

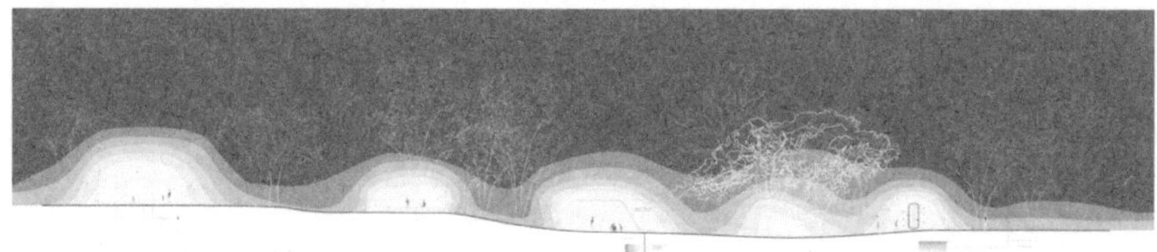

Philippe Rahm architects, *Evaporated Rooms*, Lyon, France (2011)/*Gradating Atmospheres (Heat Section)* (2012–15), Taichung Gateway Park Taiwan

Philippe Rahm

Gradating Spaces. Gradation versus Outline in Architecture

We can establish an interesting parallel between the formal demarcations of space in architecture in relation to its environment and the figure-ground-relation in a painting. The question is: How does one distinguish a figure from its setting? How does one delineate the boundaries of a space from its site? The history of art provides some interesting answers that vary according to the specific period of time, to recording techniques, representational tools and scientific knowledge. There are two strategies to delineate a figure from its environment. On the one hand, there is the earliest strategy aiming to an explicit separation between figure and ground found in the line of development that accentuated the line and hence the contours. This strategy begins with the origins of art and can be found in Egyptian frescoes and Byzantine icons. It can also be found in the academic paintings of the 19th century as well as in Edouard Manet's works, where the contours are painted with black lines and – very clearly – in the comic strips drawn in the 20th century. Here, the outline of the figure is emphasized in order to define an interior and an exterior, to separate a foreground from a background and to differentiate a figure from its context.

On the other hand, there are strategies that aim at a dissolution of the boundary between a subject and its context, or between two figures that are adjacent to each other. The strategy that interests us here is the technique known as sfumato. Sfumato was invented by Leonardo da Vinci and can best be described as "without lines or contours, like smoke". With this technique, da Vinci achieved an ethereal and undefined gradient transition effect between a figure and his background, by overlaying dozens of very thin layers of glaze containing very little pigment, each only 1 to 2 µm thick. This gave a sense of depth to the solid colours of paint. He did not have to draw contours anymore but was able to blur or veil the contours of a form in a painting and therefore to avoid sharp outlines. Blurring the outlines became more important at the end of the 19th century with the invention of photography and with Impressionist paintings. The Austrian photographer Heinrich Kühn, a key figure in international Pictorialism at the end of 19th century, worked with tonal values of photographs, that is, with a continuum from black to white instead of emphasizing the contours. According to Kühn, this allowed him to depict the most delicate play of light subtlety expressed by a succession of gradations caused or carried by light effects. Kühn established a palette of gradation while working on his studies on the gradations, and spoke of "fine gradations" that allowed the photographic medium to create an image only by changes in light tones. The photograph does not represent the outline of a figure against a background anymore. Instead, the photograph represents objects and things only by using changes in light intensity – they are thus distinguished by their ability to absorb or reflect more or less light. The Impressionists and, even more radically, the neo-Impressionists and Pointillists also abandoned clear-cut lines and contours in favor of paint-by-point colours whose distribution was based on variations in tone, intensity of colour and light. This practice anticipated the invention of the pixel used in digital imaging by Frederic Crockett Billingsley in 1965. Nowadays, we can question the first strategy regarding the outline and the contour of the object in more depth. When examining a substance under a microscope, you will find no clear delineation between one thing and another. Our knowledge of molecular, atomic and electromagnetic reality, vibration and constant communication between all things in the world abolishes the boundaries between a simple form and another form.

Our architecture belongs to this paradigm shift. The mode of tracing the contours of space, with the help of walls and floors clearly separating two spaces, one inside and one outside, can now be forgotten and be replaced by a mode of composition in which spaces are created by gradation, as expressed by Heinrich Kühn, by means of light, temperature, or humidity. Our architecture belonging to this new paradigm shift is composed with gradation in both climatic intensities and the density of chemical and physical components. Our last two projects – an apartment in Lyon, France, and a 70-hectare park in Taiwan – derive from this mode of composition.

Evaporated Rooms, 2011
An apartment for a young doctor
Architects: Philippe Rahm architectes
Design team: Renaud Pinet, Mathieu Bujnowskyj, Huguet Marina i Blasi
Client: Louis Malachane
Site area: Perrache, Lyon, France
Total floor area: 70 m^2
Design phase: January 2011 – June 2011
Construction phase: September 2011 – December 2011

For the apartment in Lyon (*Evaporated Rooms*, 2011), we used the latest sustainability recommendations for reducing environmental energy consumption in a built environment. This caused a shift from designing with a plan based on line drawings to composing in sections based on atmospheric gradations. The information we consulted advocated reducing the temperature level in spaces in which we are on the move, dressed, or protected by blankets, such as the corridor (16° Celsius), the kitchen (18° Celsius) and the bedroom (16° Celsius). In areas in which we are not in motion and not warmly dressed, such as the living room (20° Celsius) or the bathroom (22° Celsius), the heating will be turned up. If we wanted to follow these guidelines to reduce energy, we would – traditionally speaking – need to physically separate the different rooms, each with their own function, by means of walls and closed doors. This would prevent the air in rooms with different temperatures from merging into a homogenous mix, the way water does when mixed together from hot and cold taps. So to strictly follow these recommendations, we would have to abandon the free plan and spatial continuity achieved during modernity and return to the plans that were drawn up in the 19th century, when each room was separated from the other by walls and doors. We can avoid this regression by considering the intrinsic physical characteristics of air, which rises when it is warm and sinks to the ground when cold. Bearing this in mind, we can start composing rooms and spaces, or rather, begin to divide the space without using walls, which clearly delineate the different parts of a building. Instead we can compose a house by using only the spatial distribution of temperatures, humidities and luminosities in the air. This would mean designing an atmosphere, with its various thermal, humidity and light gradations, in which one moves to find a certain ambience. We propose not to draw plans of rooms and contours of spaces, but to fix the furniture and to define the furniture's usages according to particular temperatures depending on height and specific light intensities. This would create an atmosphere a little bit like a natural landscape, where you would take refuge under a tree when it rains or sit in the shade of a rock when it gets too hot. Therefore, a chair that accommodates only one person would be located at the highest level, where the air is warm, as warm as when you are under the shower without any clothes on, whereas the sofa, generally a place of interaction where people are social, would be at a somewhat lower level as its temperature would be expected to rise thanks to the increase in warmth that occurs when several individuals sit beside each other on the same piece of furniture. The kitchen floor would be placed lower still, reducing its temperature, while the bed would be found in the coldest part of the house, on the ground floor.

Gradating Atmospheres, 2012–15
Taichung Jade MeteoPark
Architects: Philippe Rahm architectes
Landscapers: Mosbach paysagistes
Local architects: Ricky Liu & Associates
Client: Taichung City Government
Site area: Taichung Gateway
Total floor area: 70 hectares
Design phase: January 2012 – June 2013
Construction phase: September 2013 – July 2015

The design composition principle of the Taichung Jade EcoPark *(Gradating Atmospheres,* 2012–15) is based on climatic variations: some areas of the park are naturally warmer, more humid and more polluted while some of them are naturally colder, drier and cleaner. We have augmented these differences of climates in order to create places that are cooler, less humid and less polluted. Using the existing conditions as a point of departure, we have defined three climatic maps. Each map specifically corresponds to a particular atmospheric parameter. The first one corresponds to air temperature, the second one describes variations in air humidity, and the third one the intensity of atmospheric pollution. Each map shows how the intensity or strength of the respective atmospheric parameter is modulated through the park. By doing so, the maps keep areas within the park from reaching excessive conditions, while making changes in climate a much more comfortable experience. The three maps intersect and overlap randomly in order to create a diversity of microclimates and a multitude of experiences in different areas of the park. At a certain place, the air will be less humid and less polluted but will still be warm, while elsewhere in the park, the air will be cooler and drier yet remain polluted. The three climatic maps vary within a gradation, ranging from a maximum degree of discomfort with regard to the atmospheric conditions that usually prevail in a city (maximum levels of pollution, humidity and heat) to more comfortable areas where levels of heat, humidity and pollution are more moderate.

To build theses three weather maps, to reduce the natural heat, humidity and pollution, we have invented an exhaustive catalog of climatic devices, which are installed in the park. Each of these devices is able to reduce one climatic parameter: heat, humidity, or pollution. A first type of these devices are trees that have specific climatic properties, for example for reducing pollution with hairy leaves, reflecting sunlight because of the white colour of the leaves, or providing increased shade thanks to the high density of their foliage, and reducing the humidity of the air with floating roots. The second type of devices are artificial, such as water jet nozzles that cool the air by evaporation, fans that increase the cooling air flow, dehumidifiers or ultrasonic repellers. Increasing the number of cooling climatic devices on a given surface will increase the quality of coolness of the place in question. The climatic devices are regrouped, densified, separated, or expanded in order to generate a gradation in the intensity of heat, humidity, or pollution. These variations in the concentration of devices generate a variety of atmospheres with different climatic properties that visitors can select and use freely at their own discretion. The devices are a contemporary extension of traditional urban and park furniture – such as fountains, kiosks and grottos – which have climatic values and are commonly found in parks.

Heat, humidity and pollution are the guidelines and founding elements in the composition of a park. With reference to these three parameters, we define how densely our devices will be dispersed in different areas of the park. The climatic devices will thus be scattered over the site in different concentrations and will give texture to the modulated climatic landscape. The varying concentrations of climatic devices throughout the landscape and in the background will be our only pieces of architecture within the park.

The distribution of programmes including public buildings, recreational areas, paths and playgrounds will naturally follow the intensities of the new climatic zones we have created. Thus the recreational areas are situated in the coolest climatic zones we have created, while sporting activities will take place in the driest areas, where the players are less likely to have problems with perspiration. Activities for families and children will be placed in the most depolluted areas, far from the road, where we find the densest concentration of depolluting devices with ozone and NOx filters, particle matter cleaners or sound absorbing devices.

Philippe Rahm (b. 1967 in Pully/Switzerland) studied architecture at the Swiss Federal Institute of Technology (ETH) in Lausanne and Zurich. His work extends the field of architecture to a cross-disciplinary art and architecture work focusing on the meteorological. Rahm has become a prominent exponent in the context of sustainability, and is working on several private and public projects in France, Germany and Taiwan. In 2002, he was chosen to represent Switzerland at the 8th Venice Architecture Biennale. He lives and works in Paris.

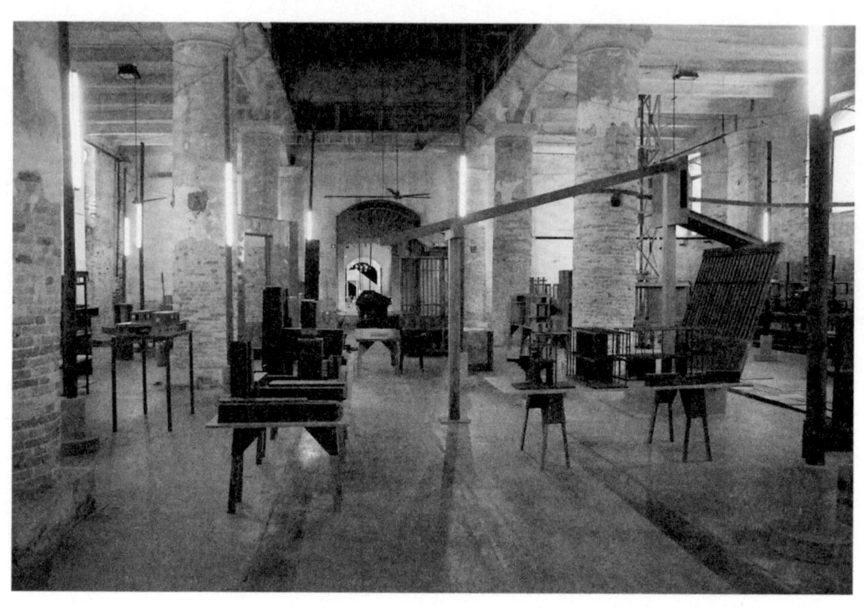

Studio Mumbai, *Work-Place*,
Venice Architecture Biennale, 2010

Bijoy Jain

Practice

Most of my work is produced through gestures, through sketches, which I then immediately make into models. It sort of shows a delicate balance in the condition of machine, man and nature, and the dependency between the three. Which one is dependent on the others at what time is really critical. And what is quite interesting for me is the fact that there is a sort of relationship – and to ask what that relationship forms. Let's take wild birds for example: herons that pull out grass in order to get at any insects that may be in the ground. I was once standing a good three to four metres away from them, and the moment I took a step in their direction, the birds moved away to maintain that distance from me. I am fascinated by what it is that creates this condition in which two distinct creatures – the human being and the bird – are able to coexist and do what they need to do. But what also fascinates me is a sort of internal gesture that allows for a certain condition. For example, if you think of a woman sweeping the floor, there is this idea of cleaning the space with a broom, of setting what could be a place in which to eat, to sit, to gather. I find the consideration of the idea of a floor particularly interesting. How do you relate all this back into your work? A lot of work is, in terms of construction, just in terms of materials that we can use, a cultural condition. At the Venice Biennale, when we were setting things up, we wanted to have this black, highly polished concrete floor and so we called in some Italian masons to do the job. It was interesting because they actually found it difficult to sit on the floor in a certain posture and do the work. We figured out that carpenters were the only ones who would be able to do that. You and I can't sit like that, but they sat hunched over for three hours without getting up, and with no pain at all. So this is a condition of a material that is embedded in a certain culture, more precisely in the way we sit. That was the first time it struck me that once we lose the way we sit and our relationship to the ground, the possibility of practising a certain technique will disappear with it. It is not the material, nor is it the manpower, but rather just the gesture of sitting, which then creates conditions for architecture. What interests me, therefore, is more the consideration of the gesture of the human body in relationship to nature and to materials, as well as the possibilities that exist in between, and somehow being able to draw the work from that space.

So there is this latent universal potential that exists, which is sort of interesting. For example, just using this idea of the gesture of sitting on the floor is something that, if we lose it, can be regained. But what counts is having faith in regaining that position. Now, regaining that position can only come through doing the work. In order to build this floor myself, a task that would require sitting on the ground for three hours, someone like me would have to begin by going through the process, and through the pain that it necessarily involves. There is no other way but to endure this struggle between pain and happiness, for want of a better word. I'm not nostalgic about tradition or about things that are old, but what interests me, I think, is what they put into it, this energy that they invest and keep there. And that is what draws us to it, the sort of embedded potential, embodied potential that you put into work. So if you ask me, despite this constant concern that we may lose our tradition, that we are losing our technique, it is important to have faith that they exist, that they will always exist as long as man exists. That is my belief.

Bijoy Jain (b. 1965 in Mumbai/India) received his master's degree in architecture from Washington University in St. Louis, USA, in 1990. He worked in Los Angeles and London between 1989 and 1995, and returned to India in 1995 to found his practice. Studio Mumbai is a human infrastructure of skilled craftsmen and architects who design and build the work directly. The essence of their work lies in the relationship between land and architecture, and in their endeavour is to show the genuine possibility of creating buildings that emerge through a process of collective dialogue and a face-to-face sharing of knowledge. In 2012, Jain became the winner of the third BSI Swiss Architectural Award.

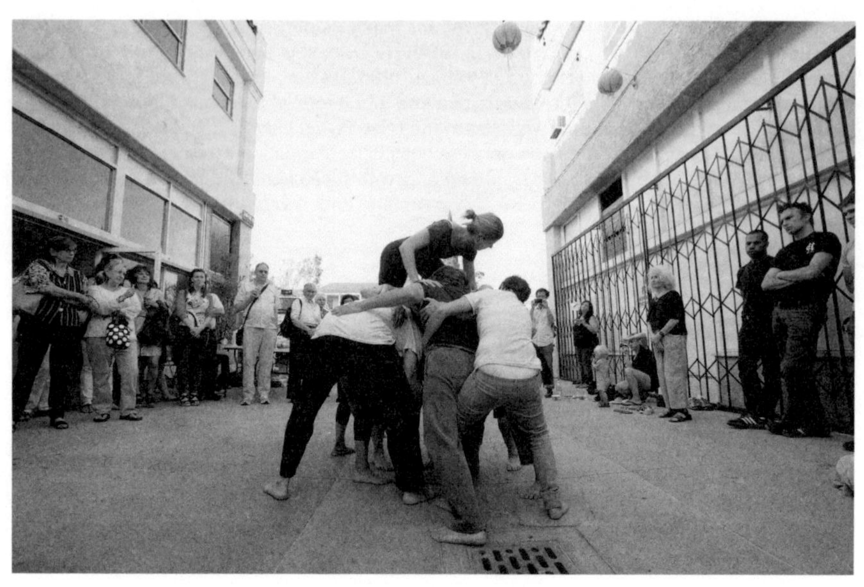

Simone Forti, *Huddle* (1961)
Performance at The BOX Gallery,
Los Angeles, 2011

Simone Forti

The Roots of Our Dancing

There seems to be an interest right now in works that I did when I was in my early twenties, when I made some pieces, including *Huddle* (1961), which I called “Dance Constructions”. This was at a time in New York when painters, poets, musicians and dancers were drinking together, having parties and talking together about art and about their work. The title, *Huddle,* refers to American football and describes the situation when the players get together, all facing to the centre, to decide on their strategy. The piece requires six to nine performers to form a tight cluster. Then they take turns, each climbing over the top of the tight group and down the other side, immediately becoming again part of the supporting mass. We have done the piece in various types of venues, including in the lobby of a theatre or in a sculpture garden, where people could see it as they walked by or around it, or sat down and looked at it from a low angle.

They could watch it for a short while or for its entire duration of ten minutes. I have noticed that in the context of the visual art world, and maybe also in the context of architecture, *Huddle* is primarily seen as a form in space, as a structure, almost as a sculpture. In fact, I also see it as a sculpture as well as a dance.

I often teach *Huddle* in dance workshops. There, it is not so much about seeing it, but about experiencing the doing of it. A wonderful part of the experience is when you are in the supporting part of the huddle and feel the climber's weight: you can feel it pass through your shoulder, through your arm, and through your hand with which you are gripping the thigh of your neighbour. Or maybe feel the weight pass through your neighbour's hand, into your leg, foot, and into the ground. So the lines of force of weight pass through the various bodies and there are these adjustments that are made intuitively and reflexively. It is a very collaborative and reflexive experience. And the climbing itself is also an experience. We have all climbed over rocks, or up into trees, but in *Huddle* it is about climbing on a medium that is responsive. It is very much a somatic physical experience. When I teach it in a dance context, it is understood that the people who did it can go into the world, do it again and teach it. I often get a snapshot via e-mail, with an attachment of a huddle from whatever part of the world. And it still looks like a huddle, and they still call it *Huddle.*

I want to talk about my motivation at that time, which was partly very personal. I had just moved to New York from San Francisco, where I had been studying with the dancer Anna Halprin. She was focusing on improvisation, on how she wanted to use it, and how she wanted to teach it. Her studio was a beautiful dance deck, which her husband, the landscape architect Lawrence Halprin, had built outdoors in the woods. Suddenly, I was in New York. Everywhere I looked, everything I saw, had been designed by humans – except if I looked straight up to see some sky. I needed to feel my simple, unstylized, body just performing the task of climbing, engaging directly with the nature of weight and mass. I had seen photographs of a performance piece by the Gutai artist Saburo Murakami. He had made a series about five frames, such as you might stretch canvas onto, but had stretched paper onto the frames instead and placed them one in front of the other. Then he just walked right through the series of sheets of stretched paper, just crashing right through them. With this piece, I realized that there could be a single action, and that it could be fully satisfying. So it seemed that I could create a dance that was a single form and that was a steady and ongoing activity.

Some time later, I happened to be living near a zoo and started observing the animals. I was interested in comparing how I walked with the way differently structured species moved. I thought it would help me to understand my own movement in a way that had nothing to do with style. I began trying out some of the movements the animals made, such as the bounding gait of a kangaroo or a rabbit. Or changing direction by swinging my head to the side, the way a bear would do.

After a while, I started noticing many instances of what seemed to be movement games, which certain individual animals were engaged in: a young chimp sticking a finger into a small hole in the ground, and leaning outwards while running round and round. And I began to feel that the roots of our own dancing are ancient, and that from those ancient roots people of different cultures have developed their various forms of dance. I think that some of the behaviour that I saw in the animals in captivity could also have happened in their natural environments. But a lot of it, I think, was a matter of passing the jail time, enriching the possibilities of this very limited, difficult situation.

Simone Forti, who was born 1935 in Florence/Italy, now lives and works in Los Angeles. After the outbreak of World War II, she escaped with her family to Los Angeles. In 1955, she moved to San Francisco, where she studied improvisation with the postmodern dancer Anna Halprin. After her relocation to New York in 1959, she began studying composition with Robert Dunn, who introduced her to the work of John Cage. For the past three decades, she has been improvising with movement and language, performing "News Animations".

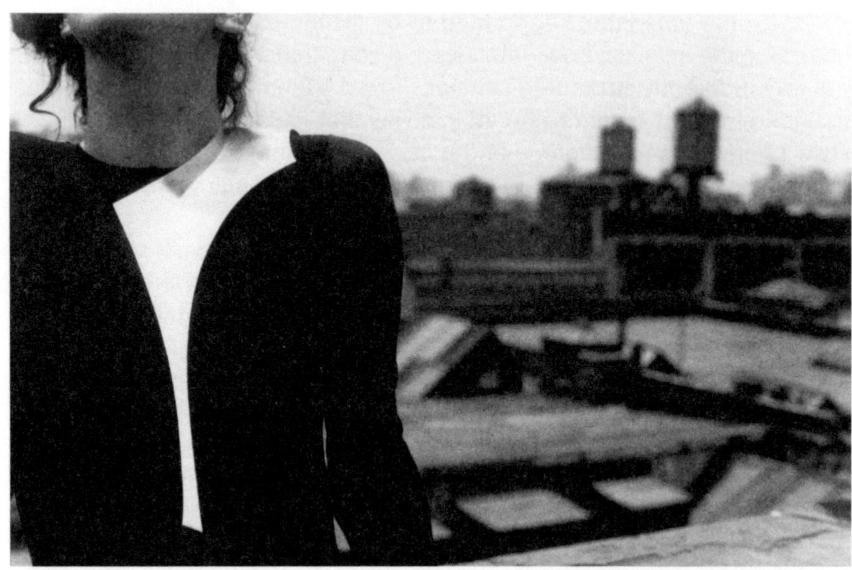

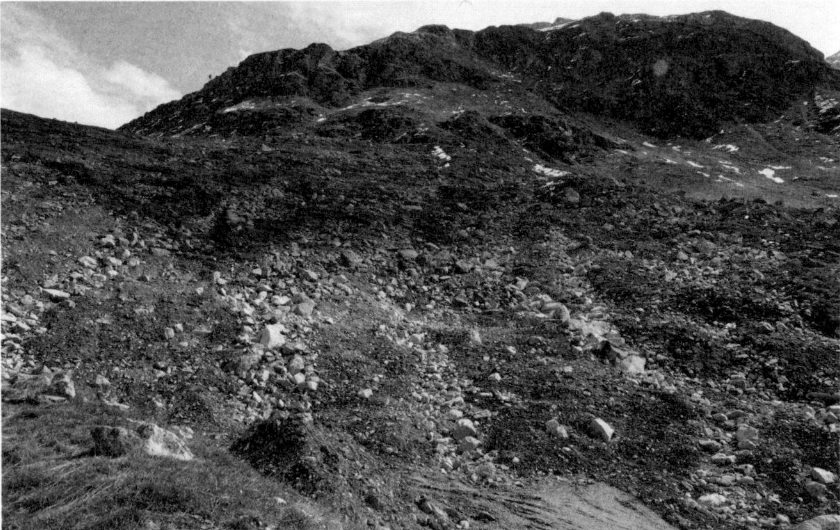

Nina von Albertini, shoulder-object in silver (1979)/a newly remodelled landscape at the Julierpass (2011)
200,000 m^3 of material were extracted for the street building project; the relief and the structural elements are adapted to the natural surroundings, in order not to appear artificial. A construction worker translated successfully my "renaturalization" ideas not with a paintbrush but with a 30-ton caterpillar

Nina von Albertini

Body Objects and Landscape

Sensibility and Responsibility

I am originally from the Engadin valley, my mother is from the Engadin valley, my culture, my roots are here, and in my life and my different activities it was always very important to me to be rooted here. So, I would like to speak about a few phases of my professional career. Early on, I was most interested in ancient jewellery and its craftsmanship. I worked with different masters in various places in Europe and the United States. I focused on ancient methods of jewellery-making and tried to apply them in contemporary forms. I had no interest in the jewellery that was fashionable in my time, preferring instead something that had to do with our here and now and with us, self-assured women. I declared my pieces to be wearable sculptures, body objects. It was mainly silverwork, such as a shoulder object with clear lines and a smooth surface, or a later object for the back, with a very simple, rectangular structure. I concentrated on expressing myself through the body and these wearable objects. In other words, I wanted to give back to women a symbol or a ritual art piece inspired by jewellery of ancient times that had a function and meant something, such as belonging to a tribe, or having a certain status. By contrast, the jewellery we had in the 1980s or 1970s was often reduced to its pecuniary value. To wear my pieces, you need a strong posture and a certain inner attitude – and so you can't wear them every day. For example, one object I created is an ear shell to put around your ear. This particular object – as all my objects – relates to the anatomy, to the shape of the body and to movement. The pieces are hard-edged and look striking, but they are actually very comfortable to wear. They also simply stand as sculptures by themselves.

By the time I had begun to exhibit my work in galleries more frequently and was successfully collaborating with the world of fashion and publishing, the type of customer had expanded. But I realized that I did not feel like selling my pieces to simply anyone, to people without a connection to the sense of my work. So I withheld my objects and decided to start studying agricultural engineering at the Swiss Federal Institute of Technology (ETH) in Zurich, which, back then, was a still conservative institution in this field. It was not easy for me after having lived in New York, Milan and Paris. But still, I had my roots here in the Engadin, with our family house, a very old patrician house with a farm, located nearby. I wanted to obtain theoretical and practical knowledge and was interested in going further into agricultural engineering. I realized that the basic resource for nature, for most ecosystems and especially for products, is the soil and its fertility. So in my studies, I concentrated more and more on soil ecology and processes – I went into soil physics. But there, modelling, statistics and analysis were the main focus, although what I wanted was to render physical and biological regeneration processes visible. For example, I wanted to show what soil compaction damage was being caused to the soil structure and its fertility. By infiltrating blue water as artificial rain on grassland surfaces of different compaction stages, I was able to show coloured flow patterns of different regeneration stages on the soil profiles. These patterns indicate the paths the water takes and where it is able to infiltrate. The youngest patterns, just after ploughing, showed a sealed plough layer and almost no interaction with deeper layers of the soil. As a consequence, the soil organisms are disturbed, and soil fertility is impoverished. This happens every time soil is ploughed or compacted by heavy machinery. But what I wanted to make clear was the potential and capacity of soil regeneration – if we just treat soil a little better, if we change the way we produce and harvest, with less heavy machinery. A flow pattern of the same piece of grassland four years after ploughing showed that the upper layer was no longer sealed and disconnected, and that the blue-tinted water was able to seep deep into the soil. Physical processes and soil organisms such as earthworms, insects, funghi and bacteria had reconquered and reopened the soil to water and air – to life.

The images I was able to analyze generated almost better results than would have been possible through physical analysis or statistics. And the most important part of my work was that I was able to show my results not only to researchers but also to farmers – and farmers would be in the position to see something they had never seen before – so in this respect my images opened up new dimensions.

After this research and the resulting images, and after I had lived in Niger for several years, I came back to a valley close to the Engadin because I had to take over our family house and farm. For me, it has always been important to combine research, experience and practice. I wanted to do further research after my return since a lot of our soil and environment is being destroyed – especially in mountainous areas like the Engadin, where we don't have many resources and the few we do have are very vulnerable. Besides, our valleys are highly populated and we have a lot of construction going on because of second homes, tourism, and therefore the pressure on land is very high. This is why I try to help people become more sensitive and knowledgeable about nature and the landscape. My collaboration with important construction projects such as roads, tunnels or hydro-energy plants aims to integrate a respectful, aesthetic, logical and site-specific handling and modelling of the environment in order to reduce negative impact. There is evidently an urgent need to show more sensitivity and knowledge when intervening in nature. This means doing much more to avoid brutality, ignorance and lack of taste.

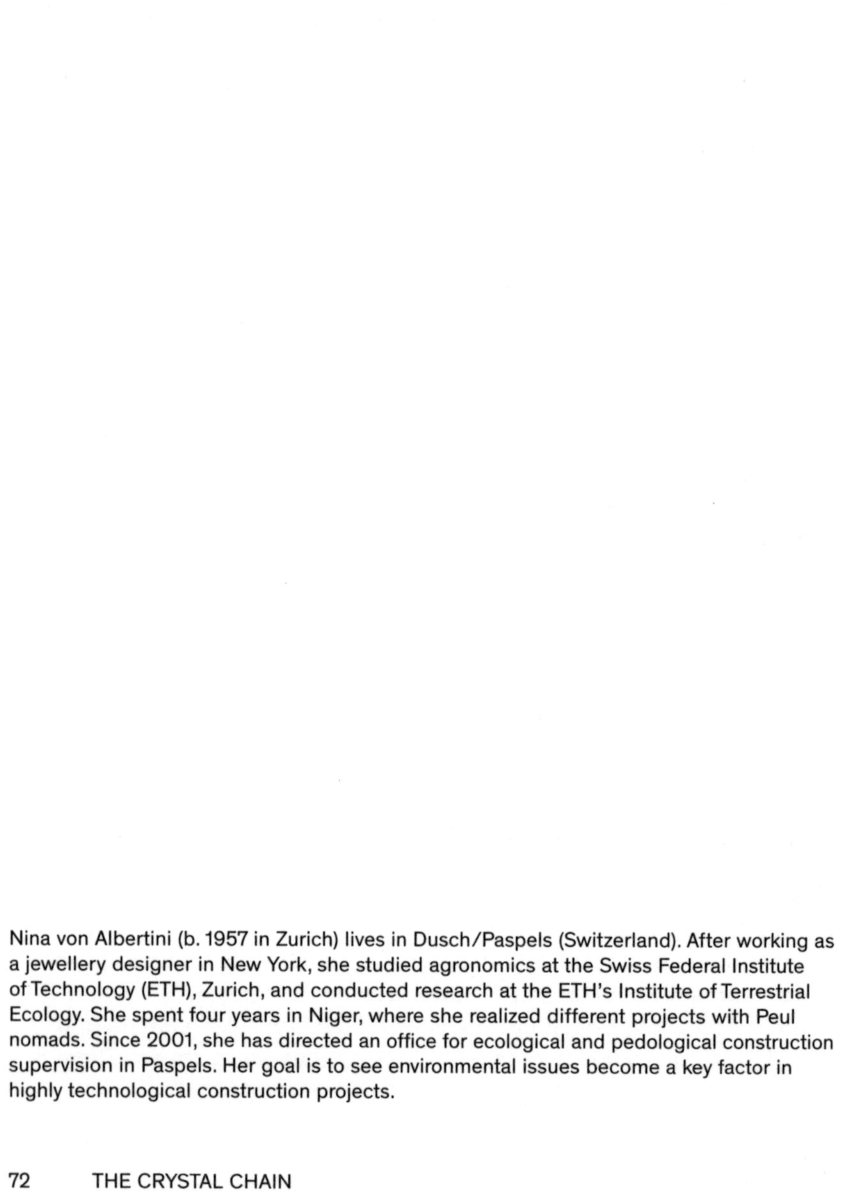

Nina von Albertini (b. 1957 in Zurich) lives in Dusch/Paspels (Switzerland). After working as a jewellery designer in New York, she studied agronomics at the Swiss Federal Institute of Technology (ETH), Zurich, and conducted research at the ETH's Institute of Terrestrial Ecology. She spent four years in Niger, where she realized different projects with Peul nomads. Since 2001, she has directed an office for ecological and pedological construction supervision in Paspels. Her goal is to see environmental issues become a key factor in highly technological construction projects.

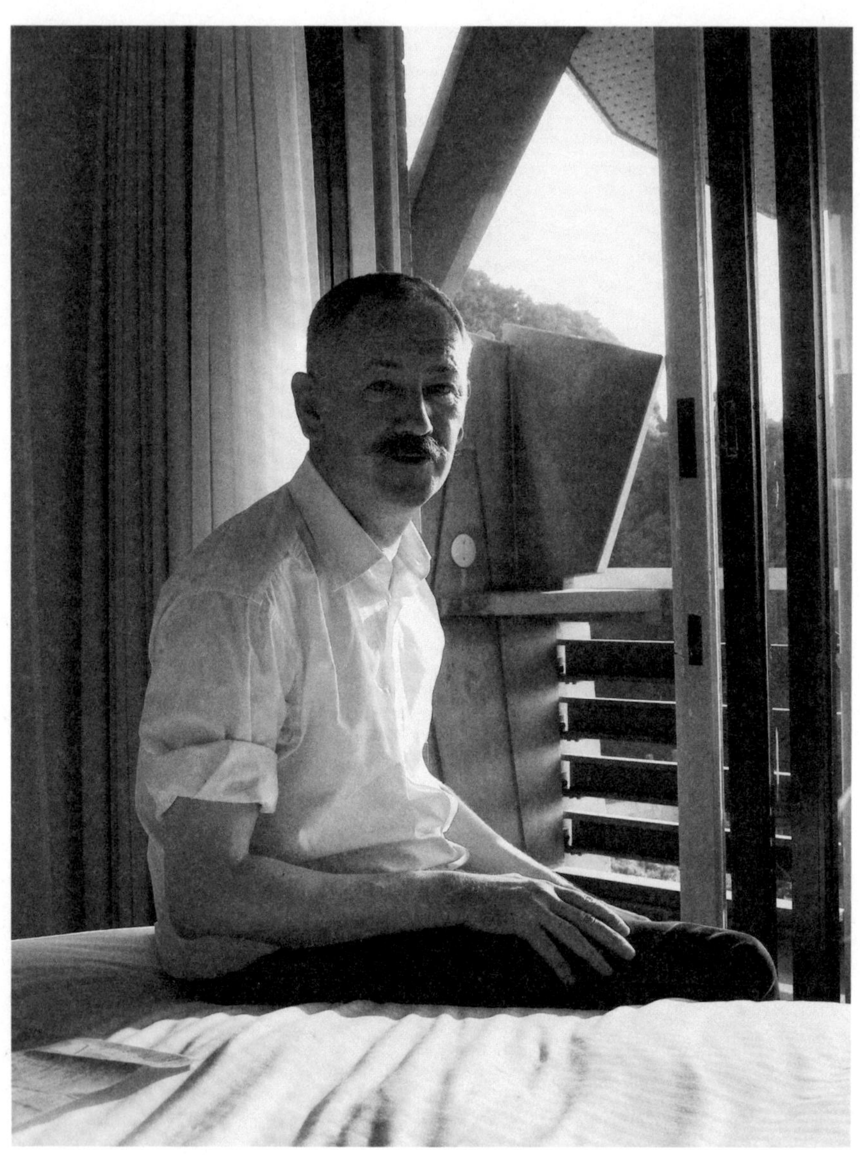

Cerith Wyn Evans

Cerith

Wyn Evans

Sitting here today and reflecting on why we are here, working together in the same room, I realized that, perhaps in contrast to the other contributions that were so erudite and considered, I thought I might, as the English would say, fly by the seat of my pants. So I hope that in a sense I'm able to respond in some way and reflect the experience of coming to the Engadin for the very first time. What I know about the Engadin actually was revealed to me anecdotally during a phone call I made to my cousin because I was concerned about her husband's health. I don't speak to her very often, so she said, "Where are you now?" because quite often I'm only concerned about her when I'm overseas and just worry about the fact that I'm far away. And so I said, "Oh, I'm in Switzerland." She said "Where abouts in Switzerland?" I said, "In a valley called the Engadin," and she said, "Oh, I know where that is. Do you know that your parents went to the Engadin?" I thought, okay, because my parents never traveled, and I think this was on the occasion of their belated honeymoon, because my grandfather died shortly after they married and so they cancelled their original honeymoon. And I said, "When would they have been there?" She said, "Well, I don't know, in the late 50s," and I said "Could it have been in 1957?" and she said "Yes, it could easily have been 1957." Then I remembered seeing photographs, slides, transparencies that my father had taken, which I got after he died – the whole collection, since he was a photographer. And I said, "Joy" – that's her name – "I don't think this is really possible" She said, "You know, you might well have been conceived in Switzerland." So, possibly, my relationship to the Engadin has been a profound one for the last fifty-two years.

Cerith Wyn Evans (b. 1958 in Llanelli, Wales) lives and works in London. He completed a foundation course at Dyfed College of Art in Wales and later studied at Saint Martins School of Art and at the Royal College of Art, London. Wyn Evans began his career as a video and film-maker of short, experimental films during the 1980s. In the early 1990s, he began to work in a wide range of media, including installation works, sculptures, photography, film and text, focusing on a conceptual practice and often combining light sources with reflective surfaces. In 2011, he was commissioned by the Vienna State Opera to design the safety curtains for the 2011/12 opera season.

MA

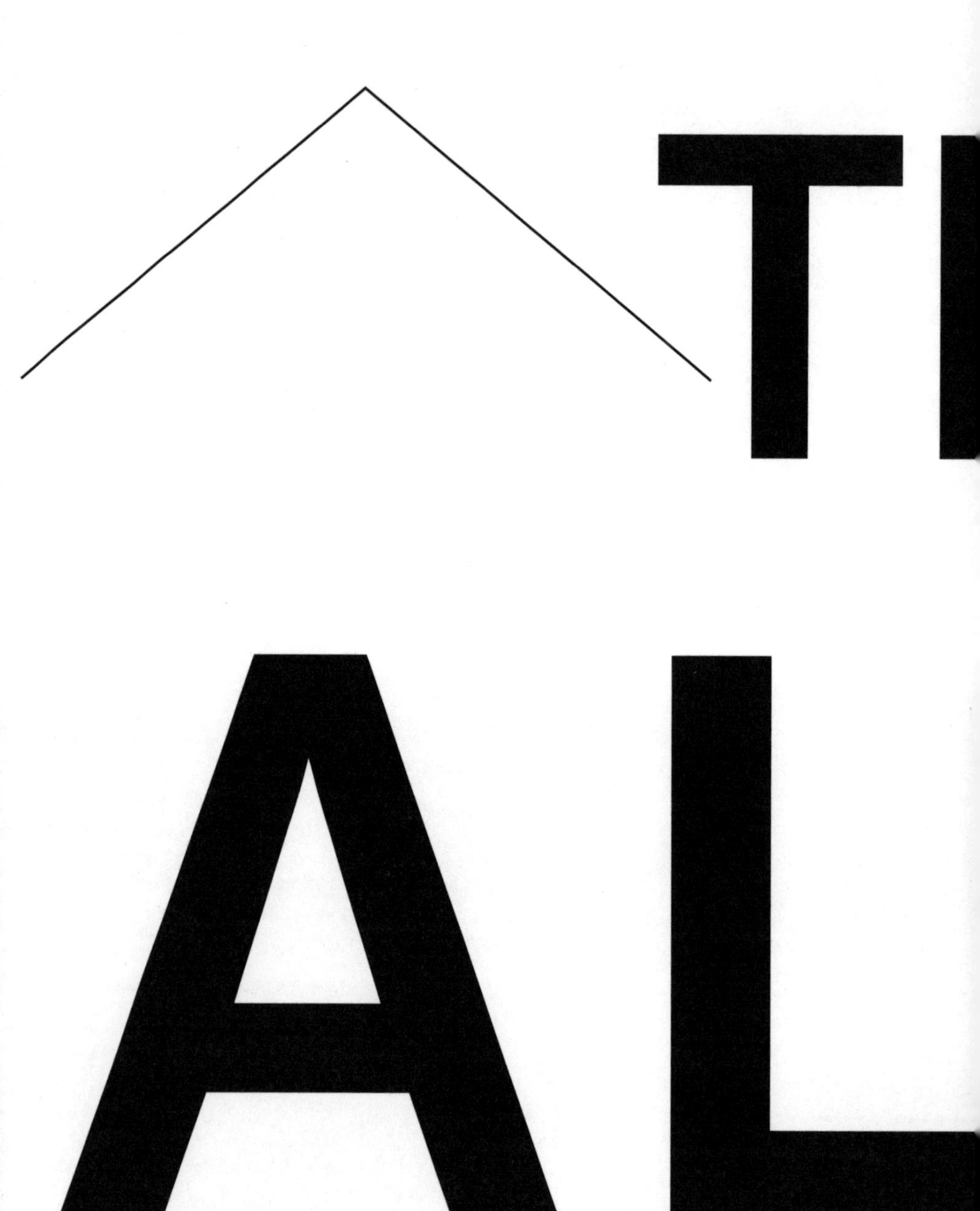

N G

IE

PS

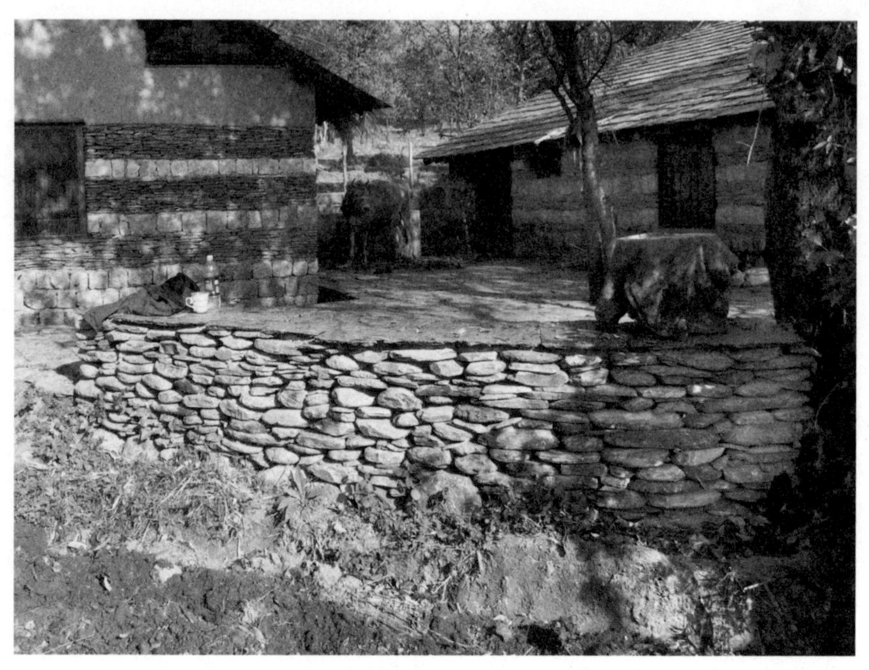

Ritu Sarin & Tenzing Sonam, *Mud Stone Slate Bamboo* (2011)
Film, colour, 17 min., White Crane Films
(film still)

Ritu Sarin and Tenzing Sonam
Work in Progress: Mud Stone Slate Bamboo – Traditional Architecture in the Himalayan State of Himachal Pradesh, India

In August 2011, we had the opportunity of presenting a short work in progress at the Engadin Art Talks. The 17-minute video, *Mud Stone Slate Bamboo,* was an attempt to capture the building process of a traditional Himalayan structure, and to evoke the timeless connection between man and nature in an architectural context.

We live in a rural area on the outskirts of Dharamshala, a small hill station in the state of Himachal Pradesh in India. As India modernizes, we see all around us an explosion of brick and concrete houses, structures that are as ubiquitous as they are ugly. The evolutionary process by which traditional architecture developed in harmony with its surroundings is being abandoned in favour of a building style that has little or no connection to the land and its environment. This has meant that the skills needed to build traditional structures are dying out as artisanal builders are slowly becoming redundant.

With this in mind, when we needed to build a small house for our cow, we decided to construct it in a completely traditional style so that we would have the opportunity to observe and document the building process. Working with a small team of artisans and using mostly mud, stone, slate and bamboo, materials that were available on site, we filmed the process over three months.

Watching the structure take shape was a fascinating experience. From the beginning, we were taken by the unhurried and meditative quality of the work – the focus of the stonecutters, the making of mud bricks, the measured laying of river stones, the artful splitting of bamboo. There was a sense that man and material were one, that the structure slowly emerging out of the ground was organic and a part of the landscape. We understood how even something as basic and simple as a cow house was imbued with centuries of tradition and wisdom, and began to appreciate the natural aesthetics of a building that is in complete harmony with its surroundings.

It seems crucial to preserve these traditional building practices. But it seems equally clear that if they are to survive, they have to be adapted to a contemporary context. Out of the meeting point between the ancient and the modern, a new architectural style could emerge that takes the best of both worlds and is aesthetically, ecologically and practically relevant.

Ritu Sarin was born in New Delhi in 1959. She studied at Miranda House, Delhi University, and at the California College of the Arts, Oakland. Tenzing Sonam, the son of Tibetan refugees, was born in Darjeeling, India, in 1959. He studied at St. Stephen's College, Delhi University, and specialized in documentary film-making at the Graduate School of Journalism, University of California, Berkeley. The couple lives in New Delhi and Dharamshala, and has been making films on Tibetan subjects for more than 20 years. Together with their film company, White Crane Films, they have documented, questioned and reflected on the issues of exile, cultural identity and political aspiration that confront the Tibetan diaspora.

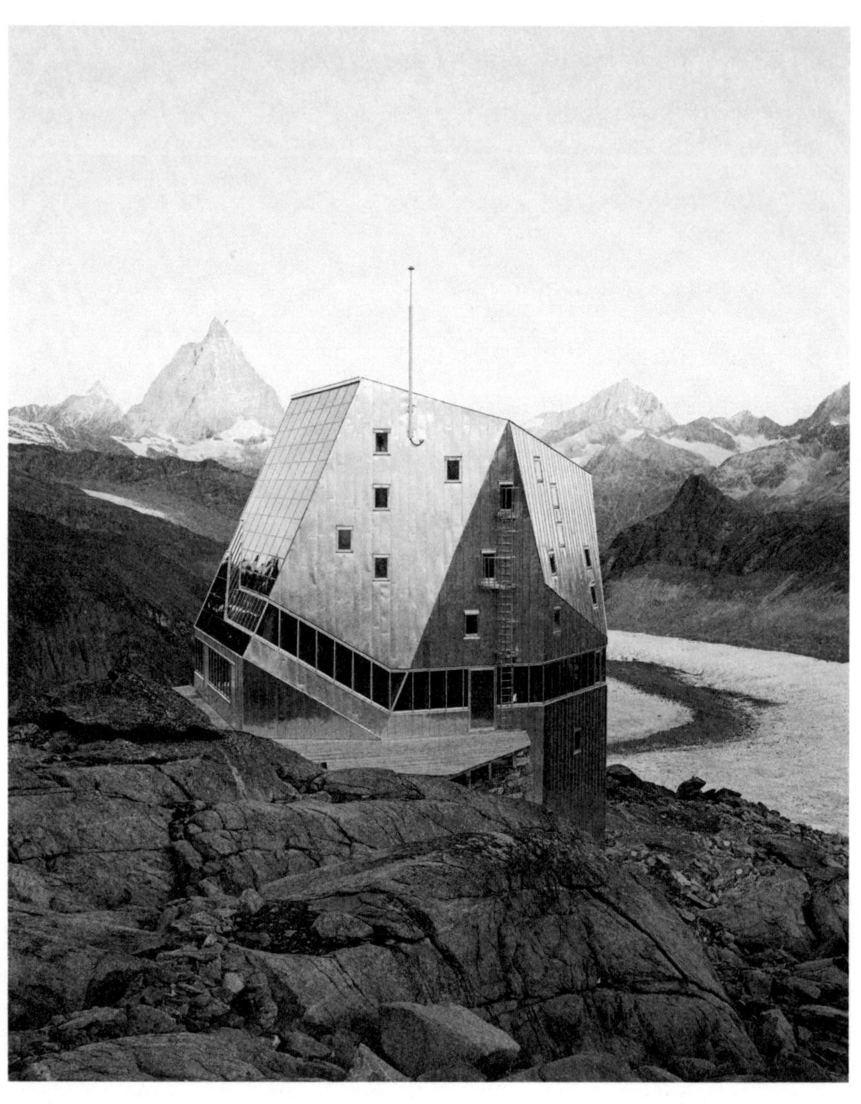

New Monte Rosa Hut SAC (opened: 2009),
view from south-east at dusk

Andrea Deplazes

The New Monte Rosa Hut, Switzerland

I would like to present the Monte Rosa Hut project of 2009 as an example of close collaboration between the Swiss Alpine Club, the Swiss Federal Institute of Technology (ETH), Zurich (in honour of their 150th anniversary), and my architectural office. The Swiss Alpine Club – our building contractor – is a club with a long tradition and the only association that is allowed to build outside so-called building zones (areas in which new buildings are permitted), or in the mountains. At the beginning of the project, I worked with students of the ETH for, let's say, the innovative part with regard to technical issues. In a later phase, I had to carry out the project in my own office because of legal questions such as insurance or guarantees. The aim of the project was to develop a sustainable building that linked architecture, sustainability and modern technology.

The Monte Rosa Hut is one in which hikers and climbers stay overnight. The building site is located at an altitude of 2,883 metres in an extremely remote mountainous area, the Monte Rosa massif. That's where you'll find the highest peak on Swiss territory, the Dufourspitze –or Dufour peak – and if you want to climb this peak, you'll need a "pit stop station", so to speak. Not far away, with an impressive infrastructure, are Zermatt and the famous Matterhorn, which attract many tourists from all over the world. But high in the mountains near the Dufour peak, you're in a completely secluded place: there is snow and a glacier, but nothing else. And this is exactly the site where the hut has been built. In fact, our hut replaced a predecessor. The first building had been a small, traditional timber hut built in 1885, which was upgraded and expanded over time, and finally mantled by a large stone wall. It eventually became too small for the increasing number of visitors able to access it easily from Zermatt: after a ride in the Gornergrat mountain railway, you can walk to the hut more or less horizontally in three to four hours. This also makes it attractive to people who don't intend to climb the Dufour peak.

We started with a research phase at the ETH Zurich. A group of students worked for four semesters on the project, and during this time, the way the project developed was like an evolutionary process. The first challenge was the location and accessibility of the site. The students had to deal with the fact that there is no road leading to the site, and no sewage station, electricity or water there. Furthermore, the Monte Rosa Hut is not a hut in the real sense of the word – not just a very simple building comparable to a bivouac – but a hut with a certain degree of comfort. Although the people who hike up there are looking for the challenge of being alone in the Alps, and of being alone in the wilderness, they still want to lodge somewhere that also provides good food and beverages, and where it is warm. Outside, it can be minus 30 to 40 degrees, but inside they want to feel free to have a fondue and enjoy a glass of wine with friends.

The ETH students had to think about how to bring building materials to the site. At the beginning, some of the students thought that, because the area is rocky, people would be able to collect the stones that were already there. Since the Swiss Alpine Club has roughly 140,000 members, it would have been an interesting experience to take them to the building site and say: Let' s collect the stones and then build this house! However, the Swiss Alpine Club said that would involve too much work and that it was not in the position to force its members to work without pay. And so we analyzed different ways to transport the material to the site. One idea was to use horses. We thought that since Switzerland had an army and mounted units, they would be able to carry the material. But the Swiss cavalry no longer exists, and our only other option was to consider using modern technology. Finally, the material was transported to Zermatt by train and from there by helicopter.

The output of the four semesters was a synthesis of many ideas. It was a project that evolved over time, with the ETH students developing a sense for the most important criteria and parameters that had to be fulfilled. And since one of their tasks was to find sponsors for the project, they always had to bear in mind the budget for the hut and come up with reasonably priced solutions. When we first talked to people about the project and explained it to them, they were, unfortunately, not very enthusiastic about it in general. So we decided to create a visualization, which turned out to be very important, because it suddenly looked much more realistic, even if at that point of the project nothing was really certain and a lot of problems had not been solved yet. Over a period of three years – and parallel to the project as it evolved – we found benefactors and sponsors who made it possible to realize the project.

Let me describe the architecture of the hut, which is very simple. It is basically a dense cluster of rooms. The ideal profile would have been a sphere, but since it is not easy to build spheres, this was not an option. Instead, the students decided to construct plain elements, or rather, they took up the idea of a sphere that had some parts cut out, so that it would look like a glass crystal. Metaphorically speaking, it was cut out in the way an orange is cut, with its internal structures organized radially. This metaphor, this comparison with an orange, allowed us to convey the idea to people who had never ever come in contact with construction issues. The most important architectonic part inside the five-storey wooden building is the staircase. Normally, a staircase would be placed in the middle of a multi-storey building because that enables you to connect as many rooms as possible to the façade and let in as much light as possible. Our plan was very unusual: we decided to use the periphery of the five-storey building for the staircase and to construct it like a cascade, with a ribbon window. As they walk to the top, people turn full circle, which gives them a 360-degree view of the Alps. But the ribbon window – and this is important – also absorbs solar heat: when the sun is shining, a lot of warm air enters the staircase, which goes all the way to the top of the building since air is rising when warm. A ventilation system conducts the warm air into the various rooms to heat them, and then directs the used air down to the technical room. There, the waste heat is recovered by means of a recuperator and is stored in a combi-system reservoir. You could in fact say that the entire building is heated by the staircase.

In the second phase, we had to plan the construction of the hut in minute detail (2008–09). A very complex timber-frame structure with almost no right angle was derived from the initial idea of a sphere. The technical room, the main entrance and the wardrobe are located in the basement. The ground floor houses the restaurant kitchen and – very important – the connection to the terrace outside. And then there are three floors of sleeping rooms, bathrooms, and so on. Since everything had to be transported by helicopter, and keeping transportation costs as low as possible was an imperative, the hut had to be a lightweight construction. We started in the autumn of 2008 with the construction of a foundation that allowed us to fix the hut firmly to the ground. This was important: the hut is so lightweight that a strong wind would otherwise blow it away. We had to anchor it like a tent construction into the rock. With the building site located at an altitude of almost 3,000 metres, an effective heat insulation became extremely important. Whereas the interior is made entirely of wood, the exterior is covered in a thin aluminium shell – a material that doesn't corrode. Although its fabrication as a building material consumes a lot of energy, its maintenance is very easy and almost nothing needs to be done for the next 50 to 60 years. Given the remote location of the building, this was an important issue.

You can compare the Monte Rosa Hut to a car with all the designed parts of the car body and the coordinated and synchronized engine. The hut is like a closed system fulfilling several needs, such as heating, electricity, water supply and wastewater treatment. Software developed by the ETH controls the technology of the building and makes possible an optimal management of energy and waste flows in the building. The south façade includes a photovoltaic system that generates its own power. Solar collectors installed in the grounds on rocks and facing south-west generate solar heat, which provides very hot water that can be stored in a combi-system reservoir and later used in the kitchen, the showers and the washing rooms. When the ice melts in summer, the water is collected and stored in a cavern. There is an internal wastewater cleaning station with a micro-filtering system that bacteriologically cleans the wastewater. The greywater is then reused to flush the toilets. The interplay of the individual components and an elaborate energy system enable the hut to achieve a self-sufficiency level of 90 per cent.

Since the opening of the Monte Rosa Hut in September 2009, many more visitors have wanted to stay than we expected. The success was overwhelming, and the hut, which was designed to accommodate single overnight stays for around 6,500 people a year, was visited by more than 10,000 people. The building services were overloaded and some of them had to be expanded. For example, the system required support from the block-type thermal power station more often than was initially expected in order to deal with extraordinary peak situations when the hut was fully booked and the weather was bad at the same time.

This project is a good example of how architects are more and more confronted and have to work with state-of-the-art technology. But how important is traditional knowledge within this development? Architecture has to deal with climatic conditions, with locations, with contexts and with gravity. Although gravity is more or less equal all over the world, climatic conditions vary enormously and account for the many typologies in architecture. I would say that the tendency to introduce the latest technology into architecture in the 20th century brings with it the danger of becoming disconnected from traditional knowledge. When I look at buildings in desert areas, I see people who protect themselves from the heat with great skill just by using shade, cooling the air with natural air ventilation, and so on. They don't use any technical devices. What is interesting in architecture is that it always depends on cultural and climatic influences. It is sometimes possible to use low-tech solutions, but occasionally there is no alternative to using high-tech components. If you have climatic conditions that demand the latest technology – as in the Monte Rosa Hut – I find it important to be part of the whole complex. It is not enough just to be the designer of the building that is then filled with technical devices. But let's not forget that – despite the fact that there are a lot of technical issues to be solved – the hut is basically still a normal building, such as a donjon or a watchtower. It's a very traditional tower in a remote landscape that I as an architect have constructed, with small windows where the sleeping rooms are.

Andrea Deplazes (b. 1960 in Chur/Switzerland) studied architecture at the Swiss Federal Institute of Technology (ETH), Zurich, and completed his studies in 1988. In the same year, he and Valentin Bearth founded the architectural studio Bearth & Deplazes Architekten AG, Chur and Zurich, which they now run with Daniel Ladner. He has been professor of architecture and construction at the ETH Zurich since 1997, and served as dean of the faculty from 2005 to 2007. His most famous project is the Monte Rosa Hut (built in 2009). He lives and works in Chur and Zurich.

THE METAPHOR PROBLEM

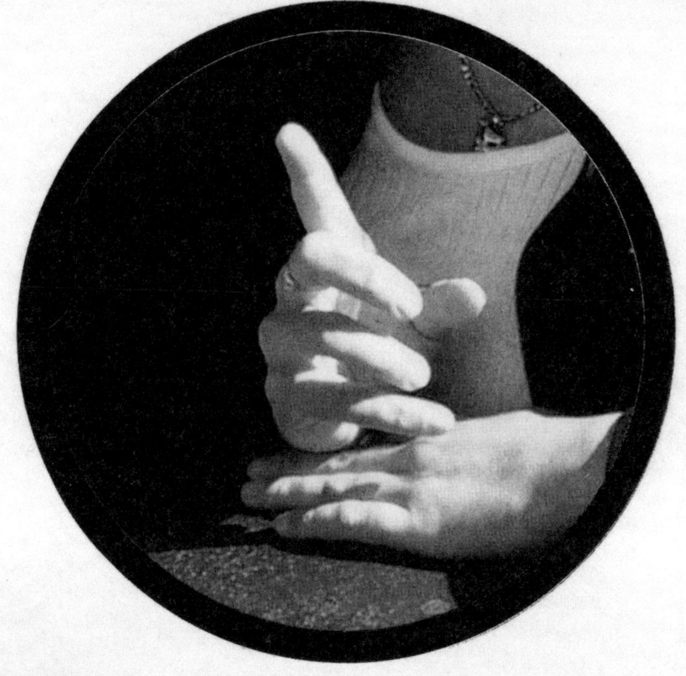

AGAIN

The Metaphor Problem (1999)
Book cover

Lawrence Weiner

COLLABORATION

AS

METAPHOR

I was asked to speak, and I have affection for this situation. I have affection for the people who made it all possible here. And I also had a successful use of the space in Zuoz when I came to work together with John Baldessari on a book Cristina Bechtler suggested. The title would be *THE METAPHOR PROBLEM AGAIN.* John and I had decided that it was time for us to make a work together; we had been close friends. We put a whole load of computers in a car in Zurich, drove through a snowstorm over the saddle and got to Zuoz. John is known for pictures, but he is very involved in the meaning of words and in words. And I think I am known for materials, but people seem to think that I am known for language, because I present them in language. So we decided that I would do the pictures, since I knew how to do that: I made movies, and John would do the language, since he knew how to do that: he could read and write. We used the hotel in Zuoz and worked with the employees. We were able to build the book around the idea of metaphor.

But also before that project, I have had a history of being able to work with other people because I have started to make certain kind of movies and music and things when I was younger. By then, I began to think: Was this a collaboration? I also had the pleasure of working with Baldessari, and with Kathryn Bigelow among others. Baldessari, Sarmento and myself did something with video and showed it in Portugal and in Miami … But this is still not a collaboration.

Maybe the word itself is what we should be talking about. “Collaboration” sounds so wonderful, it sounds appealing to everybody who has been in the ivory tower, stuck alone in a studio, or stuck in research for doing something: I would like to collaborate. Why then is “collaboration” in all four of the major European languages a dirty word? All of us have grown up with the word: *Kollaboration, collaborazionismo, collaboration*. There is a reason: collaboration is not the point. Being able to understand, what a melody line is, being able to understand what the point is – that is the point. When you collaborate, you come together to build something and place and show it in the world, an aspect that has not yet been shown. If you begin to collaborate you have already begun to compromise. The first compromise is with the dominant culture. I have really no idea why you have decided to make art. If you have decided to do mathematics or science, the dominant culture sucks. There is something wrong with it. You are not happy with the dominant culture. You are going to make something, place it in the world that makes it impossible for that dominant culture to be dominant any longer.

Collaboration is essentially when one person or more people bend to whatever is in power at the moment. That is essentially why the word has been used in times when the dominant culture was not the right thing; from Hitler to Mussolini to other things. Therefore, "collaboration" became a bad word. But in any other situation, if you are living in the Swiss Alps and the Romans were coming through, if you then accepted their culture as the dominant one – not to take sewage and plumbing as something to use – but to accept their culture, you would be a collaborator.

Everybody then looks at you and says: Lawrence, that is all very nice, intellectually and that is a very nice polito-aesthetics. Politics and aesthetics mixing together – that is all fine. No, it is not! Jazz is a collaboration. No, it is not! Jazz is not a collaboration. The acceptance of a common melody line – it is a fact that we all have to eat, sleep, defecate and do all the other things that our body tells us, and that is a melody line. Jazz is when two people, or three people, or five people, or twenty people have a reality that is simultaneous. And it is about the thing that has been troubling me for years, to the terms that we live in an Aristotelian sense. We think that a parallel existence means something. In fact, it is against everything we really would like to believe in. Parallel existence means that you have an immediate hierarchy. One thing is a reference to another. It is a shadow reference. It is a light reference. It is the problem that we have with most our major European languages. I showed a movie in Basel about that called *DIRTY EYES* (2010) and it is the people who mean well, in order to express themselves to the audience. If they want to speak French, German, Italian, etc., they have to wake up every morning and convince themselves, that "a shovel", *la pala* in Italian, is a girl. Once they have convinced themselves that "a shovel" is a girl they start to build and construct the most well-meaning propositions, concerning the relationships of human beings, male or female, this and that, political structures – but they change the grammar. Why is "a shovel" a girl? That is a collaboration with a dominant cultural structure. In the German language it is absolutely insane. It is not even a collaboration with an academy, it is a collaboration with a company that prints dictionaries. Or even with the new revision in German from 1977 that is still accredited by Duden.

And we are sitting here now; all of us have come together here. We have all come distances and map mountains. I have lung problems, so when I come to a mountain it is because I really like the people that I am coming for. Why are we accepting all of this? Collaboration is the whole major point of this. We have to understand that we are all living at exactly the same time, at exactly the same place and we are not spirals. We are concentric circles, one after the other. Every single thing is in the middle of the middle of the middle of the middle of ... And if it is not there we are nowhere, living in some dream world, living in a "Mutti-Vati culture". Looking at things during the conference was rather exciting. To watch people who were able to understand the building of a structure, and then to see what happens in the 21st century, when structures don't look the same any longer. They don't have to. That is because everything is a compromise, and everything is an essential collaboration. Our grandparents did this, our parents did this. Preset this, this one said that. Maybe if we did not listen to anybody for five minutes every day we could come up with an idea of what we have come together. And having said that: Why do people choose to work together? How do people choose to work together? I have been a very lucky artist and have been able to work with other people. I don't know how other people do it and can only think in my own terms.

One of the first rules is: Do not ever work with anybody who is not ambitious. There is a metaphor involved in this. If you are working, do not even hire anybody to help in the studio that is not ambitious. And it is not for you to question what the ambition is. If they do not want to break out of the role, the last thing you want to do is to be working with them, because it is always about having a compromise – because they have feelings.

The other problem is that the term "collaboration" carries with it an acceptance of an existing fact but a dominant code. I have recently had to retranslate certain things, because somebody is doing a book about my relationship with the German language. And my theory was to raise the German language to its own dignity so that it did not need a gender, that a stone was a stone. That it was a word. That a word in any language has a meaning, it could be Tibetan, it could be any other language you want, but the word itself has a meaning. It does not necessarily have a metaphor. This sounds a little bit odd, but in fact it is how you get through your life.

We are privileged people, and we are entrusted with showing something – not telling, but showing things in space. And we have means of doing it: we have platforms, we have stages, we have what we call galleries, we have spaces, we have performances, we even have legal rights to make performances in public and put things out in the world. We have an obligation then not to collaborate. We have an obligation to be honest, to genuinely never adapt one's work because of local feelings.

If you do not want to accept that, than you should have done every single thing your grandmother or your mother told you. Everything. Because that is what we do when we move from one culture to another: we want to be decent people, so that we will bend to something that in fact means nothing, and we will put it into a context. And we won't do this, we won't put Hebrew or Arabic on the ground. They are modern languages, I don't see why not. We won't do this, we won't do that. And then you know what happens? The minute we do it, nothing happens. The world does not come to an end. Some people will stand there and say: "My grandmother is upset." Ok, sorry, the work that artists make in fact very often does upset people's grandmothers, mothers, fathers and themselves. That is the problem with metaphor.

We live as if we understand other people's metaphors, but in fact we don't. What we understand are other people's rules, other people's codes, and maybe we are doing something that has nothing to do with this. Collaboration also implies that you will bend and accept whoever is in power at the time. You will do something that they can accept. And you are usually quite proud, and you say: "Well, I went in and I talked to them and you know, the mayor looked at me, and I made a joke. He likes football and I like football. We talked about this and we talked about that. And well, we will make it yellow instead of green." For me, it does not much matter, the yellow and the green, because I do not accept the metaphor of colours. But that immediately tells you the story. That is the anecdote. There is no other anecdote. And there is no metaphor for doing the right thing.

There is a joke in New York amongst people of my generation who are involved in what is now called civil rights and in my generation was pure common sense about the rights of certain people: that you are never supposed to be rewarded for doing the right thing, but that you should be punished for doing the wrong thing dead sure. And I think art is about those things.

But let me come back to the book *THE METAPHOR PROBLEM AGAIN* I was speaking about at the beginning. There is a first photograph focusing on a pair of hands referring to Renaissance paintings. Literally, I had simply asked a girl to put her hands that way, and when asking her if she knew what it meant she knew it – but it was different from what I knew it meant. After the photograph was taken, I asked several people what the pair of hands meant to them and it had twenty-five different meanings. It was then that I realized that we live in a world where we are convinced we understand the metaphors of things. And we think very often that our intentions are good, and everyone will understand them, which is not true. I think all of this stuff is like taking for granted and just do it. And not worry so much about what the metaphor is.

For the next documenta, there is a series of booklets in preparation by Carolyn Christov-Bakargiev and Bettina Funcke called *100 NOTES – 100 THOUGHTS*, for which I contributed a book called "If In Fact There Is a Context." One of the reasons that I haven chosen language and made art eventually was that you could then have it translated into any language, because at the end my work is all material relationships to each other. And a stone is a stone is a stone. And a piece of wood is the same piece of wood. It looks differently, that is the only problem. You mill it in Switzerland, you mill it in Scandinavia, Italy, Japan, Tibet, any place – it looks differently. In fact it floats in the water, with one exception of wood – the so-called ironwood – that sinks to the bottom. But essentially all wood floats. If I could translate what it was into language then it would take away the two big problems in art: that everybody knows what a piece of wood looks like, but it does not look like what everybody else thinks it looks like, because it is in another place. My work could then move across boundaries without being exotic. It would take away this idea that the artist got it right. When you are talking about two pieces of stone, or about a piece of stone and a piece of wood there is no right and there is no wrong. Every work I have ever done could be built. But in fact, once I will have built it, it is very hard in our culture and in most cultures to say that it is just the way it could be and not the way it should be. There is a big problem that nobody likes to substitute the "c" for the "s". I guess the "s" has a real precedence.

If art is supposed to be showing people what their position in the world can be, how – if they wake up in the morning – can artists relate themselves to the value structures around them and have some sense of dignity? And the word is dignity. If you don't do something, because then a gallery owner would not like your work or a museum curator would tell you to do something, then you really had to change your job. We are lucky right now. We have hundreds, thousand of artists who have attended a school and want to be artists. This is maybe a time when art really can change the world. There is a group all over the world of reasonably educated people who can communicate with each other. This is a time now to start pushing this collaboration crab out of the way. This is a time to say that we don't know the metaphor. All we know is what is put onto the table sits on the table, and that each reality has its own dignity. It is a concentric circle, and we can go back into history for that. That major question is: How many angels can dance on a pinhead? The point is with quantum mechanics. And the nicest thing is: there is no quantum mathematics. It does not work. With quantum mechanics, as sculptors, as artists it is infinite what can dance on a pinhead, as long as they are concentric. The pinhead is infinite. That is the answer. And that is what I try to do with the book.

I was a lot in the mountains. In my youth I was very much involved with extremes. I remember once climbing up the glacier near Bodø to build a piece for Jack Wendler, the art gallery owner who cofounded the fine arts journal *Art Monthly*. He raised the money, got me on a plane and flew me to Bodø, which is in Norway not far from Saltstraumen, the world's most powerful maelstrom. And there is a glacier that leads over into Sweden. I decided I would vandalize a glacier for Lucy Lippard, which is a piece that she owned and I would just go across the glacier. Yes, I have been in the mountains a lot. I am fascinated by it. In my later stage of my continuing youth, my lungs went down and I have a great trouble in the altitude. So, I don't do it much anymore. But when I am in there … I just came from Aspen, where I am fascinated as well by the same thing: the mountains. And the mountains here are very pretty. You realize it when you are standing outside. It is just gorgeous. And I like the fact that in any given moment it changes – just like that. And that is what art is about. Art is about doing something that any given moment changes, because it does not have any rules.

Lawrence Weiner (b. 1942 in the Bronx, New York City) lives and works in New York and Amsterdam. He is one of the primary figures associated with the emergence of conceptual art in the 1960s. He studied literature and philosophy at Hunter College for less than a year before hitchhiking across the country and doing different jobs, mostly around seaports. He has defined art as a representation of relationships in the physical world and considers language to be his primary material. His work is often manifested outside the gallery context.

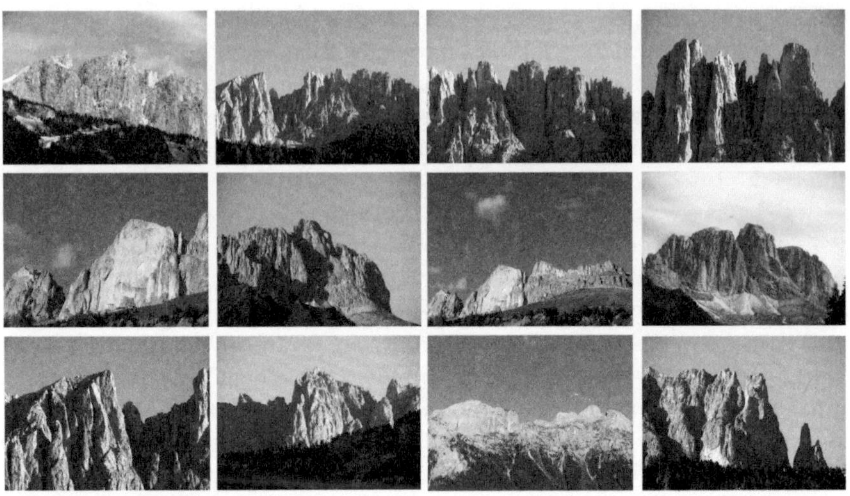

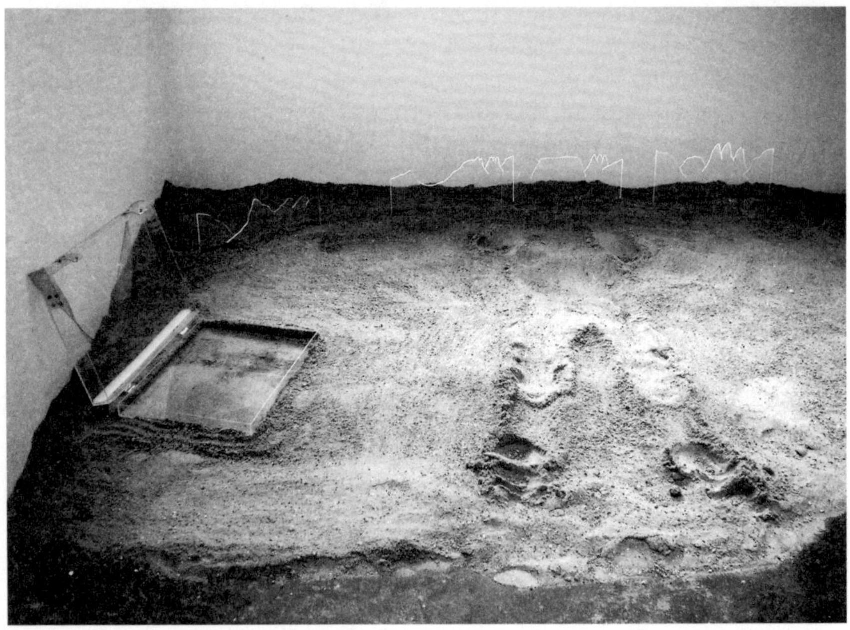

Gianni Pettena, *La mia scuola d'architettura* (2011)/*Paesaggi della memoria* (1986), Castello Aragonese, Otranto

Gianni Pettena

On Architecture

I had never faced my work as an artist, or as an architect, in relation to mountains until I got the invitation to this convention. It was an occasion for me to start a kind of a therapy, which is still going on. I had never thought that my work had any references to my origins, the Dolomites. The Dolomites are the mountains where I started to hike and climb in my teens, and after my teens, I begun to swim in the mountain lakes. Maybe my work is a continuous reaction to the power of those mountains. Actually, they have – consciously or not – always been monuments for me, always a kind of abstract architecture. From an architectural point of view, the scale of the mountains has always been challenging to me. This is why I had to hike and to climb them. I always wanted to reach the peak and look around from there.

The fact that I studied architecture was somehow related to my fatherbeing a philosopher and writer: I wanted to do something complementary. I wanted to learn a visual language and to communicate through it. So I decided to study architecture, which was not always easy for me, but I was a "bravo bambino" who tried to finish his studies and who eventually got his diploma. Already in the second year of architecture, I had become friends with people from the art world. I was living in Florence and driving my Fiat 500 up to Turin, to visit Gian Enzo Sperone's gallery, then to Milan to the Galleria Franco Toselli, and to Rome to Fabio Sargentini's gallery L'attico. And in my studio there were always magazines about art and architecture. Unfortunately, I absolutely did not like the kind of architecture I was taught at university school. The idea of architecture I had in mind was comparable to the idea of a girl I loved and adored. It would have to be a language through which I could communicate. Instead, the architecture they were teaching you at university was supposed to be a machine. Nobody was telling you how to communicate with that visual language, but everybody was telling you how to put together a structure, how to connect different floors, and how to make a structure that hosted practical functions. In Florence, I admired the drawings of Antonio Sant'Elia, which were incredibly influential in the history of architecture, by the way. The projects he sketched were never realized, and for this reason, such an approach would not be of interest at the university. Even today you find architecture magazines that publish only architecture that has been built or that has been shaped and drawn in a way that makes it possible to build it. An experimental architecture that speaks about concepts, that refuses the so-called duty to accomplish practical functions, structures, even an investment of capital and a return on investment, is never published. Little by little, my architecture was becoming more and more something handmade or rather experimental and not necessarily bound to be built.

A year and a half after my graduation as an architect, I was invited as an artist in residence to the United States for the first time. Being a European means that you never have – metaphorically speaking – a blank sheet of paper, you are always dealing with the heavy presence of the past. Thus, you have constantly to deal with the context, and to find layers of traces of previous interventions. In principle, this was fine for me. Still, there was always a desire to find a blank sheet of paper, which is why I became interested in deserts. If you are raised as a European architect, you believe that deserts might be the blank sheet of paper you are looking for, but in fact they are not. First of all, deserts are not dead. And secondly, they are the architectures of the nomads. The Navajo people, for example, use Monument Valley as a place to maintain their traditions and perform ceremonies. The villages are somewhere else. Only hogans are built in the valley itself, and they are made by hand. They consist of tree trunks covered with clay and earth. The most basic conceptual level of making architecture can therefore be discovered in nature, precisely because you do not need to build a screen between you and the context. If you are a nomad, you are part of that context just as much as any other animal that stays only seasonally in an area and therefore has to adapt quickly to climate changes and a lack of water – or, more generally speaking, to a change in context.

As soon as you transform your nomadic situation into a settled one, then you start to build a screen between you and the context. You begin to be detached from the context. Nature and you become interrelated insofar as nature is contingent on your cultivations, and the change of nature influences in turn the way people and animals live. In the 1950s and 1960s, the hippies were somehow imitating nomadic people, while at the same time referring to Buckminster Fuller. They started to erect buildings that were very similar to the hogans of the Navajo people. By doing so, they were trying to go back in time to find ancestors who were not considered to have converted the planet into a rubbish dump or wasteland. They were looking for ancestors who were environmentally aware and would follow a nomadic approach to context. I travelled to the south-west and visited many handmade houses by those hippies and spent a lot of time with them. Their houses had nothing to do with the tradition of architecture built by trained architects. For me, it was the first time in the 20th century that people – very often people educated in the visual arts – were not using architects to build their own homes, but were building the houses by themselves instead. At the same time, many of the visual artists I met disapproved of architects, because, for example, they thought that architects were banalizing the relation of people to the urban context. Architects were not accepted in the art world as far as I remember. Maybe I was accepted. I had an exhibition at the John Weber Gallery at 420 West Broadway, New York, as early as 1972. Furthermore, I was a close friend of Robert Smithson and we had many conversations about our self-concept. He was educated as an artist, whereas I had been educated as an architect in Europe, but I was very much interested in the field between architecture and art. We discovered that we were taking the same direction in spite of the differences. Some of the land artists, like Smithson, were in my view inventing a new approach to the context. They were inventing a new path in the history of architecture. In fact, the visual artists who faced architectural problems in scale and in concepts were the most interesting contributors to the field of architecture. There is no architect I can recall, except perhaps Peter Zumthor later on, who followed this specific approach and digested the languages these artists were suggesting. The land artists were not burdened with the whole history of architecture, but were just very spontaneously dealing with the context and making quotations, notations and metaphors. From my perspective, one of the reasons for the development of land art is that the artists were living in megalopolises like Los Angeles or New York and needed to reinvent an alphabet to enable them to deal with an urban context. For this purpose, they developed their tools and went to the deserts. The only artist who did anything with regard to context in towns was Allan Kaprow, who somehow dealt with the context of the outside and the inside.

Interestingly, Smithson thought of himself as the legitimate successor to the landscape architect Frederick Law Olmsted, who had co-designed Central Park. I did not know much about Olmsted until Smithson – I think it was in the early 1970s – took me on a walk in Central Park. He had just written an article on Olmsted for *Artforum*[1] – one of a number of really beautiful articles. He was sort of constantly publishing in *Artforum* in those two or three years. Thirty years after my walk with Smithson in Central Park, I had the chance to show original presentation drawings of Olmsted, from Central Park to Prospect Park,[2] at the Galleria degli Uffizi in Florence and to publish a book about his work. Having somehow invented the public park within an urban context, he was also the inventor of the concept of the natural park.

Coming back to the topic of mountains, I must admit that I have unrealized and realized projects, but strangely enough not in a context dealing with my background. The Dolomites, where I grew up, were never a context for a work of mine. Except for one piece I made for an exhibition around 20 years ago in Otranto, a city in southern Italy. Since I was born in Bolzano, not far from the border with Austria, I thought at the time that I had better be prepared when the time came for me to go to the other side of Italy. I brought with me a suitcase containing cut-outs of the mountains of my childhood that I had made by memory, just as I remembered them. In Otranto, I put the plexiglass cut-outs on a floor covered with sand and I lay down to contemplate them *(Landscapes of Memory,* Castello Aragonese, Otranto, 1987). This is the only work that is directly related to the Alpine context. But somehow, consciously or not – very often unconsciously – I discovered, thanks to your invitation, that many of my works have to do with memory. They somehow express the will to confront myself even with the scale of the mountains where I was raised. The scale of the mountains is a scale you cannot confront. You will always lose thiskind of confrontation, not only because of the dimensions, naturally, but also because what nature builds as buildings is something you cannot challenge. Nature will always win.

1 Robert Smithson, "Frederick Law Olmsted and the Dialectical Landscape", in: *Artforum* 62 (February 1973).
2 Gianni Pettena and Frederick Law Olmsted, *L'origine del parco urbano e del parco naturale contemporaneo,* Florence: Centro DI 1996.

Gianni Pettena (b. 1940 in Bolzano/Italy) studied architecture in Florence and has been involved in the study and practice of experimental architectural activity since the late 1960s. Together with Archizoom, Superstudio and UFO, he was one of the founders of the Architettura Radicale movement in Italy. He has lectured in the USA and in Europe, has worked as a critic, and has written books on the expanded idea of architecture. He is professor of history of contemporary art and architecture at the University of Florence, where he lives. Pettena has exhibited his work at the Venice Biennale, the Barbican Centre in London, the Mori Museum in Tokyo, the Centre Pompidou in Paris and Metz, the Secession in Vienna, and the Frac Centre in Orleans. His works are found at the Centre Pompidou, the Frac Centre and in many other public and private collections.

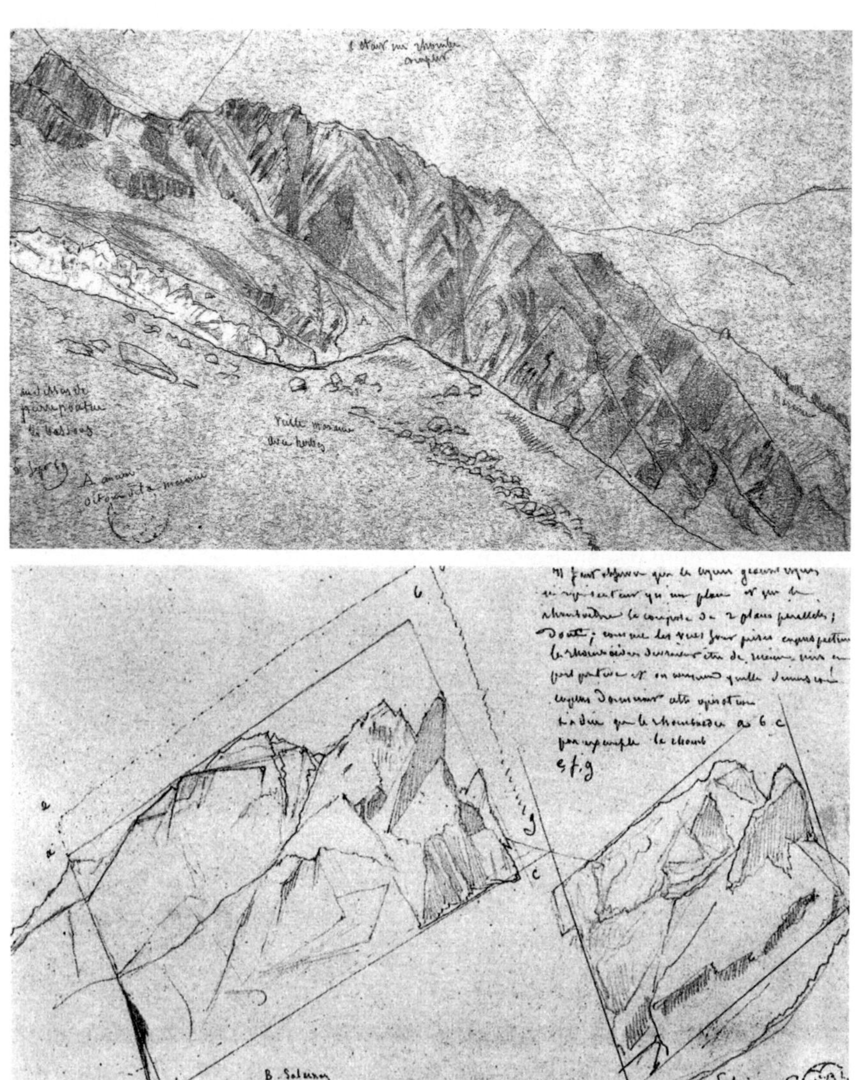

Fig. 1: Pierre A. Frey & Lise Grenier (eds.), *Viollet-le-Duc et la Montagne*, Grenoble: Glénat, 1993, p. 30
Fig. 2: Viollet-le-Duc, *Rhomboèdres, sommets, structure ancienne reconstituée* (n.d.)
Pencil, 15.5 × 23.9 cm

Jan von Brevern

Mountains as Ruins, or: How to Reconstruct the History of the Alps with Drawings

In the summer of 1875, the Mont Blanc area was the destination of the French Geological Society's yearly trip. The regular members of the *Société Géologique* were accompanied by an unusual guest: the architect and historian Eugène Emmanuel Viollet-le-Duc, famous for his spectacular restorations of Gothic monuments, among them Notre-Dame in Paris. One of the highlights of the trip was an excursion to a medium peak just west of Chamonix, which offered a particularly impressive view of the Mont Blanc chain and its glaciers. "M. Viollet-le-Duc had the kindness to explain Mont Blanc to us," Alphonse Favre, president of the *Société Géologique de France*, later wrote in his report. "There is, according to this scholar, a close relation between certain parts of geology and architecture; Mont Blanc is a ruin; one can retrieve its original form by following the same principles that are used in the restoration of a monument."[1]

Having an architect explain Mont Blanc to them probably didn't happen very often to the geologists. On the other hand, it seems that they were interested in *any* new idea on the building principles of mountains. By the second half of the 19th century, geology found itself in a crisis. A unifying theory on orogenesis – the process of how mountains are formed – was still nowhere in sight. Geologists were desperately looking for local or global patterns in the distribution of mountain chains. Where did the forces originate that were able to lift up huge masses of rocks such as the Alps? "Wie seid ihr Berge und Thäler entstanden?" – *How did your mountains and valleys come into being?* – the prominent Swiss geologist Albert Heim asked in 1881.[2] This was *the* big question in geology – more or less unsolved, one might add, until a century later, when the theory of plate tectonics was finally accepted in the 1960s.[3]

Viollet-le-Duc's approach to geology points to a methodical problem that geologists where confronted with in the mid-19th century. In short, the problem could be put as follows: geology was an empirical science that drew much of its reputation from the following: geologists travelling around with their hammers, identifying minerals, strata and fossils, taking samples, making observations. Likewise, it was clear that these empirical studies had to lead to theories about the history of the earth. But during the 19th century, there seemed to be an unbridgeable gap between observation and theory: how could one, for example, find out something about the history of Mont Blanc by simply *observing it*? Wouldn't one just scratch the surface of a phenomenon that was mostly subterraneous, and maybe much larger than one could overlook?[4]

But as the geology historian Martin Rudwick has pointed out, there was a solution to this problem: it was called *images*. The establishment of the geological sciences was very closely connected to the development of a visual language.[5] With sections for example, scientists could virtually *look into* the mountains, incorporating their empirical findings and trying to generalize them. Views, maps and sections were, as Rudwick pointed out, *thought experiments* – very speculative more often than not, but absolutely necessary for a science that had only very limited access to its object, the earth's crust.

Viollet-le-Duc, to come back to him, made use of images in his geological studies as probably no one before him. As an architect, he was very familiar with the use of plans and sections. As you all know, floor plans were used by architects very early on. A drawing by Villard de Honnecourt from the 13th century shows a section through the walls of the Laon Cathedral *and* a projection of its roof structure. An image like this is a highly theoretical construct – it gives you an understanding of a building that would otherwise be impossible. This is what you could call the "epistemic power" of images: they sometimes make something visible, bring elements together, or reveal a structure that would otherwise stay unnoticed.[6]

Viollet-le-Duc's whole approach to Mont Blanc was rooted in a deep trust in the epistemic power of images – and especially of drawings. Between 1868 and 1875, Viollet-le-Duc travelled every summer to Chamonix and made hundreds of drawings in the area. With them, he believed he could actually enter into the history of Mont Blanc.[7]

So what did Viollet-le-Duc mean by "restoring the original form of mountains"? One of his drawings represents of a part of the Les Bossons glacier, and there is a small patch of ice visible on the left (see figure 1). But Viollet-le-Duc is more interested in the rock formation in the background. At first sight, this seems to be a pretty straightforward depiction of the rocks, but when one looks closer, one can identify at least two specifics. To the lower right side, the rocks follow a strangely regular pattern, as if consisting of perfect rhombuses. And above the rock formation, there are two faint pencil lines, forming a triangle with its top outside the image. There is also a small note: "C'était un rhombe complet" – *this was an entire rhombus*.

What do this pattern and this note mean? Viollet-le-Duc takes the analogy of architecture and geology very seriously. He looks at mountains in the same way as he looks at buildings. And he is convinced that mountains, like buildings, must have an inner regular structure. He supposes that during the time when the earth cooled down, its outer crust must have crystallized into geometric forms, just like the basaltic formations that could be found, for example, at the Giant's Causeway in Ireland. A very popular analogy to what happened to the earth's crust as it cooled down was that of a shrinking apple with its wrinkled skin.

Viollet-le-Duc's other hypothesis is, very much in conformity with the geological theories of his time, that over the many million years of their existence, mountains were worn down by atmospheric and glacial influences. Therefore, he is convinced that they must once have been much bigger, that they are now, as he puts it, "ruins" of their former selves. One of his illustrations shows this ideal process of ruination in four steps, from a pretty regular and smooth form on top to their present appearance on the bottom. In another illustration, a section, he superimposes the present form of a mountain with a rhombic pattern, showing its supposed original size and inner structure.

These are general illustrations, explaining the principle, but not depicting any actual mountain. But if it became possible to see the rhombic structures on real mountains, Viollet-le-Duc would be able to reconstruct their former appearance. This is where a drawing as a powerful research instrument comes in. In his drawings, Viollet-le-Duc tries to identify geometric patterns, and uses the outlines of mountains as a starting point for lines that represent their supposed original outlines. The "entire rhombus" is supposed to show what these rocks once looked like. This is one of the advantages of a drawing: you can include things that *are* there and things that you believe *were* there on the same piece of paper. It makes not only spatial dimensions visible, but also temporal ones. For Viollet-le-Duc, a drawing becomes something that allows a view into the past of the Alps.

The main problem for Viollet-le-Duc, though, is to actually *see* those rhombic rock structures. It is, no wonder, very hard to identify them with the naked eye. At one point, he makes the telling statement that the rock's "general structure is very hard to recognize close at hand", but at the same time "can be only imperfectly seen at a distance". So there is basically *no* point of view from which the structures are visible. To overcome this problem, he makes use of a very peculiar instrument, the so-called *téléiconographe*, which he describes in a small passage in his book on Mont Blanc, published in 1876:

"One of my confrères, M. Révoil, conceived the idea a few years ago of applying the prism of the camera lucida to the telescope, to effect the drawing of general views at long distance and to a large scale."[8] This combination of camera lucida, a much-used drawing instrument during the 19th century, telescope and drawing table is crucial for Viollet-le-Duc's project.[9] The *téléiconographe* is needed, not so much to improve his sight, but to alter it – and to connect eye, hand and mind. With its help, he identifies the geometric patterns and the former outlines of the mountains in the Mont Blanc massif. In a way, he seems to be able to look into the past of the mountains through the instrument – as if he were a astronomer, looking into the past life of stars with his telescope.

This is very obvious in a small drawing that was probably made around 1870 (see figure 2). Again, he identifies a rhombic structure, and again he uses the outlines he can see as starting points for his pencil lines showing the former extension of these mountains. Drawing and seeing are very closely connected here. The *téléiconographe* produces a kind of "feedback": it allows Viollet-le-Duc to draw the outlines and to look at the mountain at the same time – so that after a while, he really does *see* the rhombic structures. In another drawing, his project of reconstructing the Mont Blanc massif becomes even clearer. On top of this sheet, Viollet-le-Duc wrote an explanation: "the white indicates the ancient glacier, the blue the present glaciers; the red the present summits, ruins of the ancient ones."

Mountains as ruins – that is a powerful metaphor, allowing new ways of thinking and seeing.[10] To look at Mont Blanc as a ruin and to look at it in the usual way are two completely different things. Everything there becomes a trace of its former being. The red outlines and the blue (or violet) patches are what everybody would have seen – everything else is a product of this metaphor, of the *téléiconographe* and of the drawing process. As Viollet-le-Duc once wrote, drawing is the only way to properly learn seeing – and seeing is knowing. In French, this sounds even better: "Voir, c'est savoir."[11]

1 Favre, Alphonse, "Réunion extraordinaire", in: *Bulletin de la Société Géologique de France* 3 (1875), pp. 145–46.
2 Heim, Albert, *Die Gebirge*, Basel: Schweighauserische Verlagsbuchhandlung, 1881, p. 3.
3 See Oldroyd, David Roger, *Thinking about the earth. A history of ideas in geology*, London: Athlone 1996.
4 On the historical problem of observation, see Fiorentini, Erna (ed.), *Observing nature – representing experience. The osmotic dynamics of Romanticism, 1800-1850*, Berlin: Reimer 2007.
5 Rudwick, Martin J. S., "The Emergence of a Visual Language for Geological Science 1760–1840", in: *History of Science* 14, no. 23 (1976), pp. 149–95.
6 There is a great deal of literature on this question; see, for example, Bettina Heintz and Jörg Huber (eds.), *Mit dem Auge denken. Strategien der Sichtbarmachung in wissenschaftlichen und virtuellen Welten*, Zurich: Edition Voldemeer 2001; Kelley Wilder, *Photography and Science*, London: Reaktion Books 2009.

7 See the catalogues by Pierre A. Frey (ed.), *Viollet-le-Duc et le massif du Mont-Blanc 1868-1879*, Lausanne: Payot 1988; Pierre A. Frey and Lise Grenier (eds.), *Viollet-le-Duc et la Montagne*, Grenoble: Glénat 1993. See also André Corboz, "Schlussfolgerungen aus der Geologie: Von Viollet-le-Duc bis Bruno Taut", in: *Die Kunst, Stadt und Land zum Sprechen zu bringen*, ed. André Corboz, Basel: Birkhäuser 2001, pp. 201–18.

8 Viollet-le-Duc, Eugène Emmanuel, *Mont Blanc. A treatise on its geodesical and geological constitution, its transformations; and the ancient and recent state of its glaciers*. Translated by Benjamin Bucknall, London 1877, p. 8.

9 See Young Lee, Paula. "'The rational point of view': Eugène Emmanuel Viollet-le-Duc and the *camera lucida*", in: *Landscapes of memory and experience*, ed. Jan Birksted, London: Spon Press 2000, pp. 63–76.

10 This metaphor has its own history; see Gordon Leslie Davies, *The Earth in Decay. A History of British Geomorphology 1578-1878*, London 1969.

11 Viollet-le-Duc, Eugène Emmanuel, *Histoire d'un dessinateur. Comment on apprend à dessiner*, Paris: Hetzel 1879, p. 302.

Jan von Brevern (b. 1975) studied art history, philosophy and Italian literature in Hamburg, Naples and Berlin. He was an assistant at the Swiss Federal Institute of Technology (ETH), Zurich, where he wrote his PhD: "Blicke von Nirgendwo. Geologie in Bildern bei Ruskin, Viollet-le-Duc und Civiale" (Fink 2012). He specializes in the history of photography and the cultural history of nature. Since 2010, he has been teaching at the Kunsthistorisches Institut, Freie Universität Berlin, and was a scholar at the Getty Research Institute in Los Angeles from 2012 to 2013.

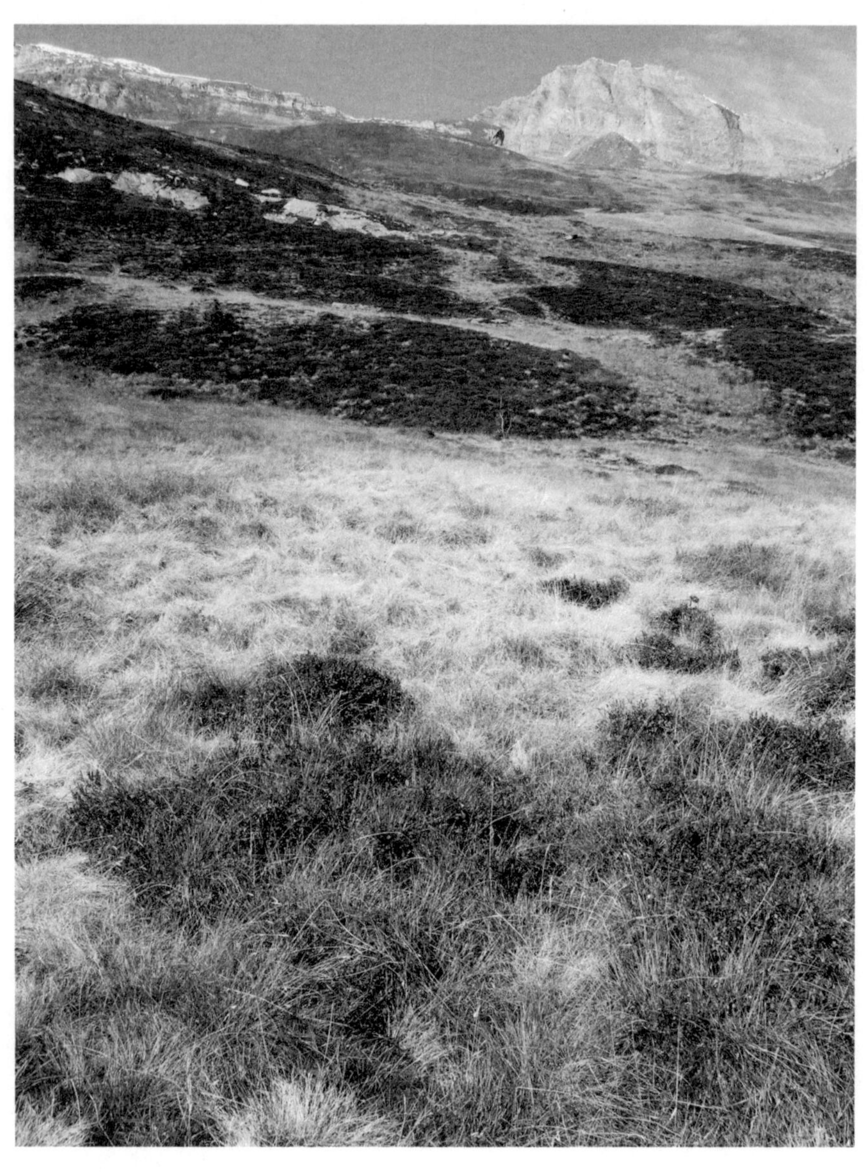

Annalisa & Peter Zumthor, *Landschaftshotel Alp Bidanätsch* (project not yet realized)

Annalisa & Peter Zumthor

in Conversation with Philip Ursprung

Peter Zumthor Annalisa and I have a dream. I don't exactly know when this dream started; it must have been a long time ago. So we share this dream, and would like to talk about how this dream could become real.

There was a time when I loved palace hotels. Around twenty or thirty years ago, I could afford to go to such castles and palaces for the first time and I – a small guy – could share that bourgeois pleasure of being in a big palace. But now, I really love beach hotels. I think they are great. The ideal beach hotel for me is right on the waterfront. There is sand and there is water, all for us, for me. And there is this beautiful horizon. I think it is amazing to have this long line of water and the sky. But I also really love city hotels. When I go to the city, there is this exquisite, nice, small city hotel, very elegant, which makes me feel I am at the centre of the things happening in this urban kind of excitement. The people working in such a hotel are completely informed about what is going on in the city. They know about the galleries, the movies and everything. They have a small restaurant where I can eat. For the big meals, they tell me to go out, and of course they also know the in-places. City hotels are great! There is of course another kind of hotel I really like: the mountain hotel. I love mountain hotels, and what I especially like about them is the sense of space of the mountains. Everybody knows about it, but for me it is always good to feel it. You are in a valley, and you are in a space, everything is space, it is not a vast expanse and there is this solid mass of rock or earth. And the most amazing thing is that you can climb up. So you have one perspective if you are down in the valley, and then you go up, and up and up and up, and all of a sudden, my experience is that I feel calm, or as Annalisa would say: she feels strong. Well, she grew up 1,400 metres above sea level, so when she gets to 1,400 metres above sea level, she starts to feel really strong – and I feel the same way.

Our dream is to build a mountain hotel. It is called Alp Hotel. For English speakers, I should perhaps explain the difference between *Alpen* and *Alp*. *Die Alpen* are the mountain range, whereas *die Alp* is the highest agricultural area on a mountain. No grass or hay is harvested there, but it is used as a pasture in the summer. The farmers bring their cattle up here to graze during the summer, and take them down again in the autumn. So our dream is not an Alpine hotel but an *Alp* hotel – located on one of these Alpine pastures.

Our hotel will be on the Bidanätsch Alp – one of 14 Alps that belong to the community of Vals. There is this small town, Vals, and if you go up the mountain there you will find 14 Alps, and Bidanätsch is one of them. From there, you are surrounded by an incredibly beautiful landscape. There is the mountain Piz Aul, which you can also see from Lugnez valley behind it. If you walked across the mountain, you would come down to the small village of Vrin, situated at the end of Lugnez, and could visit the architect Gion Caminada. When farmers here give directions for the valley, they don't say "north" and "south" – the way Americans do – but "in" and "out". "In" is used for going up the valley, "out" for going down the valley. "In" the valley, there is the Güfnerhorn glacier, and also the huge artificial lake Zerfreila with its dam wall. "Out" the valley, far out, there are the Flims and Laax mountains. Nearer, but still in the direction of "out" the valley, is Piz Tomül, and below that, the Tomül Alp. Across the valley, there are few, if any, traces of obvious civilization. You can see where the tree line ends, and where the Ampervreila Alp is located. It is nice to know the names of the various places and I could talk for an hour about what you would find if you walked around there.

It will not be possible to drive up to the Bidanätsch Alp Hotel: you will have to leave your car down in the valley and walk up. We will provide possibilities to bring up anyone who is unable to make it on foot. There is a big plain on the lower part of the Bidanätsch Alp and that is where our dream hotel will be. It is not yet there in reality, but you will see that we already know a lot about it. I am even using this conference to get to know more about it by talking to one another, finding out what will be there, and how it would work.

Annalisa wrote a text for me about the design of the architecture, and I would like to read the first passage to you:

Being in the landscape, at the edge of the forest. Silence. Peace. The sound of the meadow. Wind. Water. Goats. Sheep. Jackdaws. Golden eagles. Dawn. The early morning air. Twilight. Sky. Snow. Grass. Velvety moss. Tiny trees. Martagon lilies. Eyebright. Boulders. Stones. Rocks. Grey dolomite. Wood. Mountains, large in scale. Place, location, topography, the folded surface of the earth. Fog. Cloud formations. Winter storms.

Summer morning. Summer mornings at almost 2,000 metres are refreshing. I love starting in the morning by bathing in the air on my wooden terrace. Stretching, breathing, gazing; every morning, regardless of the weather. I love the 20-minute walk up to the stable before breakfast. On the way, I pass the walled garden, the greenhouse and the chicken coop of the hotel. Little wooden bridges cross three streams. I am alone in the landscape. I see mountains, Alpine pastures, woods. The dairyman, "Senn", is milking the cows in the hotel stable. The smell of the fresh milk fills the air.

I love the warmth of the cows. On the way back, I dip into the ice-cold water of the second stream, in the pond near the small waterfall.

Images of architectural settings, spaces or rooms:
Our Bidanätsch Alp Hotel has several buildings. There is a breakfast veranda. All of the guests enjoy the view. A long wooden structure. The kitchen in the rear in the mountain. There is a wooden bathhouse. Warm water, steam. Bathing in the landscape. There is a large wooden tub, filled with water. It is outside on stilts. You can bathe there summer and winter. The water is always warm enough. There is a large wooden platform, to lie on, to play on, to dance on, a place for outdoor events, events at night, food, music, theatre, full moon, sun umbrellas in the summer, the luxury of a wooden balcony warmed by the sun in the winter snow. There is a library. There is a library of landscape – where the landscape is present as a sensual experience and a subject of reflection. I see an architectural core of books, magazines and films, literary, scientific and artistic contributions on the subject. The core is surrounded by a wooden veranda, facing all directions. Here I find a spot to read, write, draw or talk with friends.

The Bidanätsch Alp Hotel has buildings with rooms for guests. Four or five pick-up sticks cut into the landscape tracing the lay of the land with the pasture passing through, underneath them. I lie in bed, in my room, above me the roof, the sky, underneath me the land, the earth.

So those are some of the spaces and things we talk about and dream about when planning our Bidanätsch Alp Hotel. We could go on for another hour but that might be boring, and we don't want to reveal all our ideas. What we want is for you to come and visit us in a couple of years.

Let's do a little note on architecture:
I would like to talk about the so-called "Ifang", which comes from the German word "einfangen" (to catch). An "Ifang" is a special enclosure that farmers build high up in the mountains – 2,000 metres and above. They keep their cattle there, overnight for example. They look like pieces of land art. Amazing things.

Elementary architecture:
Elementary constructions of wood and stone, expansive geometries lying quietly in the landscape. The topography remains unchanged. The architecture is inspired by the clear form and large scale of the walled pastures on the Vals Alps.

The next chapter by Annalisa is called “People in the landscape”.

Annalisa Zumthor A while back I had a vision: suddenly, in the middle of the afternoon, a detached picture in my mind of a man striding across the landscape, in a blue work shirt. He was striding and floating at the same time. He was tall and resembled my father. I realized then that someone was looking after the landscape. The image, it was like a message, gave me a sense of peace. I have to think of the image and the feeling it gave me whenever I try to envision the Bidanätsch Alp Hotel. I think about how the hotel will cultivate the Alp and look after the landscape, how the landscape is subject to ceaseless change. I think about how the work of human beings will be inscribed in that landscape, respectfully, the way it used to be. The people who run the Alp are part of the hotel. Bidanätsch Alp Hotel and Bidanätsch Alp are a unit. The delight in running these operations is tangible and shared with the guests. All parts of the building are accessible. There are guided tours on the Alp, in the garden, in the greenhouse, in the goat pen or hen house, even the laundry is always open to everybody. People are invited to help everywhere, to pick berries, to hang out the laundry, or to fold the bed sheets.

While snow shovelling, a remembrance:
It is silent, one doesn’t even hear the running water of the fountain. Snow. It has snowed. To stay a little bit longer in bed with this thrill of anticipation of snow. Finally, it is here. First father, who is shovelling snow, then the voice of the neighbour. She is shovelling snow, too. Then to open the window and to see if it is true. Before you see snow, you can smell it. Sparkling air. Snow air.

Spalar naiv, ün’algordanza:
Id ha naivü. Star amo ün mumaintin in let, cun tuot quell plaschair sülla naiv. A la fin e’la gnüda. Uossa bap chi spala naiv davant chà, lura la vusch da la vaschina. Eir ella scua davent la naiv. Ün sigl our da let, divrir la fneistra per verer schi’d ais vaira. Avant co tilla vair, la naiv, tilla savurast. Che bellezza d’ün ajer! Ajer das naiv!

PZ So this is a little bit of how we work on that project. As you can see, it is about trying to create emotional spaces, trying to fulfil some dreams we think should come true. It reflects 30 years of living in this area. It is nice to think that people can come on holiday, but at the same time, local people have something to construct and are given work – they can make a living. We think it is nice that all of this comes from the inside and not from outside. It also shows you maybe a little bit of designing, my way of designing, which comes from the inside, which is programme and form. Programme and form – always developed at the same time – may in the end result in a form.

The translator of this text wrote to me: "As I said in my last message, I would love to lie in that wooden tub with the fog rolling in and the sun peeking through the clouds."

Philip Ursprung Thank you very much, Annalisa and Peter. This is a very unusual kind of architectural presentation. This genre is usually about presenting buildings: I made this, I made that ... I think this is the first architecture lecture I have witnessed in which no building was actually presented.

Can you say something about your design process? You mentioned that you alternate between programme and form, programme and form. At what moment does an image materialize in your mind? Are you following a fixed image in your mind, which you won't show us, so that we don't copy it? Or will it gradually evolve during the design?

PZ I think that when you listen to some of these texts, you will maybe get an image of how this could look. That is exactly what it is all about, that is how we work: we provoke images. We talk, and we talk in the office, we talk to you, to the audience, to provoke images. That is why I like my translator writing back: "I'd like to be in this tub, man, do it!" This is how we work. I remember that when the former urban planner of Zurich, Franz Eberhard, read our text a couple of weeks ago, he said: "First I thought I had to go through all this paper, but where was the project, god dam!?" But when he started to read, he said:" And then I began to understand: this is the project; it's not yet a drawing of a building, it is this imagination." So this whole process is the most beautiful thing, I think, in my profession. Imagination should not be brought into a form too early. Keep it open!

PU Once the form comes into play, do you stick to that form, or is it possible to erase it completely and go another way? I am interested in the kind of experimental process you follow. Are you following a given path, or can you interrupt the process and radically start anew?

PZ Annalisa would say that it always changes. But for me, it is really important to have a sort of basic theme, or a basic atmosphere. With the Bidanätsch Alp, for example, I have a feeling for the whole thing.

We both have it – it is not completely identical. Based on this, a lot of things can be brought into the process and can disappear, of course. Concretely, if I look at the images I have – which we have not talked about – let's say, if I look at the image of this platform, a hundred by a hundred metres, made of wood, flat, on the Alp, shading devices, midnight dinners, moonlight parties – maybe only one, because it is always too cold, you can only make a few a year – if this is such a strong image for me, I have a feeling that it will always stay. But I am not sure. I have a feeling, but ask me in three years, or let's see, three years from now. Maybe you will find a version of this. It is subject to change, so it is like a process of getting clearer and more precise. It is about big emotions. I like big emotions, and I like to do emotional spaces, which appeal to me and to you and to everybody. Not as an abstract theory, but as emotional space.

PU I would say that there is great scepticism in your work towards the very idea of abstraction. I would argue that there is no such thing as a general concept that works every time.

One of the typical elements of your work is that it takes time, often a very long time. I know some of your collaborators, and on my last visit they said: "Oh, that's good because the next time you come we will probably have finished the door, which we have been working on for one and a half years." And I remember I was there when you said: "Yes, I think we have it now. Let's start with the door handle next." In this very, very long time that you use, there must be a moment when you say: "That's it, now it's finished, now it's ok." How can you tell when something is definite, when a project has ended, that it has been realized?

PZ All of a sudden, it starts to feel right. But the problemis that it can have felt right five times before. And then two weeks later I come back and say: "Guys, it's no good." It has to feel right and moreover, this feeling has to stay with me. I check it with this kind of going back to a naïve state of mind about the project. I work on something, and if I am too close to it, I don't have a critical distance. For example, two weeks ago, I was in Los Angeles. I woke up at five in the morning, then all my projects went through my mind – this is beautiful, I can work in bed – and I realized that the project in Haldenstein with three houses had become far too complicated. I decided just to do one house instead of three. I went home and I threw this out. Now I think it is ok, but I needed this moment of not being in on it.

I am fast; I am incredibly fast. Usually, I get bored if somebody tries to explain something to me, and I say: "Yeah, I know what you want to say, this, this …" But building is something else. These buildings stand there afterwards, for some time. So they better be good.

PU Annalisa, we have never talked about your part in this design process, and this is actually the first time that I have witnessed it in public. I saw it the last time I was in the studio and you were also there, and you were asked what you thought. Has this always been a method throughout Peter's career, or is it a rather new phenomenon? What is your role in all this?

AZ It has always been like this. I am like a sparring partner. I can say: "Yes, it is good or not good", and he believes me. When it is not good, he starts again, more or less. That is my role, and it is a nice role.

PU I like the start of your presentation when you say, that it is a hotel on the Alp, not in the Alps, it is not an Alpine hotel, but an Alp hotel. This is again not an abstraction. You are not evoking an abstract concept, but a concrete economic reality. Futhermore, it is a reality that you, Annalisa, know very well. You were raised in this Alpine area and you speak the language. Does Peter understand the Alps, or is he still somewhat a stranger?

AZ He is like a local farmer now. We have been talking about this project for maybe two years, and we have walked to the site many times. We also talk a lot about the work that could be done there. The Alp is somehow dying a little bit, so it is also a revival for the Alp. This is a great motivation to do a project there. We talk a lot about the Alpine area, and of course Peter has been living in this canton for 30 years, and did the inventory of the "Maiensässe" (lowest part of the mountain pasture) in Soglio. This means that in his early years he learned a lot about the land use of the Alps.[1]

PU Is the method also truly based on real mapping procedures? Do you know the connections, the economic functions of the site you are working with here?

PZ I think we worked on this a lot. I mean, I was working for the canton authority and I looked at all the villages in the whole canton for ten years. I was driving around trying to understand the structures, and sometimes trying to understand what couldn't be understood. This included not only the forms, but also the economy. We are very concerned about the economy with regard to forms of tourism and forms of agriculture. As Annalisa says, this kind of Alp agriculture is – as everybody knows – in danger. It can only survive because in Zurich we make, or rather Switzerland makes, a lot of money in other businesses. And that is why we can keep all of these beautiful things, but we have to find new forms. So we think that our hotel will maintain the Alp.

PU Of course, on a general level of architectural discussion, this is a very new point that you are bringing into play. A few years ago, the ETH Studio Basel published a widely discussed book: a portrait of Switzerland as a completely urban reality.[2] The authors Jacques Herzog, Roger Diener, Marcel Meili, Pierre de Meuron and Christian Schmid brought into play the concept of the "Alpine wasteland" ("Die Alpine Brache"), because – according to their thesis – it is too expensive to maintain this desert and keep it in shape just for tourists. The consequence would be simply to leave it alone, and to move the inhabitants to urban centres. What do you think about this concept of the "Alpine Brache"?

PZ I think this could happen to a certain degree, but somehow I would love it if some of these things could continue as living structures – without being subsidized by Zurich or by any other part of the country. So we have to think of what could be done. I like the idea that I am from the city, and I am from the mountain. We are all from the city and all from the mountain. We are all up here, and all in Los Angeles. Let's try to find things that come out of the existing agricultural or touristic structures, and go on with this, so that not everything is sort of superimposed from the outside. If I am in this area of our canton, there will be – as everybody knows – more superimposition: works of art, Engadin Art Talks, and all these things that maybe come from Zurich to the Engadin, or – as the "Bündner" (people from Grisons) say – from the lowlands to the upper lands, which is perfect. But there should also be a flow in the other direction. So there should be life here. We are here, and we are trying to do something.

PU There is something rather typical about your projects: there is always a human perspective. The scale of the human seems to be essential. Is this sort of yourself, or do you abstract from yourself and try to imagine that you are someone else?

PZ Building houses, doing buildings, or working on cities and so on has to do with our lives. An architect cannot change a lot, but where we live and what we have are important. I don't know why but I never set out to use architecture as something that might help me in my career, as something that would help me to write a beautiful book on the philosophy of architecture, or even make me rich. There was always a passion to make an emotional space, something we can all use, and I found that if I can use it, if it is good enough for me, then it is good enough for other people. I guess this is a very straightforward kind of approach. Maybe I am a classical architect?

AZ The motivation for me is beauty as well. Two weeks ago, we were in a touristy place that was terribly ugly. To do this project in Vals also means doing something beautiful and of high quality. This is a strong motivation, too, because Vals has become an extraordinary place with the Therme. It is this thermal bath, but the rest is normal, which I like, and hopefully it will stay normal. And when they introduce some touristic structures, I hope those structures will be nice and of high quality. Besides, it is a new way to run the Bidanätsch Alp. The other Alps in Vals work very well, but this one lacks good soil. So it is difficult and a very strong challenge at the same time. But it is also about beauty and quality.

PZ I'm glad she added that because many important things in the canton are of a really low quality, and that really is a big pain. There is often not much planning, and if you go to small villages, things are often done on a layman's level, with local people coming together and saying: "Let's do something for tourism." Then they print a new leaflet or something with some nice coloured images. It is of course also a pioneering work up on the Alp. More and more young people are leaving the region; they should come back and work with us. This is what we are trying to do. But to do this work, to make Alp architecture of high quality in these communal structures and cantonal structures, is hard work.

AZ But it is also very encouraging to see Gion Caminada and a lot of young architects at work. When I travel, for example to Lugnez, I see very beautiful buildings in every village. It is a kind of a virus.

PZ This is true. You have to remember the situation when I started here 30, 40 years ago. I was not allowed to build my first three projects because of aesthetical reasons. I went to court and they said: "No. No way.

For aesthetical reasons, no way." This has changed, and many good young architects are now working in this canton, so we are getting somewhere.

Hans Ulrich Obrist Before, you mentioned the notion of calmness, plus you and Annalisa referred to notions of calm, strength and peace when you go above a certain height in the mountains. I was wondering if these experiences, which are so specific to you and to the geography here, can be brought into the city? It was very fascinating working with you on the Serpentine Gallery Pavilion in London (2011), where you built this temporary *hortus conclusus* in Kensington Gardens. Julia Peyton-Jones and I got many SMS texts and emails from people all over the world who had visited your pavilion, and very often they described it as an oasis of peace in the city, a zone of calmness in the city. Can these qualities you describe and which you are searching for with this hotel and with many other projects be brought into the city?

PZ I think that landscape and nature will be an issue in architecture. My feeling is that what I am doing in the cities and up here – nature, landscape and understanding it and taking part in its development – is important. So I think of gardens in the city. I am doing a project in Holland now, and I see it as being all about gardens and all about people growing vegetables, having flowers and living with the plants. For me, doing the *hortus conclusus* in London and doing the hotel on the edge of the ski run in Vals is sort of the same thing. I think it is good for all of us to go up there and experience these things and to learn about them. Twenty years ago, we wanted to protect landscapes, to protect everything. But I think we should participate more actively in the landscape – and not just say that the Alps are all disappearing and the trees will come and grow there. The only alternative is, as mentioned before, the Swiss income made in Zurich and Basel. It helps to keep the Alps open. I like the idea of an active interaction with landscape. This is better than mere protection. People want to live up here.

Vals has a ski lift that goes all the way to Dachberg. The Blue Zone we are in is part of the ski development. It is a great ski lift; not comparable to the ski areas in Klosters, Davos, and so on, but still, it is nice to go skiing there. The ski company can barely make it, and yet a lot of hotels and small pensions and things depend on this little skiing on the hill. I wouldn't say that this is its main purpose, but I wouldn't mind if the skiers and the people who operate ski tours stayed there. I personally love to be up there in the winter – even without the skiing, as I am not a skier.

The Alp hotel should be more than just good quality. It should be comparable to what we did in the hotel in Vals, near the Therme, ten years ago. The idea was to make a hotel that was affordable for normal people with a good job and for young people not yet earning so much. It is not going to be exactly a youth hostel, nor is it going to be a mountain cabin. It needs a certain kind of exclusiveness, and for that you have to pay a certain price, I'm afraid.

HUO I remember when we spoke about hotels, and not only about this hotel project of yours, but your vision in general in London, we spoke a lot about poetry and music. You both have a very strong connection to literature and a very strong connection to music. And you spoke about this vision also of a hotel being a place where there would be poetry readings, where there could be concerts. Is that something that would also play a role here in this project?

PZ Yes, a big role, and it should be focused on the place and should take the place as its starting point. But of course, not everything comes from the place, as we know. Some things come from the outside. It is always a combination of the local and the alien. We have friends who want to participate with their musicians, and others who are poets and artists. This is sort of natural, in a way. What is really important to me is the connection to the local economy. It is about trying to fit into the local economy of the valley and have a good level of tourism there.

1 A great deal of information about the land use of the Alps can be found in Richard Weiss, *Das Alpwesen Graubündens*, Erlenbach-Zürich: Eugen Rentsch Verlag 1941.
2 Roger Diener, Jacques Herzog, Marcel Meili Pierre de Meuron and Christian Schmid, *Die Schweiz. Ein städtebauliches Portrait*, 2005.

Peter Zumthor (b. 1943 in Basel) trained as a cabinetmaker in his father's workshop, and as a designer and architect at the Kunstgewerbeschule Basel and at Pratt Institute, New York. He worked at the Department for the Preservation of Monuments in the canton of Graubünden for ten years. In 1979, he established his own studio in Haldenstein, Switzerland. Zumthor won the Pritzker Prize in 2009 and was awarded the RIBA Royal Gold Medal in 2013. He is known for his exploration of the tactile and sensory qualities of spaces and materials (e.g. Therme Vals, 1996).

Annalisa Zumthor-Cuorad (b. 1947 in Susch/Switzerland) worked as a teacher at a school for mentally and physically disabled children. She has written short prose works in Romansh and has worked as an editor for the Romansh literary journal *Litteratura*. Before joining the Atelier Zumthor in 2009, she worked as co-director of the Hotel Therme in Vals for nearly ten years.

Philip Ursprung (b. 1963 in Baltimore) studied art history, history and German literature in Geneva, Vienna and Berlin. He received his PhD at the Freie Universität, Berlin. He was professor of modern and contemporary art at the University of Zurich, and visiting professor at Columbia University, New York, and the Barcelona Institute of Architecture. Since 2011, he has been professor of the history of art and architecture at the Swiss Federal Institute of Technology (ETH), Zurich. He edited the 2002 collection of essays *Herzog & de Meuron: Natural History*, and his book *Allan Kaprow, Robert Smithson and the Limits to Art* was published by University of California Press in 2013.

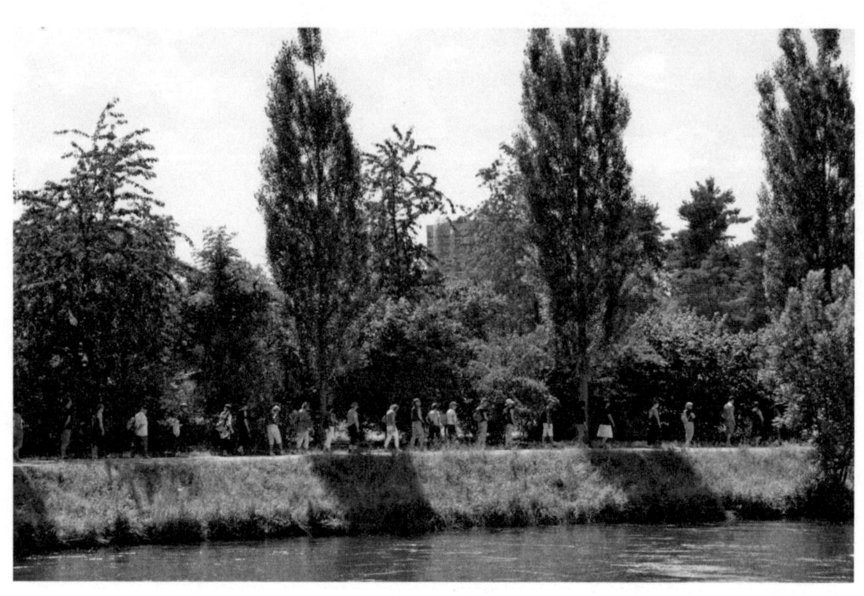

Hamish Fulton, *Limmat Art Walk* (2012)
On the occasion of *Art and the City* –
in Zurich

Hamish Fulton

On Mapping (the Alps)

Hans Ulrich Obrist You did your very first walk – which was called *The 2nd of February* – in 1967. And ever since then you have undertaken walks all over the world. As you said once: "I do not make sculpture in the landscape involving permanent alterations and changes to the earth and its surface, as my intention more and more is to be influenced by nature. And nature, the natural environment, is not man-made. My art is a passive protest against urban societies that alienate people from the world of nature." This idea of protest also leads to many of the very political works you have created from the beginning. Let me just mention a recent one: *Slowalk (in support of Ai Weiwei)*, which took place on 30 April 2011 at Tate Modern in London.

Hamish Fulton The question that seems to come out from the Engadin Art Talks, from the discussions we have had so far, in relation to the way that I think, is: to build or not to build. This sounds a bit Shakespearean, but it is the question. Although we have a question, it has to remain blank: I have no images; I have nothing. "Nothing" is comprised of seven letters and "no thing" is comprised of seven letters, too. All my art is about walking. And you can undertake walks in different ways. One is to determine the number of days to be walked before you start, as for example for a walk from Zuoz to the Mediterranean Sea. You can make a good estimation about how long that will take, but we can't be sure about the exact number of days. That means that one way of having a distance on a walk is a time distance. And I used the number seven.

Then there is also the question of my opinions. I am not a land artist. My opinion is that I am not against other people who make land art. That is not the question. The issue is that I don't want to be associated with land art. And that is an opinion, and an opinion is a seven-letter word. Back in the early 1970s, a book was published called *The Limits to Growth*[1]; quite a famous document. This title sounds very interesting to me, from my perspective, which is coming from the position of experience. When I say that walking is an art form in its own right, there is absolutely no need to refer to it as a minor category of land art. But in the early 1970s, there were two criticisms of my work: first, that I was a land artist, and secondly, that I was a romantic, that my art was influenced by the Romantics. The criticisms said that my art was romantic, nostalgic and escapist. When you turn some of these from the negative you can see the positive. On YouTube there is a film by a Tibetan lama pointing at a bone. It is a dog bone and it is just an amazing, large dog bone. He has a dog. The dog looks at the dog bone and likes the look of the dog bone. The lama looks at the bone, too, but he does not feel the same way as the dog.

This is like an opinion, a different response to different positions when looking at the very same object.

So through the early 1970s into the 1970s then, what was I going to be influenced by? Here, we are surrounded by mountains, and it is important to say that I am actually more influenced by real mountains than by conceptual mountains. But there is also the question of being inspired and influenced by other human beings, which I think is very important. I would like to read an excerpt from a text that was published in bulletin number 109 of *Art and Project* in 1979, in Amsterdam, where I had an exhibition. It is not my writing, but the writing of Reinhold Messner, the great, legendary, influential Alpinist from South Tyrol. He and Peter Habeler made the first ascent above 8,000 metres. In this piece of writing,

Messner speaks, let´s say, from the point of view of literature, in a very poetic and very romantic way. A lot of people would condemn his writing style – this is again the condemnation of poetry and romanticism – but in fact he is not writing from an apartment at sea level in a big city. He is actually talking about being one of the first two people to ascend to 8,000 metres without bottled oxygen in 1975. And at that time, which is not so long ago, people were convinced that your brain would be damaged if you went to 8,000 metres without bottled oxygen. Messner wrote:

"We arrived at the ridge between the north-west face and the south-east flank and looking over the eastern summit of the hidden peak, we were treated to a stupendous panorama of Tibet, which surpassed anything I had ever seen before; a mountain landscape in grey and white fanning out from crest to crest into eternity. Ridges like the petrified waves of a gigantic sea. To the left, the highest peaks in the Karakorum: the eight-thousanders, Gasherbrum II, Broad Peak, K2 – frontier mountains between Tibet and Pakistan. The irrational thrust into the blue, blank sky staggers the mind, heightens the sense of loftiness and isolation. The isolation was, in fact, overwhelming. When I thought about it, how long it took, how long it had taken us to arrive at this point, it seemed we had reached eternity. It was a still and quiet space. I have always sought solitude. For many years I have been developing independence to its standard and now, at last, I have found the inner peace to survive it. Up here, close to the summit, the world stands still in time, the raging of the wind and the humming from the heart of the mountain, blanket of the life of the valleys – these surging sounds and changing colours of the serrated scene come together on our summit. Come together in black and white. The atmosphere was impregnated with silence. Not the silence of death, but the liberating silence of infinity, light and carefree. All sounds were like deep silence. Each movement was neither work, nor action, merely being. And being was freedom. And freedom was older than time."

I think this sounds incredibly romantic and yet it is about a real experience.

I would like to jump forward in time to the year 1997, when I was invited to Missoula Montana to undertake a walk and an exhibition. I was influenced by people I met there who were either climbers or wildlife film-makers. But the influence was not reciprocated. When they saw my exhibition, they were not interested at all. This is quite illuminating regarding the idea of what walking can include. Walking is not necessarily located inside the field of art; it also goes out to other fields. And so, through time,

I have realized that I can meet and talk with people from a variety of disciplines about the action of walking.

In 1999, I was invited to Anchorage, where I held an exhibition in the Museum of History and Art in Anchorage. And for that, I undertook a walk in the Rangel Saint Elias Region of Alaska. I went with a guide. We went into a region that for me, personally, is still the wildest landscape I have ever been in. Even in the United States, where everybody loves four-wheel-drive vehicles, it is not possible to drive there; you have to fly. And then you take a single-engine craft with large wheels, which are soft so the plane can land on gravel by a river. When the ice melts, the river rises and the marks that you have left, the indentations from the wheels, begin to disappear. In Rangel Saint Elias, I was influenced by grizzly and black bears, which are really wild bears. They are not comparable to the ones you find in Glacier National Park in Montana, where they have been trashed and have an interest in hamburgers.

As I get older, I begin to think that I want more influence and more experience. There is this sort of connection between becoming older – older means approaching death – and wanting to have these bigger physical experiences. In 1999, I had an exhibition in Zuoz at the Galerie Tschudi. The architect Hans-Jörg Ruch bought some work, and I used the money to pay to join a commercial expedition to climb Cho Oyu, the sixth-highest mountain in the world, one of the fourteen 8,000-metre peaks. This was an incredible experience for me, because it was – in relation to the Reinhold Messner story that I read – my own personal journey to 8,000 metres without bottled oxygen. It was very powerful and sort of changed my mind about a lot of different things, which I cannot explain right at this moment, but a very powerful experience in terms of giant kinds of views. So I would say that I am at the beginning of a sort of "mountain decade", of an interest in mountains. Mountains are in a sense useless and therefore very appealing to me. I know that the Austrian economy is sort of based on the skiing industry in the country's mountainous regions. But then on the other side, you can have the influence from deep ecology as opposed to shallow ecology. And I had the great privilege of meeting Arne Næss. He is no longer alive, but I met him, and I had a two-hour walk with him when he was 93 years of age. And Næss is instrumental in this thinking of deep ecology. Deep ecology means the connection between human beings and all forms of life, not merely cows, sheep, and so on, but also insects. And then we can also refer to *Silent Spring* (1962) by Rachel Carson, or to Aldo Leopold. There are all these names, people who thought very strongly about all forms of life on the planet. Næss was a great

Norwegian philosopher and also a mountaineer and he has these comments to make, which I will read from his *Mountains and Mythology*:[2]

"A mountain is the nearest to heaven. Or, mountains touch heaven and they are therefore considered to be the centre, in the sense of the meeting place between the heavenly and the earthly. The unreachable, the passage to the beyond, transcendence may be possible or not possible for humans, the highly valued unclimableness of mountains symbolizes the unreachableness of the absolute, absolute virtue of power or also immortality." Næss then continues: "All the major ideals which man struggles towards are more or less unattainable. Only his hypocrisy and untruthfulness can give the passing sense of having reached the ideal. This holds good of truth also in the sense of scientific truth. Research is search for truth. Science or knowledge is the sense of truth arrived at, is an ideal, not anything accomplished."

The issue of finding out for yourself, the first-hand experience, the witness account, this is part of how I feel about taking walks. They are not theoretical. I transform an idea into an experience reality. I am not a mountaineer, not a climber. And I do not know anything about Alpine-style climbing, but nevertheless, these people have influenced and expanded my way of thinking and considering my work.

In 2003, I went to South America and walked to the top of Aconcagua, which is the highest mountain of South America. It is a little under 7,000 metres. This is absolutely walking and not climbing, and over the last 200 metres in vertical height you can feel the real impact of the lack of oxygen. Then in 2004, I went to Denali and joined a commercial expedition. I climbed Denali, the highest mountain in North America, because of a personal and private idea about a comment on land art. Because land art in a sense started – some people would say – in the United States and the alteration of the landscape by land art made me think. I did a little bit of research to see if any other artists had summited, had really gone to the top of Denali, and I found out that nobody had climbed Denali as a contemporary artist so far. So I thought I would like to make this private contribution to the history of art by doing that. I went with another person who was not an artist. We do not look any different, but inside my head I am an artist.

Moving on in time to 2007, when I went on a walk in Switzerland from the Zurich region to the Engadin, I made a wall painting called *Water from the mountains*, which was exhibited at the Häusler Contemporary Gallery in Zurich. The title consists of 21 letters and it was a 21-day walk. I am not going to read the whole text, only the part of it that says:

"A 21-day walking journey on pavements, bicycle paths, tracks, footpaths, rocks and snow, starting by encircling Obersee and Zurichsee. So then I walked around the two lakes there, and then I walked from there to the Engadin and then I walked up and down seven small mountains, including Piz Julier and Piz Err, for example. And then I returned to the Zurich region and I walked again, going the other way around the two lakes, to sort of complete the walk."

Later in 2007, I went with my daughter to Tibet – we both independently have an interest in Tibet – to Mount Kailash. It is a too long a story to explain everything about Mount Kailash, but it was a great ambition and I had probably had the idea for 30 years. We had a list of Tibetan monasteries that we wanted to visit. In Tibet, they have a thing called "Cora", which means "walking around a sacred sight", which could be a mountain, like Mount Kailash, or which could be walking around the Chua Choa Kang monastery in Lhasa. It could be walking in Ganden monastery; it could be walking in Drepon monastery. Of course, these are all historic places related to China invading Tibet in 1950. My opinion is that Tibet in fact is a Chinese prison. So we wanted to take these walks and some of the walks were indoors, which is also interesting, this sort of change of landscape to indoor walking. I think you can also walk indoors. I met a man in Italy who had smashed his legs in a motorcycle accident. And his greatest ambition in recovery was to walk the 17 steps from his bed to the toilet.

In 2008, I began to think of going to Mount Everest, Chomolungma, which is the native Tibetan name for Mount Everest, the highest mountain in the world. And again with the aid of Häusler Contemporary Gallery I was able to work with a series of financial supporters, because it costs a lot of money to do this expedition. In 2008, I went to Nepal and summited three smaller mountains of around 6,100 metres in altitude, just to prepare my mind, because it is mental as well as physical going to Mount Everest. I was eventually able to join a commercial expedition of a company called Adventure Consultants, one of the two companies alongside Mountain Madness that are mentioned in the Jon Krakauer's book *Into Thin Air. A Personal Account of the Mt. Everest Disaster* (1997). There is all this notoriety attached to it, and a lot of people do not like the idea of going up Mount Everest. They think it is a way of trashing the environment. People say that you step over dead bodies, that there are piles of empty oxygen cylinders at the end of the South Col, and that there are mountains of trash. They say that you are just parading your Western arrogance through the beautiful Himalayas. So that is absolutely a point of view, by non-climbers.

And then there is the point of view of climbers going on the route I took with three other people: the south-east ridge, also called the "yak" route, which is a derogatory term by climbers. But in fact any serious climber knows that anybody can die for any reason on Mount Everest. No matter how good a climber you are, it is actually a serious environment to be in. In this case, we went with bottled oxygen and that was a very serious commitment. And in no way was I let down when I arrived at the summit. I do not share the point of view that there is an anticlimax when you arrive at the summit. I did not feel like that at all. It is important to say that the summit is only half way, because on Mount Everest the trick is then to return to the lower levels. Many people – relatively speaking in terms of the numbers of people who have summited Mount Everest – can make mistakes. You have to be sure the oxygen pipe does not freeze. Mine froze many times, and I had to use a carabiner to drop the ice out otherwise I would not have been able to breath. It was a very powerful experience.

Another person who has influenced me is Doug Scott. He is more or less in the same category as Reinhold Messner but from England. On 17 November 2010, he gave a presentation called *First on Everest,* in which he included all kinds of different people who had made these particular journeys on Mount Everest. One of them was the Australian Tim Macartney-Snape, who walked from sea level to the summit. So he walked from the coast of India to the summit of Mount Everest. Another person is the great Swiss Alpinist Erhard Loretan, who also gave a presentation on that same November day. Loretan was a very small, thin, short person but he was one of the world's greatest Alpinists. Unfortunately, he was killed in a mountaineering accident in Switzerland on 28 April, his 52nd birthday.

It is possible to have all these influences but the last one is actually the issue: you can die in the mountains. The mountains do not kill you. You go there and you get into a situation yourself and then you finish your days on this planet in the mountains.

HUO I have read about you distinguishing "mountain time" from human time. Perhaps you could talk a little more about "mountain time" and explain to what extent it is different to city time. Besides, I would be interested to hear how you translate your experiences into books, because books play a very important role in your work. Ever since the early seventies, you have done great artist books, like *Hollow Lane* (1972) and it is something that continues to this day.

HF There is the issue of an ancient time of forms that are not human and then there is the human lifespan. The relationship between these times is that a human being has the possibility to make a huge impact on the environment, on mountains. Mountains have existed for millions and millions of years and it is poignant how the world is being destroyed at the moment and that people are not willing to protect the environment. I think it is *the* major issue at the moment. Of course, since we are human beings, we concentrate on the economy. But we could also say that mountains are living wards. They affect human life: they change the weather and there is the water from the mountains that we drink. Half the world´s population does not get enough water because the glaciers are melting and so on – which is very much bound up with global warming.

Coming back to your question about the books, they make it possible to stage a portable exhibition without having huge space expenses, transport costs, and so on. A book is simply a convenient way to offer people an intimate exhibition.

HUO You have mentioned that the more time passes the more you want to have a bigger physical experience. I was wondering, now that you have walked all these big mountains, whether there are any unrealized walks? Walks that are too long or too big to be realized?

HF I think there is no chance of my going on very high mountains anymore, because it is like a roll of the dice. I am not doing that anymore. You mentioned the walk in support of Ai Wei Wei in Tate Modern, which is an indoor walk and which opens a huge space to work in. You can have the space of a huge mountain, but you can also have the ideal space or an indoor space, where different kinds of experiences are possible. I find communal walking with other people really interesting. I spoke to a lot of people after the Tate walk in support of Ai Wei Wei and I found everything they said really interesting. It was a walk on the indoor ramp of Tate Modern and there were 99 people. The shape of the indoor ramp is a rectangle and people were lined on all four sides of it. They walked across the rectangle, but whichever side, long or short, they were walking, it had to take them half an hour. It lasted two hours and comprised four crossings in total. The reason I did the walk, which had nothing to do with my understanding of Ai Wei Wei's artwork, was entirely to support the man's courage. Some days ago, I heard some details about the cell that Ai Wei Wei was in: it measured four metres by four metres and, depending on what I was reading, he actually walked five to seven hours every day, covering something like 15 miles. I also kind of privately made a connection between these two walks.

I did a whole series of seven paces, which were somehow my shortest walks. Walks that were just seven paces, in different places, different times, comparable to the first seven steps and the last seven steps. You take your first seven steps, as a baby, and then you take your last seven steps. It is a kind of a distance that most people can do, a kind of a real-life reality.

HUO I read that some of your walks, such as the *Margate Walk*, have to be made in complete silence. Since our talks are related to the Alps and to the mountains, I was wondering if there is conversation on the walks you described – from walks on smaller mountains to Mount Everest.

HF My way of viewing the walks is that one walk exists in comparison to another, so I did a walk with no talking for 14 days. I think talking and not talking are part of the same story. I have met incredible people on journeys and have had really interesting conversations. Especially when you are in a tent with five people and it is snowing outside, you start to talk about nearly everything. I met the American environmentalist John Francis, who is nicknamed "the planetwalker". When he saw two oil tankers collide near San Francisco in the early 1970s, which created an enormous oil spill, he decided first not to ride any motorized vehicle and then not to talk at all for 17 years. When he finally did speak again, he explained to people the biological feeling and response in himself: he was talking, but the person who was speaking was like three metres behind him, which was a very strange biological feeling.

1 Meadows, Donella H., Dennis L. Meadows, Jorgen Randers and William W. Behrens III, *The Limits to Growth,* New York: Universe Books 1972.

2 Published in *The Sacred Mountains of Asia,* John Einarsen (ed.), Shambhala Publications 1995.

Hamish Fulton was born in London in 1946. He studied at Hammersmith College of Art, at St. Martins School of Art and at the Royal College of Art, London. The conceptual artist and photographer is known for his walks, which leave no mark or intervention on the land through which he travels. According to Fulton, art doesn't need to be materialized into an artwork. He has – especially in recent years – also painted on exhibition walls and worked on concrete poetry. He lives and works in Canterbury.

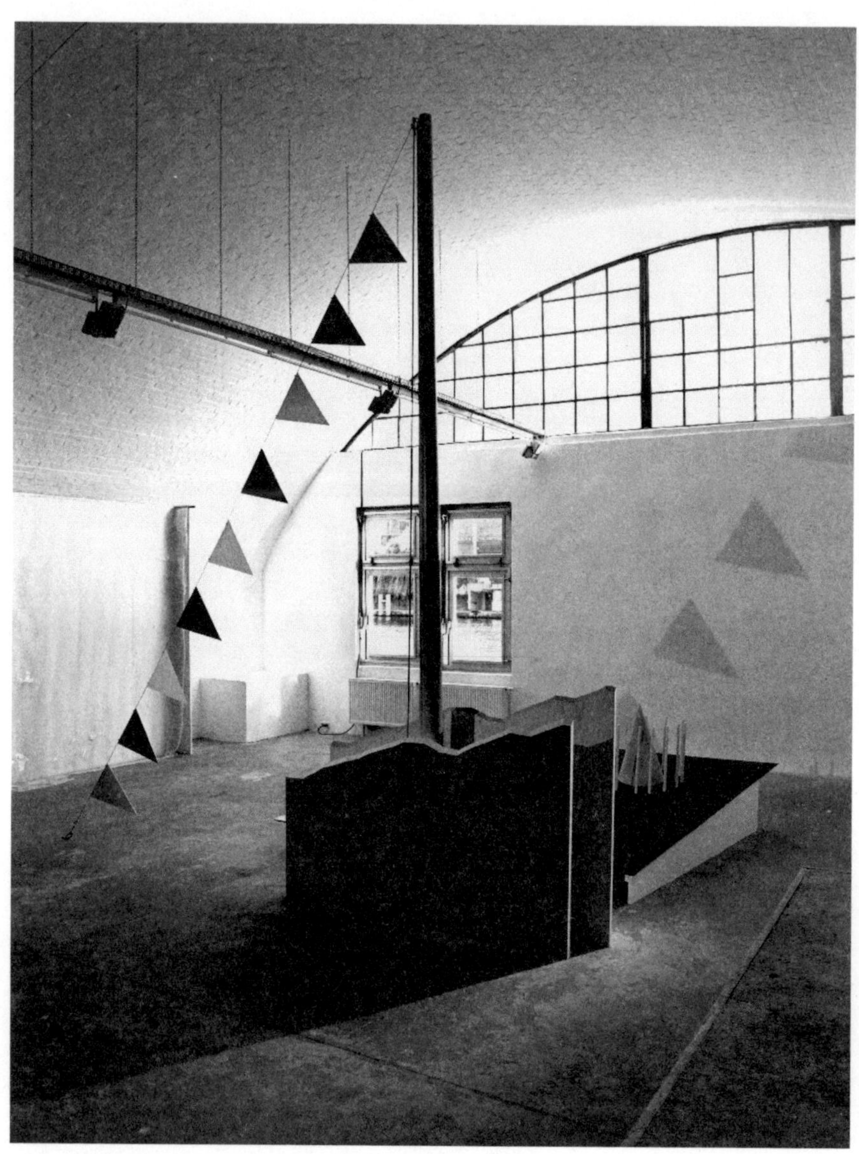

Nairy Baghramian, *The Iron Table* (2002)
Painted wood, painted metal, sand, wire cable, synthetic cable, mast, 2 spotlights, 320 × 540 × 530 cm

Nairy Baghramian

With My Back to the World

A Lecture on Landscapes (Collected Thoughts, Kenya, 2011)

The overview that one has on mountaintops lets us observe the landscape from a bird's-eye perspective. Looking down from "high-up" viewing platforms in the mountains gives us the illusion of an endless, horizontal landscape below, an illusion that is also part of any landscape in a desert or by the sea. This horizontal point of view is the starting point of my talk and takes us over the mountains to other far-off landscapes. So I am not going to talk about going up but rather about looking around. As in perspective painting – all degrees might thus connect at one vanishing point or another on various horizons.

The invitation to this symposium triggered an avalanche of memories of all kinds of stories about artists, authors and musicians, and in particular their concrete search for utopian places in the real world. I think these places can in a sense be thought of as quasi vanishing points. In the past, approaching a vanishing point often involved something like the desire for loneliness and also trying to catch the reflection of one's spirit in nature – regardless of the kind of nature: Alps, ocean shores or sand. These kinds of ideas can be found, for example, in the writings of Friedrich Nietzsche and Martin Heidegger, the paintings of Caspar David Friedrich, or in the life and work of artists like Georgia O'Keeffe and Agnes Martin. What is going on here is arguably a kind of parallel collective motivation by avant-gardes of the past century involving the use of distance from urban centres to try to generate a new social culture of their own – perhaps alone, but often in intimate correspondence with their friends.

One of my favourite examples of this are the Bowles. In the 1940s and 1950s, Jane Bowles, who was known as a rather wilful figure in modern literature, lived with Paul Bowles in North Africa in a loving gay and lesbian marriage of convenience. They surrounded themselves with a circle of well-known international intellectuals and artists such as William S. Burroughs, Truman Capote, David Herbert, Peggy Guggenheim, Marguerite McBey to name but a few. They were driven by the old desire for a different sphere of civilization and thus reset their compasses. The fantastical and ethnographic projections of past generations of European travellers were cast aside in favour of their new desire for a pure, abstract and engaged life amongst others. They did this despite the fact that it sometimes led to a panorama of looming dilemmas and personal erosion. For them it was a time when the psychology of interpersonal relationships, and impressions about the outside and politics, inextricably permeated each other. By the way, what the Bowles and actually all of the rest of the examples I wish to mention here have in common is that they don't involve the solitary figure looking out at a landscape, but rather the idea of a circle of friends who tried to shape the landscapes of their choosing.

A short fragment from Jane Bowles's notebooks for an unfinished short story, "The Iron Table", really impressed me with its incredible barren clarity, and in 2003, it became the departure point for one of my first sculptures. The notes sketch a conversation between a woman and a man about their wish to see the desert as a consequential place of Uncivilization. Their imaginings are debated within a fine choreography of indefinite evasions and particular denials.

"... There are places where the culture has remained untouched, he announced as if for the first time.
If we went into the desert you wouldn't have to face all this. Wouldn't you love that? ...
... He knew she had no desire to go to the desert, and that she believed it was not possible to continue trying to escape from the Industrial Revolution ...
... The whole civilization is going to pieces, he said.
Her voice was sorrowful. I know it. Her answer to his ceaseless complaining about the West had become increasingly unpredictable ..."[1]

The design for my sculpture grew out of the idea of a construction of a kind of "think piece", but one that skips over the idea of scenery and stage – an artificial tableau embodying Bowles's abstruse motives. The surreal proportions of my work *The Iron Table* (2003) play with the relationship between cultural projections, desire and artificial design as a synonym for attempts to model existence.

But now, before I lose myself too much in the horizon, I would like to go down a little path by quoting a passage from *The Autobiography of Alice B. Toklas* by Gertrude Stein:

"I myself had no liking for violence and have always enjoyed the pleasures of needlework and gardening. I am fond of paintings, furniture, tapestry, houses and flowers, even vegetables and fruit-trees. I like a view but I like to sit with my back turned to it."[2]

And my last word is dedicated to my dearest friend, Janette Laverrière, a Swiss designer and interior architect who, whenever a conversation dragged on or got too long, would love to interrupt and say: "It's so beautiful up there in the mountains of Switzerland."

(The text is an excerpt.)

1 Jane Bowles, "The Iron Table", in: *My Sister's Hand in Mine: The Collected Works of Jane Bowles,* New York: Farrar, Straus & Giroux 1966.
2 Gertrude Stein, *The Autobiography of Alice B. Toklas,* San Diego: Harcourt, Brace & Co. 1933.

The artist Nairy Baghramian was born in Isfahan, Iran, in 1971 and relocated to Germany in her teens. She lives and works in Berlin, and is known for her sculptural installations, texts and photographs. Her work refers to the repertoire of modernist forms in architecture and set design and is characterized by its technical precision. In 2011, she was represented at the 54th Venice Biennale.

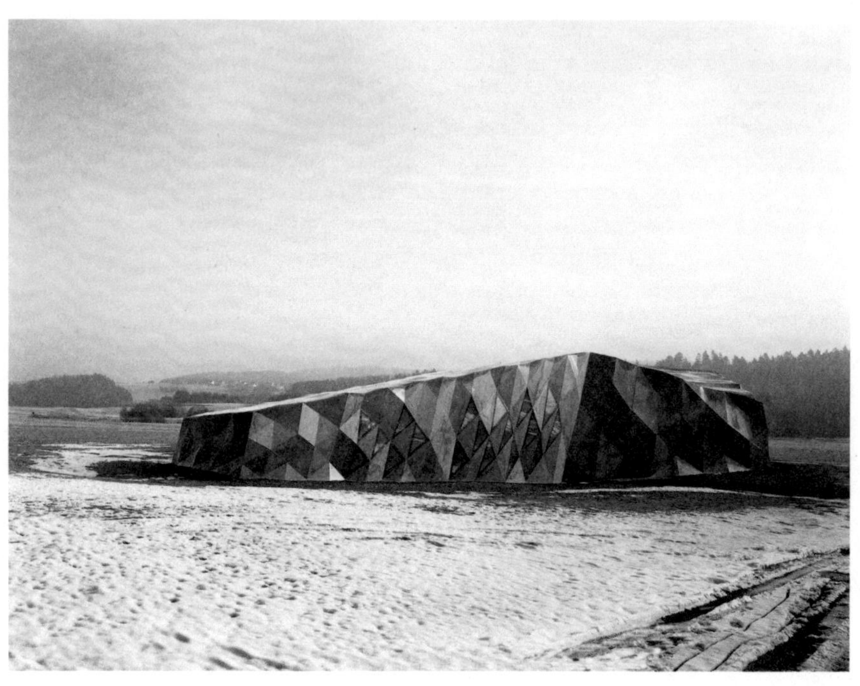

Nikolaus Hirsch, Wolfgang Lorch & Andrea Wandel, *Hinzert Document Centre* (2005)

Nikolaus Hirsch

Mountain as Prison

The Hinzert Document Centre

Mountains are a topos for tourism, nature, health; a self-chosen, mostly temporary refuge for a better life. What was once perceived as harsh and repellant seems to be increasingly familiar and domesticized. Yet there is a counter-history to the process of tourism, to weekend trips and holidays in the mountains: the trajectories of exile and prison. The forced exile in contrast to the self-chosen refuge. In other words: the mountain as prison.

PRECARIOUS IDYLL

The landscape around the village of Hinzert, 30 km from the Luxembourg border, seems like an idyll. Located in the Hunsrück, a German *Mittelgebirge*, characterized by rather low, smooth hills and agriculturally used fields. Yet this perception depends on the perspective. What seems like an idyll to the eyes of today's tourist, was once a harsh environment, a mountain prison. No original trace hints at Hinzert's use between 1939 and 1945, when the site was a Special Camp for political prisoners from more than 20 European countries.

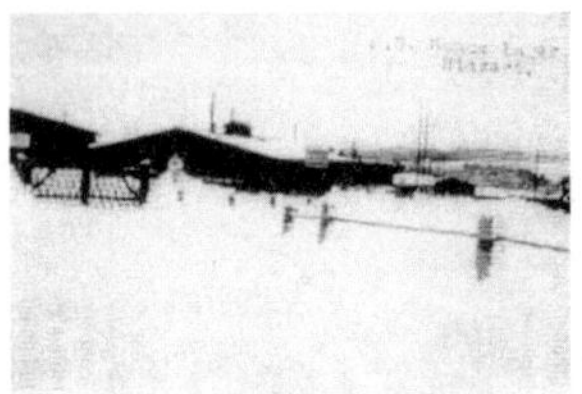

Fig. 1: The Hinzert Camp in winter

The Hinzert camp was first established in 1938 to house workers who were building the West Wall, a gigantic fortification against the "arch-enemy": France. However, the camp burned down on 16 August 1939, and was rebuilt in October 1939 as a police detention and re-education camp, or *Polizeihaft- und Erziehungslager des Reichsarbeitsdienstes (RAD)*, for prisoners condemned to light sentences (under 14 days) and for workers who had demonstrated what the Nazi regime termed "anti-social behaviour". These men were put to work on the West Wall and other military infrastructure projects in preparation for the war on the western front.

On 1 July 1940, the camp was placed under the jurisdiction of the Inspector of Concentration Camps. After Germany invaded Belgium, the Netherlands, Luxembourg and France in 1940, Hinzert became a camp for political prisoners from those countries, and from other states that would later be occupied by the Wehrmacht (such as the Soviet Union, Greece, Yugoslavia and other European countries). Hinzert, a tiny, unknown place in an unspectacular mountain area, became part of a complex geopolitical network, a topos within a vast topography of terror.

NATURE AND TORTURE

Located on the Hochwald plateau, and overlooking the Hunsrück mountain range, the Hinzert camp was named after the nearest village. At an altitude of 550 m, the plateau is exposed to strong wind, heavy rain and snow, and glacial temperatures in winter.

An access road that initially bordered the prisoners' cemetery led to a first area guarded by the SS. This area contained seven buildings, a guard post, the camp's "Kommandantur" (commandant's office), a garage, workshops, the officers' mess and two buildings to house the SS. This area was decorated with floral and garden arrangements. Prisoners were kept in an adjacent area measuring approximately 200 × 200 m, bordered by a three-metre-high barbed wire fence with watchtowers. The prisoners' area also contained the camp commander's quarters, the clothing workshop, the carpenter's area, the quarantine area, the morgue, a disinfection area and the "cloakroom", where the prisoners' belongings were kept.

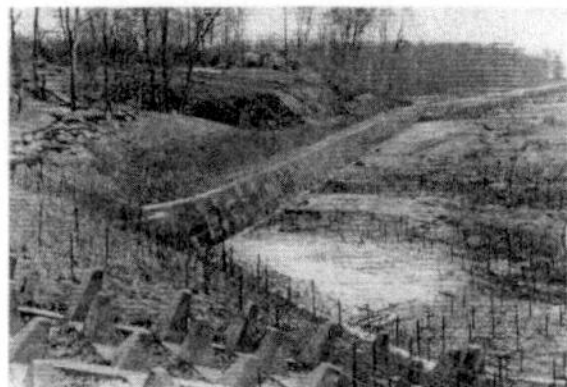

Fig. 2: Forced labour at the West Wall

Prisoners were housed in four buildings, each barrack containing two rooms that in turn contained 26 bunk beds for a total theoretical capacity of 208 prisoners. Later, straw mattresses were added to increase the total capacity to 560. Certain rooms were reserved for a particular category of prisoners, such as the so-called Night and Fog prisoners from France.

DISAPPEARING IN NIGHT AND FOG

How do people disappear? In Richard Wagner's *Rheingold*, the dwarf Alberich, who guards the treasure of the Nibelungen, tries out his new helmet, the "Tarnhelm", and says: "Seid Nacht und Nebel gleich!" (Resemble night and fog!) – in other words, become invisible and leave no trace. In a direct reference to this, the Wehrmacht High Command issued the "Nacht und Nebel-Dekret" (Night and Fog decree) on 7 December 1941. Almost 2,000 Frenchmen along with Belgian and Dutch members of national resistance groups were deported to Hinzert between May 1942 and October 1943. The "Nacht und Nebel" prisoners (known as "NN" prisoners) were supposed to disappear without trace and be deported to Germany in utmost secrecy. Family members received no information about their whereabouts, and NN prisoners were strictly forbidden to write letters.

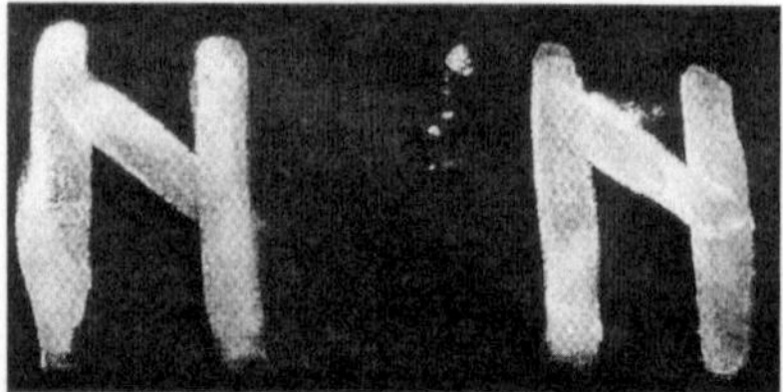

Fig. 3: Nacht und Nebel (Night and Fog)

"NN", the code name used in official papers, was explicit in its double meaning: aside from being the the abbreviation for "Nacht und Nebel" directive, a term also used by Alain Resnais in his 1955 documentary on the Nazi death camps, it could also be read as *nullum nomen* ("without name"). This is the countermodel to tourists and their search for individuality, or even reinvention of identity. The NN programme exposed the prisoners to an agenda whose ultimate aim was the loss of identity. The mountains became a place of anonymity, almost without witnesses.

Yet, the "Tarnhelm" plan did not fully work out. There were survivors and witnesses. Night and Fog was turned into daylight. Research and legal action were initiated. The French Fondation pour la Mémoire de la Déportation estimates that approximately 1,500 Night and Fog prisoners were sent to Hinzert; at least 804 of them died and 390 survived to return to France. And then the post-Nuremberg era of testimony began: human rights trials, humanitarian education. Today, the witnesses, now in their nineties, are passing away. A paradigm shift is taking place: a move from oral history to documentary history. A shift from witnessing and speaking to collecting and exhibiting.

REAPPEARING: FROM ORAL HISTORY TO THE DOCUMENT CENTRE

What are the implications of the move from the human body to an institutional body? What are the spatial effects of the shift from the witness-oriented experience to the exhibition-based condition? The first and obvious answer is that the paradigm shift implies a process of musealization. Almost by necessity it initiates a conservationist agenda that preserves the documents, objects, images and papers that are meant to embody the memory. A new, decontextualized environment has to be created. Now the witnesses tell their stories from flat screens. Suddenly the objects are asked to speak. In fact – according to Bruno Latour's theory of a "Dingpolitik" (thing-based politics) – they become "things" rather than "objects". They leave behind the status of neutral, remote, objectifiable items and become active and performative.

What, then, is the thingness of architecture? Should the Hinzert Document Centre, which houses these active things, now speak as well? Or asked the other way round: is there an option for the architectural envelope to be silent at all? Maybe neither one nor the other applies – with architecture finding itself in a grey in-between zone. It is neither able to simulate a historical reconstruction nor is it a neutral, ahistorical container. Instead, the architectural project addresses the political and territorial deformations of the landscape: a document centre including archives, research library, seminar and exhibition spaces, designed as an unconventional, almost topological building that seamlessly blends intuition and rational design strategies.

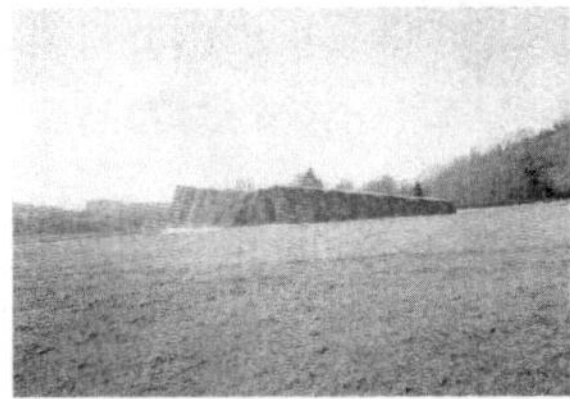

Fig. 4: Nikolaus Hirsch, Wolfgang Lorch, Andrea Wandel: Hinzert Document Centre

The 43-metre-long structure occupies a slope, rising from two to seven metres in height. The all-in-one structure, roof and façade, consists of more than 3,000 different triangular plates of 12-millimetre Corten steel. These were welded together in a workshop to form 12 large elements that were then assembled on site. The angles between the individual panels were calculated to ensure that the elements have an adequate structural height and that the entire construction forms a rigid folded plate.

The reddish brown envelope encases an elongated exhibition space, a seminar room, a library, an archive and offices, with lines of sight giving the impression of a single spatial unit. The design process was developed from the inside towards the outside. Around the central exhibition-archive space, a series of "pockets" contain archive units, research cells and large exhibition objects that push the volume outwards into the landscape. As a shelter that protects historic material and relics, the Document Centre is a rather introverted building, opening up to the landscape only on the valley side. The opening defines the exact position of the building in the landscape and describes a precise viewpoint: a cross-fade mapping from a historical photography of the camp to the contemporary perspective of an idyllic agricultural scenery.

THE PANORAMA: DOCUMENTS AND DOCUMENTARIES

As much as the exhibition is informed by the results of more than 60 years of legal investigations, historical research and archival work, the status of a "document" in a document centre remains ambiguous. The condition of the exhibits ranges from lost material, original papers and objects preserved under glass to the vast majority of reproduced archival and photographic sources. Since they are not bound to a particular exhibition medium, the reproductions raise new architectural-curatorial questions regarding their material condition and how to define their size. Unlike the distinct, objectlike quality of the original material, we decided to treat these new reproductive elements not as separate objects but to link them directly to the architectural space, almost like a contemporary form of fresco.

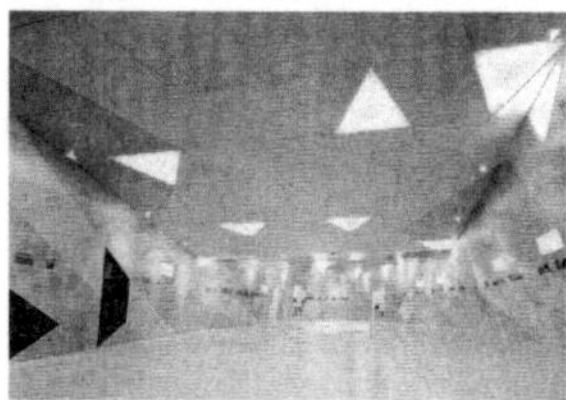

Fig. 5: Nikolaus Hirsch, Wolfgang Lorch, Andrea Wandel: interior panorama, Hinzert Document Centre

The inner skin consists of triangular, birch plywood panels, in which photographs and text are inscribed by a direct printing process. The grain of the wood interacts with the grid of the printing process. Following the logic of a triangular map, this new historiography forms a continuous envelope. Photographs, text, diagrams and trajectories of the prisoners' itineraries. Mapping all over. Documenting again and again until a new panorama emerges. Yet the ambiguity remains – this panorama is not so much the illustration of an ultimate historiographic truth as it is a construction of history that selects and organizes the material with a contemporary intention. Somewhere between document and documentary.

Nikolaus Hirsch is a Frankfurt-based architect, curator and director of the Städelschule and Portikus. His work includes the award-winning Dresden Synagogue, Hinzert Document Centre, unitednationsplaza, European Kunsthalle, Cybermohalla Hub in Delhi, and the Land Workshop in Chiang Mai. Hirsch curated *ErsatzStadt: Representations of the Urban* at the Volksbühne Berlin, *Cultural Agencies* in Istanbul, numerous exhibitions at Portikus, and the *Gwangju Folly* project in Korea. He is the author of the books *On Boundaries* and *Institution Building* and co-editor of the *Critical Spatial Practice* series.

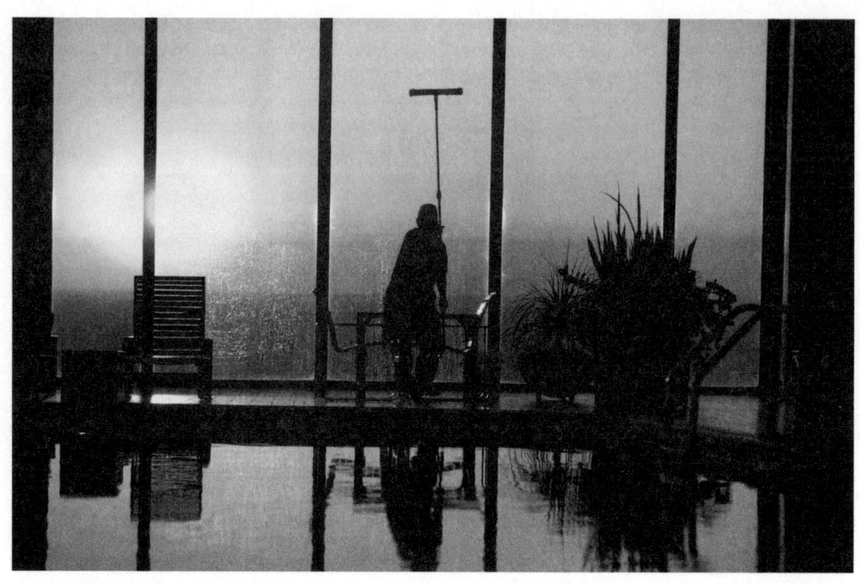

Sarah Morris, *Chicago* (2011)
Film, colour, 68 min. (film still)

Sarah Morris

The Arrogance of Power

I have seven points that I can talk about in relation to mapping and the idea of perspective. But aside from my personal history and production in Switzerland, I think one important point is the idea that all places are interlinked, that there is a "pile-up" of cities, of people, of places and of conversations. Meaning, there is no way to isolate the Alps, and there is no way to isolate a specific place.

Before I start with my seven points, I would like to tell you an anecdote. When I was making my film *Beijing* (2008), I naively went to China several times and had many conversations with officials, in order to film and get into this very specific moment I wanted to capture during the Olympics in Beijing. During my stays, I heard a lot of "yes", but actually I did not know that "yes" in China means "no." I kept on going to China and then I got a call recommending that I should go to Switzerland instead. So actually, the core aspect of the film came from a set of conversations

I had with Uli Sigg, a collector of Chinese art and a former ambassador to China and North Korea, with Hans Ulrich Obrist and with a lot of people in Lausanne from the IOC. I did go back to Switzerland, which is – as some people would say – ironic; but it is not just ironic, it is also a fact that Switzerland controls a lot of situations. Another anecdote is the tape I use in my works of art. It is called 3MX and is sold only in Switzerland – you cannot get it in America. It is an automotive tape and that is what I use for mapping the paintings. All the coordinates on the paintings are made with this sort of tool.

As I go through this sort of methodology or if you want to call it a mapping that I use when I am thinking about my work, I will sort of touch on my new film *Chicago* (2011) every now and again. I had always been thinking of doing a film about this city because there were a number of very interesting people and histories that I wanted to explore.

Number one, I would say: mapping for me means "simultaneously from many perspectives." It is sort of a schizophrenic activity, where you are looking at coordinates from within, from without, from various people's perspectives within a city. You are looking at very minor details and you are looking at the panorama. I am flicking between these different points all the time and there is no sort of stasis. In this regard, I would mention that Charles and Ray Eames's movie *Powers of Ten* (first version: 1968; final version: 1977) was very influential for me. It was filmed in Chicago and was made for IBM. I was fascinated by their idea to begin filming with a couple picnicking in a park in Chicago and then slowly zoom out ten metres (101), then 100 metres (102) and further out into space, before returning to the man and zooming in further and further into his hand and finally into his cells. By zooming out and then in, they were sort of exploding the sense of perspective. A Swiss reference that I would like to mention is Vladimir Nabokov because he has a very particular way of doing the same thing. In *Transparent Things* (1972), for example, he uses a character in a Swiss hotel. He starts to write about the character, then focuses on the pencil and then on the carbon – how carbon was made and how carbon in pencils was invented in Shakespeare's time – and finally goes back again into the narrative flow. These are two important references in terms of how one imagines a place, and how one pictures being in space and time.

My second point is: using people. I do not mean this in a pejorative or derogatory sense, but I think that people are extremely important in how you approach a place. I do this by creating lists of not only places or situations I want to be in, but people I want to meet and have conversations with. People who can lead me to an image, people who might be an image, or people who might refuse to be an image, but might educate me about how to approach an image. In relation to what I was mentioning earlier, this means that the conversations I had about making *Beijing* were all somehow obtuse. Some of these people do not appear in the film, like Uli Sigg, but were absolutely important in advising me on how to approach certain situations, which I am very thankful for. It is this idea of people as makers, or as portals into the identity of place. I did a film on Robert Towne *(Robert Towne,* 2006), who was the screenwriter of *Chinatown* (1974) and one with Dr. Georg Sieber (*1972,* 2008), a police psychologist at the 1972 Olympic Games, who was in charge of the security and had to prepare the security training, but obviously failed. And as I started to think about Chicago, I was very interested in the invention of *Playboy* magazine, Hugh Hefner and Nabokov, whose short stories were published in *Playboy*, Barack Obama, Mayor Daley, *Ebony* magazine, John Johnson, the Kennedys, Robert R. Wilson, who designed the first particle accelerator at the Fermilab near Chicago, which is parallel to the one in Switzerland.

Point three is to try to examine or think about industrial processes and production in places, what is going on economically somewhere? What is embedded in the surface of place? What are the functions of the spaces that you are looking at, that you are occupying, that you are moving through? In Chicago, for instance, there is this massive history not only of meatpacking, but also of publishing. When I started to do my research, I noticed the dwindling, dying industry of the printed word, which was in a way very fascinating. I did not known that many American newspapers are printed in Chicago. There is one compound for the *Chicago Tribune* of about ten acres. That's where *The Wall Street Journal*, *The New York Times*, the *Miami Tribune* and so on are printed. So I started to investigate the publishing world, but also the advertising world, and food production. Of course, in contrast to this is the consumption of these things, whether or not they are produced in a dwindling or increasing pattern. Anyhow, these are important elements if you think about a place, about citizens and their flow. I filmed in several of these places in Chicago. There is, for example, a scene we shot in the headquarters of *Ebony* magazine, where they allowed me to shoot a board meeting while they were on a conference call with the White House, which I thought was charged.

Point four is that the issue of meatpacking and industrial production brought me to the question of whether it is possible to do a map without literature – which I think it is not. Whenever I think about Chicago, I also always think about that very important book *The Jungle* (1906) by Upton

Sinclair. The book triggered the whole concept of muckraking and a massive change in industrial production prompted by legislation, and at the same time, it also invoked the idea of failure.

The concept of failure is my fifth point: failure past and present. What does failure look like? How do you embrace failure? How do you use it as a motor, as a device to crack the surface of something in order to make an image or a series of images? I think that is what I am constantly trying to do. With this concept, I am referring to social failure. I have always been interested in moments in which things break down historically. When I was trying to make the film *Beijing* – which was so difficult to organize even aside from the language issues, with all the incredible bureaucracy that could drive you insane – I started thinking about my own failure. How was I going to make this film? Would it maybe all fall apart? I started thinking about the Olympics as a failure, because we all know it is. At the same time, I started thinking about the Black September of 1972 and began to read a lot about it. I went to Munich and had dinner with Dr. Georg Sieber, who was a psychologist and crowd choreographer and very much involved in the work of Munich's police force in the late 1960s. The police wanted to control demonstrations and their flow, and his idea was to give the demonstrators a platform and a microphone, which was very progressive and worked very well. He was someone from the political left who ended up in the police and who also created a company called Intelligenz Transfer Systems, which advises governments, companies and architects how buildings should be made in order to be secure. My film *1972*, which I mentioned above, is definitely not a documentary. You certainly do not have to believe every word Sieber is saying. I had to make a piece that contextualized this idea of failure because I honestly think that Beijing is a failure – not in relation to China, just in relation to the fact that we are all complicit. I am not excluding myself in any way.

Point six needs to be seen in relation to failure, artistic and otherwise. Post-Watergate, this subterranean concept of surface could be defined as archiving, tunnels, documentation, the narcissism that led to Richard Nixon's demise, his undoing, which brings me to the title of my talk, which is called "The Arrogance of Power." Anthony Summers wrote a book, an extremely good biography of Nixon, called *The Arrogance of Power: The Secret World of Nixon* (2000). I think this idea of never trusting a surface is very present in my generation. It is a belief that emebedded within a surface are all the things that would lead to the surface's demise. This is almost a contradiction in terms, because you have its failure, its lack of resolution and a regenerative splintering into new images.

So a surface is never just a surface; it always leads to something else. And again, it is the idea of a chain, or a series of moments. It is a notion that nothing is really static, but that things are constantly in flux. This applies not only to people, but also to cities and places.

Point seven is the role of fantasy in relation to mapping. I think about this a lot. I try to come up with a list, for example places I want to be, rooms I want to be in, people I want to meet, or conversations I want to have. I think this involves a sense of projection into the future, which I would call fantasy. In relation to Chicago, I would like to talk about Mies van der Rohe and fantasy. His fantasy is linked to Berlin and to Germany, and it is also linked to his dream of modernity: to his 1920s' drawings of the glass skyscraper and to his idea of not only creating an image of America, but the reality of how America should look. He played this amazing fantasy out in Chicago. You see it everywhere you go in Chicago: the post office, the bank, the school, the apartment block, the convention centre. You have this sort of cinematic effort to stage, to control the flow of citizens and their production and their movements. I think from this effect, again, you have this transparency of surface, transparency of form.

Sarah Morris (b. 1967 in London) grew up in Rhode Island. The American artist lives and works in New York and London. Since the mid-1990s, she has been making complex abstract paintings with household gloss and, non-narrative films. In both media, she is concerned with architecture, the psychology of urban environments and their surfaces.

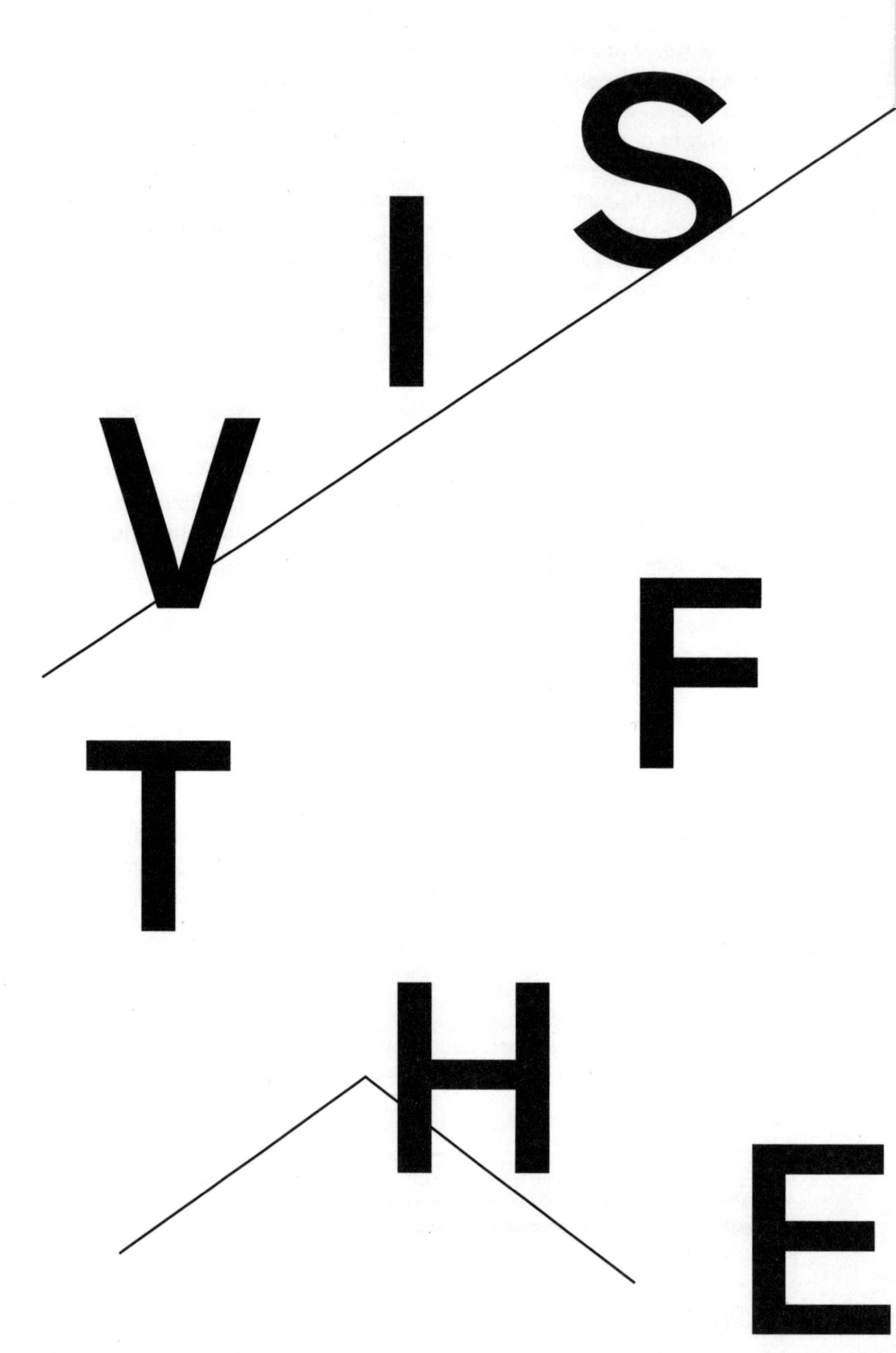
S
I
V
F
T
H
E

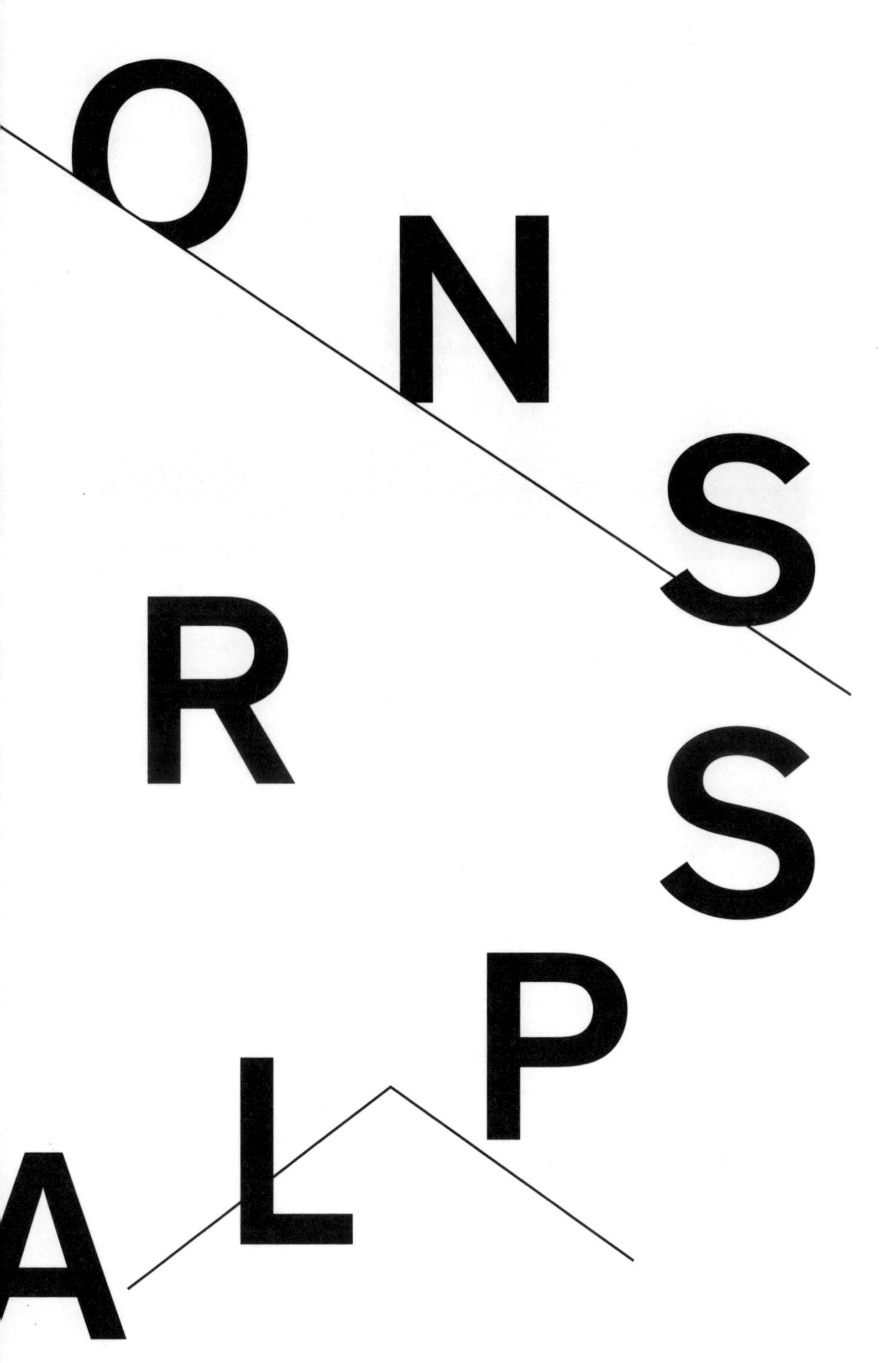
O
N
S
R
S
P
L
A

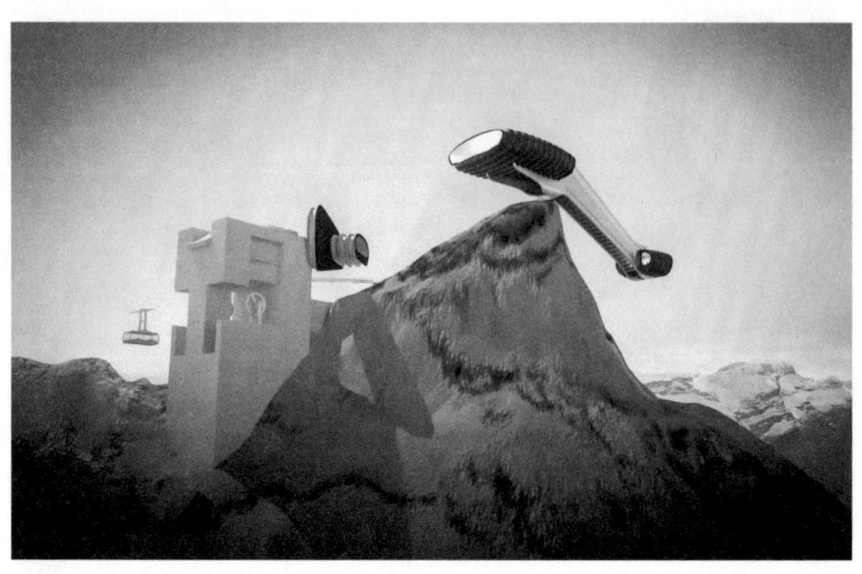

Ron Arad Architects, *Les Diablerets/ Switzerland* (2007, unrealized project)

Ron Arad

"I don't care how much it costs – my only problem is who is going to pay for it" (and other problems)

When I was persuaded by Hans Ulrich Obrist to participate in the Engadin Art Talks in the middle or end of August, I did not know that I would be totally involved in something completely different. So I flew from Jerusalem – or rather Tel Aviv, because Jerusalem does not have an airport – where I am involved in the installation *720°*. In fact right now, I am more interested in that than in some abortive work I did few years ago that had to do with the Alps … Anyhow, I will now present the project that I was asked to do in 2007 by Bernie Ecclestone. It was a partnership between Swarovski, Formula One Management, and Red Bull Extreme Sport Division. They brought me to Les Diablerets, which is a Swiss ski region near the border between the French and Swiss Alps, and not too far away from Gstaad. Close to the summit there is a ski lift and motor room designed by Mario Botta, and the idea of the project was to connect the ski lift with the summit 3,000 metres above sea level. When I got there, I couldn't see anything.

It was all white, and there was really nothing to see because it was foggy. So we had to go back to the studio and build a model of the Alps. The ski area on this mountain is bankrupt; it loses money every day and they wanted us to do something spectacular there – a landmark panoramic gallery and restaurant on the peak. As Swarovski was involved, I was tempted for a moment to do some crystal things, but that idea did not last very long. Then I thought that when you go to a place with a 360-degree panoramic view, it would be nice to do just the opposite and offer not the panoramic view but something like a panning shot instead. I wanted to evoke the feeling of being in a camera. The idea was to have a balancing space. The escalator would be the arm and lead to the restaurant. Both would rotate as one element, taking around 40 minutes for a complete turn. But it did not happen, and the reason it did not happen was that although it could have been built entirely off-site, it failed to get planning permission. Like any other project in architecture, it did not automatically get planning permission. That scared the people who had commissioned it and then they did not have the stamina to go for it. Bernie Ecclestone said this famous sentence, famous to me: "I don't care how much it costs – my only problem is who is going to pay for it." And it would not have cost more than a yacht that any one of you might have parked somewhere. As Swarovski was supposed to have a shop there, I thought: let's do a camera obscura so that you can see the Alps upside down before people buy any crystals. But then the project was stopped. And that was how my one and only involvement with the Alps came to a halt as well.

Ron Arad (b. 1951 in Tel Aviv) studied at the Jerusalem Academy of Art and at the Architectural Association in London. He established the design and architecture bureau Ron Arad Associates in 1994. Arad, who is based in London, was professor of design at the Hochschule in Vienna (1994–97) and at the Royal College of Art in London (1997–2009). He is one of the most influential industrial designers today and is known for his experimentation with materials and his radical reconception of the form and structure of furniture.

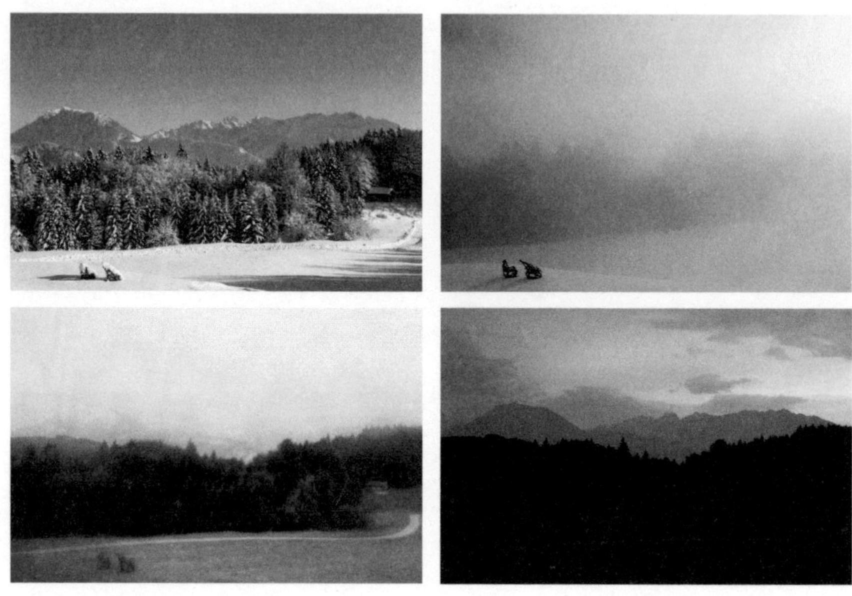

Rolf & Maryam Sachs, photographs from the series
The Wild Emperor (2004)

Rolf Sachs

Alpine Thoughts and a Project

I am very attached to the Engadin, and I am particularly attached to the school hall we are in now because I went to school here for eight years. It was a time when I did some of my first creative works: I made the stages for the theatre plays or for the Sankt Nicholas presentation, which took place here. But it is also the hall in which I was decorated with my sports' awards and had to hold my acceptance speech for being elected "School Captain". This was a great honour and a very special moment in a young man's life.

Today, I would like to speak about the photographic project *The Wild Emperor*, which I did with my wife, Maryam, in 2004. It is – to sum it up briefly – a photographic timeline. A fixed camera took panoramic photographs from our family's mountain lodge in Bavaria. From there, you have an incredible view. At a distance of about 17 km you can see two impressive mountain peaks: one is called *Der Wilde Kaiser* (The Wild Emperor), and the other *Der Zahme Kaiser* (The Tame Emperor). Kitzbühel is located behind these two mountains, meaning that our lodge is actually situated in Germany, yet the landscape you see belongs mostly to Austria. The landscape is dominated by the far-off peaks, and this is why changes in the scenery are particularly clearly visible. The landscape looks different depending on the weather conditions, on the time of the day or on the season. Our idea was to catch such different atmospheres with a camera. To do so, we installed, on the balcony of the lodge, a little shelter that was equipped with a climatic system, a heating system and a humidity extractor, and placed the camera in it. For one year, this camera took photographs every ten and a half minutes – in total around 50,000 pictures. Many people asked me why we chose this timing, and the reason was that we absolutely wanted to avoid regular intervals.

In fact, I had already dreamed of such a photographic timeline when I was still young, but back then, it was technically not possible to do it the way we did it in 2004: we used a 15 MPx Kodak professional DCS SLR R/n digital camera to take the pictures automatically. The photographs were immediately downloaded to a computer located in the house. None of the pictures has been edited in any way on the computer – although we had, in principle, the possibility to process the digital pictures, we did not want to do so.

We wanted to accentuate the depth of the pictorial space, so we put two chairs that I had conceived in the foreground. Interestingly, many of the photographs remind people of other artists: some of the pictures recall Hiroshi Sugimoto's photographs, others call to mind Caspar David Friedrich's paintings, or, when it was raining heavily and the pictures looked blurred, the photographs that were created are reminiscent of paintings by Gerhard Richter. Some of the pictures are sepia-toned, making them look like historical photographs but in fact the camera had simply captured a sandstorm. A sandstorm in the mountains – here in the Engadin, too – is very rare and happens only every ten or 15 years. It is surprising that the whole day during which the camera took photographs, the pictures did not look so different from each other: all were sepia-toned, which gave the impression that they were taken in black and white. Only when you look ed very carefully at the trees were you able to discern some green spots. It is indeed incredible that light can change a landscape so dramatically. I was expecting the photographs to be quite interesting, but I have to admit that the variety of atmospheres we were able to depict was a surprise even to me.

Rolf Sachs (b. 1955 in Lausanne/Switzerland) is a conceptual artist and designer whose work never fails to intrigue and surprise audiences, pushing them to question preconceptions. His approach is playful and inventive, and encourages human interaction, as well as emotional and sensory reactions. His work moves across art and design, objects, visual media and spaces; from furniture and lighting, architectural installations to set designs for opera and ballet. He is a member of the Board of Trustees of the London Design Museum, the International Advisory Board of Tate Modern, and Sotheby's. In 1994, he and his wife, Maryam, and their three children moved to London, where he founded his studio Rolf Sachs Func'tion.

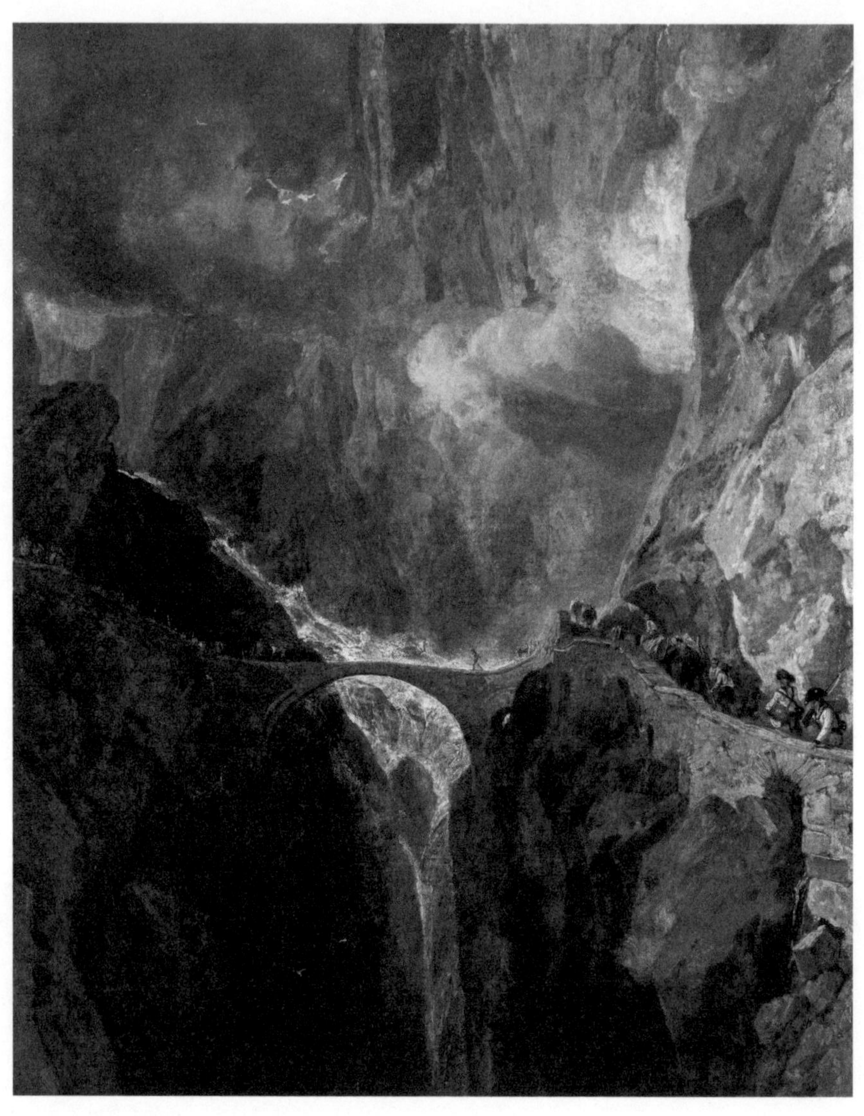

Joseph Mallord William Turner,
The Devil's Bridge, St. Gotthard (c.1803/04)
Oil on canvas, 80 × 64.1 cm, private collection

Christophe Girot

Topology: Sensing the Alps with Point Clouds

I would like to show you a conceptual revolution in the way of looking at the Alps. The devices we have been using have allowed us to map the Gotthard Pass electronically in 3D. This is a big research project we have been doing and it is leading to an extraordinary conceptual revolution in the way we perceive Alpine space today. What I find interesting in these results is that we will be able to create pictures that are actually a field of points of information, a physical and visualized model. Each pixel in the model generated by a terrestrial laser scanner is linked to seven satellites delivering a very precise geographic position. You can move inside the model with great precision, to within a centimetre accuracy in the X, Y and Z coordinates. You can also choose to see close-ups of any rock or plant in the whole Alpine valley.

There is a word I want to propose that presently belongs to the field of pure mathematics and philosophy. It goes back to the Greek notion of topos and of logos: the word is topology. Topology is basically a form of intelligence about the continuity of landscape and surfaces. I think we should bring that word into the current discussion about the intelligence of place, because we tend to think of landscapes just as objects and fragments. On the contrary, I would like to be able to model space entirely – in which a variety of objects could come into play. With regard to mountains, when we talk about topology, it is obviously a field of accidents and breaks in continuity. Part of our work on the Gotthard Pass was done in collaboration with the architect Christian Sumi of the University of Mendrisio and my Laboratory at the Swiss Federal Institute of Technology (ETH), Zurich. What is happening currently in the Gotthard is quite interesting with the high-speed rail system under construction. After its completion, it will be the longest tunnel in the world with a distance of 57 kilometres: despite its length, you will be able to cross the entire Gotthard range in less than 15 minutes. The streamlined tunnel will efficiently link Milan to Zurich as if they were on flat terrain. Ironically speaking, you have the convenience of not having to look at the Alps anymore and can look through a black tunnel instead. So what is my point? The point is that we are arriving at a specific moment in history when we can cross the Alps without a view. What would John Ruskin think of that?

To put this research in place, my fellow researchers and I benefited from the support given by the Swiss National Science Foundation. Together with my fellow colleague ETH Professor Adrienne Grêt-Regamey, we got equipment worth half a million Swiss francs and founded the LVML (Landscape Visualization & Modeling Lab). Support of this kind does not usually go to landscape architects, but to dam, tunnel and bridge engineers.

The equipment we use detects and geo-positions a hairline crack in a wall a kilometre away. These are state-of-the-art machines, and we have perverted them for the sake of landscape architecture, actually reconsidering Alpine space altogether. We have almost finished this Alpine model and are thinking of exhibiting it, because we think it represents a conceptual revolution.

I would like to refer to the famous painting *The Devil's Bridge, St. Gotthard* (c.1803/04) by William Turner. He was an atmospheric and gaseous painter. In a way, the two English painters Ruskin and Turner, together with the English Alpine Club, are the makers of the Swiss Alps aesthetic as we know it today. The Swiss picked up whatever the English brought to them and let it grow into a very profitable business, changing desolate Alpine valleys into gold. The railway is an English invention and the whole Swiss Alpine concept is a product of the early train lines. We all know that and we have benefited enormously from it: St. Moritz is a perfect example of this miracle – there are many poor valleys in the Alps that have never managed to reach that level of notoriety. This could not have happened without the red trains of the Rhaetian Railway. My point is that this model we have been building is not about a picture, not about a photograph, and not about a video but about a physical body. It is composed of a field of electronic dots, a sort of topographic veil that work almost like raindrops defining the skin of the entire Alpine environment. It brings relativity into the way we can view a valley, and can be either dangerous for bad architects or very beneficial for good ones, showing good site planning strategies. Topology is going to allow us to look at our environment in a completely different way.

I think that we are through with the dominance of one-point perspective, we are through with the Albertian revolution that has held for 500 years, influencing even Romantics like Caspar David Friedrich. The one-point view is gone, whereas in our model, all becomes visually relative. We can look through the mountains as if they were a diaphanous skin. The real revolution is that every place, every picture and every dot in the model is a determined reference point. Any spot or patch on a rock becomes a point of information that is clearly positioned. Unlike conventional representations, which feature only height lines and maps, our model maps the entire vertical face of a mountain precisely. I can give you the exact position within a centimetre where any object, any house or any foot has left its mark. The machine that we have at our disposal has a range of one and a half kilometres, and we can draw contour lines around a cigarette butt discarded on the ground a kilometre away. This is a very diabolical device. This is why I refer to *The Devil's Bridge* as a symbol of deep perceptual and representational changes. We use a variety of techniques like drones, which take pictures while flying over the Alps, and which are combined with other tools such as the terrestrial laser scanner and LiDAR scanners that produce complex data sets turned into digital terrain models. The laser scanner looks like a robot. It sees matter and positions at the speed of light everything upon the surface of the earth within a single scan. It also generates pictures of extraordinary beauty. They look like an aquatint or a print of some forest, but every pixel dot composing the image is linked to seven satellites. You can move around a site, without flying. When you do a campaign on site, you gather a hundred views and then you throw all these pictures into the computer, and then the pixels migrate and make up the model of the entire skin of the mountain. The result is a 3D point cloud of extremely high precision that can be embedded with newer projects. This new way of creating models and of perceiving a landscape is opening up a conceptual revolution.

Christophe Frédéric Girot (b. 1957 in Paris) holds two masters from the University of California, Berkeley, one in architecture and one in landscape architecture. He was professor and head of the Department of Landscape Design at the École Nationale Supérieure du Paysage in Versailles, France (1990–2000). Since 2001, he has been a professor at the Swiss Federal Institute of Technology (ETH), Zurich, where he founded the Institute of Landscape Architecture in 2005. His research addresses new topological methods in landscape design, new media in landscape analysis, and the theory of landscape design.

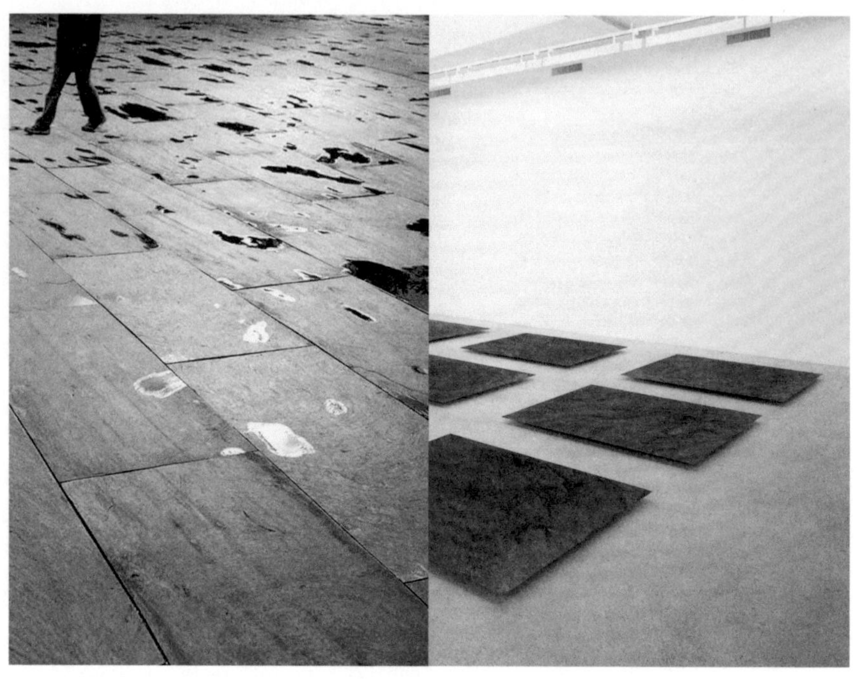

Hans Danuser, *Beverin Slate Platform* (2001, architecture project)/*Erosion* (work in progress since 2001, floor installation with photography)

Hans Danuser

The EROSION PROJECTS and Visions for the Arts

I have had the opportunity to create three major projects in the Alps. One outstanding example is the *DENKLABOR VILLA GARBALD* in Val Bregaglia. It was more than just a project, it was a project that was realized, and it was a concept based on art.

Today, I want to speak about my *EROSION PROJECTS* ... because, before developing any visions for the Alps, I feel it is important ... and interesting ... to take a look at the Alps themselves. After all, the image that urban people have formed of the Alps over the centuries has always been ... ultimately ... a view of the Alps seen from a distance: at times heightened ... *überhöht* ... at times spectacular, yet always immovable ... The Alps as a natural phenomenon that is unchanging and stable ... and in a political sense: the Alps as a safe haven. But that was not how I experienced the Alps as a child.

Meine Erfahrung als Kind war eine andere. Unser Spielplatz, oder vielleicht besser gesagt, „unsere Welt" an freien Schulnachmittagen am Fusse der Maschänzerrüfe am Scaläratobel nahe bei Chur sah jedes Mal wenn wir wiederkamen, anders aus. Unsere Spuren von vor Tagen zuvor waren verwischt, selten noch unversehrt und präzise gezeichnet, immer aber mit Spuren von Erosion oder ganz weggebrochen.

Our playground – or perhaps I should say "our world" – was constantly changing. Whenever we clambered down to the Maschänzer mountain stream in the Scalära gorge near Chur – on our free afternoons after school – it looked different. Any traces we had left on previous days had been blurred; they were rarely intact or precisely drawn. They were invariably marked by erosion or had broken away completely.

In the nineties, when the fall of Eastern Bloc Communism exposed the erosion of Western values, too, these memories came back to me …

… and I began my project of observing and exploring the Alps through photography and studying the process of erosion. I am not interested in such spectacular events as landslides and rockfalls ... I am interested in ordinary, everyday changes – in erosion.

One part of the *EROSION PROJECT* is a photographic work with the title *EROSION* (Floor Installation with Photography, work in progress since 2001). In the photographic erosion cycle, I started by focusing on the Alpine slate mountains. These geological layers in the Grison region run through the Churer Rheintal valley, the "Rätikon", and to the Domleschg all the way until the Beverin massiv. The reason I concentrated on slate and slate mountains is because slate occurs in nature, in the landscape, in forms that range from stable rock formations to the very finest dust.

Auf Schiefer und die Schiefergebirge konzentrierte ich mich, da der Schiefer in der Natur, in der Landschaft, vorkommt. Schiefer zeigt sich im Schiefergebirge vom stabilen Fels bis zum feinsten Staub. Jede Nuance lässt sich fotografisch sichtbar aufzeichnen und dadurch verliere ich als Betrachter die Sicherheit der Proportionalität, die Sicherheit der eigenen Distanz zum Objekt. Ich bin unsicher, ob es ein Überflug ist, oder ich mich ganz nah am Boden bewege... Every nuance can be captured visibly in a photograph. Looking at the photograph, I am no longer certain of the proportions or my distance from the object. I am not sure whether it is an aerial view or whether I am right down on the ground.

Slate is an interesting material for photography because its tactile quality and colour are reminiscent of pencil lead, and both have similarities with the dark and light shading of a silver bromide print in analogue photography … *Der Schiefer als Material ist auch interessant für die Fotografie, da er in seiner Taktilität und Farbe an das Graphit eines Bleistiftes erinnert, und beides findet eine Analogie im einzelnen Silberbromid-Kristall eines fotografisch analog beschichteten Hell-Dunkel-Papieres.*

Each tableau is 1.5 m by 1.4 m, and the installation of the tableaux with the photographs is arranged in an exhibition that you can – and indeed are expected to – walk around between the tableaux. The photographs are arranged on the floor, not at the wall, so it breaks down the binding, hierarchical order of images. All become equal, and – as visitors walk through the landscape of images – the entire installation itself is set in motion … Depending on the architectural setting in which I show these works, and depending on the flooring in which the photographs are laid out, our perception of the erosion changes. The installation has between six and 18 tableaux. In addition to the Alps, I began taking photographs in the slate mountains of Wales, England, Portugal and Germany, and a few in the south of the United States and in northern China ...

Allen Orten ist gemeinsam, dass sich die Landschaft, das Gebirge, tagtäglich verändert. Letztlich müsste man jeden Tag eine neue Karte zeichnen. What all those places have in common is that the mountains are constantly changing from day to day. Ultimately, a new map would have to be drawn every day …

The second project I am presenting is the *BEVERIN SLATE PLATFORM* (2001) in the valley called Domleschg. It is an art in architecture project, perhaps even a boundary-crossing project, in which the art itself became architecture. It was while I was researching for the competition that I came across the name of Richard La Nicca, an early 19th-century engineer, who began a project in the Grison Alps that was in every sense visionary. His work forms the base for the *BEVERIN SLATE PLATFORM.* It could be said, with a little bit of exaggeration, that this platform project has been a work in process from 1820 to 2000. Again, the focus here is on slate, and its layered qualities. This time, however, it is all about the material itself, as stone, and in the case of La Nicca, in the form of the controlled exploitation of erosion … *bei La Nicca in Form kontrollierter Nutzbarmachung von Erosion.*

Die Ausgangslage, das Setting, the starting point … The Beverin clinic is one of the two major psychiatric clinics in the Grison region. It was originally designed and built between 1895 and 1900, and was architectonically remodelled and radically modernized between 1997 and 2000 to meet today's standards of psychiatric care. This involved the conservation of existing historical architecture on the one hand, and new buildings on the other. The question, in terms of art, was an open-ended one.

Where should art be placed on the campus and what material should be used by the artist? … *Dies ist selten, dass die Positionierung der Kunst im architektonischen Setting und auch das Medium der Kunst frei gewählt werden kann…*

While I was researching for the project, I discovered La Nicca's plans and drawings in the Grison state archives. In the early 19th century, the river Rhine meandered through the Domleschg plains, often causing floods. *Er mäanderte über die ganze Ebene, die Dörfer waren am Rande situiert, die ganze Ebene war in dem Sinne nicht genutzte Landschaft.* In 1820, under the leadership of engineer Richard La Nicca, work began on straightening the course of the Rhine and shoring up the land on either side with slate sand from the Beverin to make it suitable for agricultural use … *Sie haben beide Seiten mit Schiefersand aus dem Beverin-Gebiet aufgeschwemmt…* It was a land reclamation project on a vast scale, begun in 1820 and completed when I made the Beverin slate platform.

Mein Wettbewerbsvorschlag im Bereich der Kunst, der auch realisiert wurde… My proposal, which was eventually implemented, is intended to mark the new clinic centre of the architecturally sprawling clinic campus and to create a meeting place for visitors and patients by placing the two central buildings on a slate platform … *Indem ich die beiden Zentrumsgebäude auf die Schiefertafel stellte.* What I did was to make the slate underground of the campus visible by raising the slate platform slightly above the level of the campus ground – and with the platform, the centre of the complex with the two buildings. The slate platform is composed of individual slabs measuring 1 m x 2 m. The entire slate surface with the two buildings on it is raised by approximately 20 to 30 cm above the surrounding area. 20 to 30 cm are quite a step; you have to go up to the platform. One of the buildings is new with a reception area, a restaurant and café, as well as a conference room. The delivery area is underground. The building opposite it is a theatre that was built in 1895 as part of the psychiatric campus, as part of psychiatric care.

So this slate platform functions not only as a public space, but also as a stage. We also tend to associate slate with writing slates that were once used in schools … and even today slate is a symbol of communication … so the area is visibly a place of meeting, interaction and communication … and another detail of the design of the platform is that it continues inside the new building: it flows under the glass façade into the interior. Depending on the angle of the sun, the slate can sometimes reflect like a lake. Slate is vulnerable … *Schiefer ist verletzlich. Er hinterlässt Spuren und zeichnet die Zeit…* Slate leaves traces that show the passage of time.

In rain and thunderstorms, the slate platform itself becomes a landscape ... *In Regen und Gewitter wird die Schiefertafel selbst wieder zur Landschaft.* All of that was expected and envisaged ...
in a way ... but what did come as a surprise was the way rain or a thunderstorm could transform the platform into an image. And so, the slate platform generates ever-changing images of vast dimensions ... In a way, the biggest photographs I ever did ... close to 2,000 m^2.

The Alps are constantly in flux ... *Die Alpen sind permanent in Bewegung... Bis in die höchsten Ebenen und Bergspitzen sind sie vermessen, meist eine Kulturlandschaft. Und dennoch zeigen sie sich jeden Tag anders. Meine Erfahrung zeigt, der eigene Standort/Standpunkt in dieser Landschaft ist instabil und brüchig. Oben und unten, nah und fern fliessen ineinander über, und Sicherheiten können jederzeit wegrutschen. Projekte in den Alpen haben nur Erfolg, wenn sie diese Bewegung und die Erosionsprozesse nicht nur aushalten, sondern damit arbeiten.*

The Alps have been surveyed, mapped and charted to the very pinnacle of their highest summits, and all their man-made environments. And yet, they look different every day. In my experience, it is our own standpoint within this landscape that is unstable and fragile: high and low, up and down, far and near – all converge and blend together; our certainties might be swept away at any moment. Projects in the Alps cannot be successful unless they not only endure this flux and these processes of erosion, but actually work with them. I have dedicated the Beverin slate platform to La Nicca, one of the real great visionaries of the Grison region.

Hans Danuser (b. 1953 in Chur/Switzerland) lives in Zurich and New York. After working as an assistant to Zurich-based German advertising and fashion photographer Michael Lieb in the early 1970s, he began to experiment with light-sensitive emulsion at the Swiss Federal Institute of Technology (ETH), Zurich. Danuser is one of the pioneers of contemporary photography in Switzerland. He became internationally known through his "IN VIVO" cycle (1980–89) and set a milestone in 20th-century architectural photography with his radically subjective photographs of Peter Zumthor's buildings.

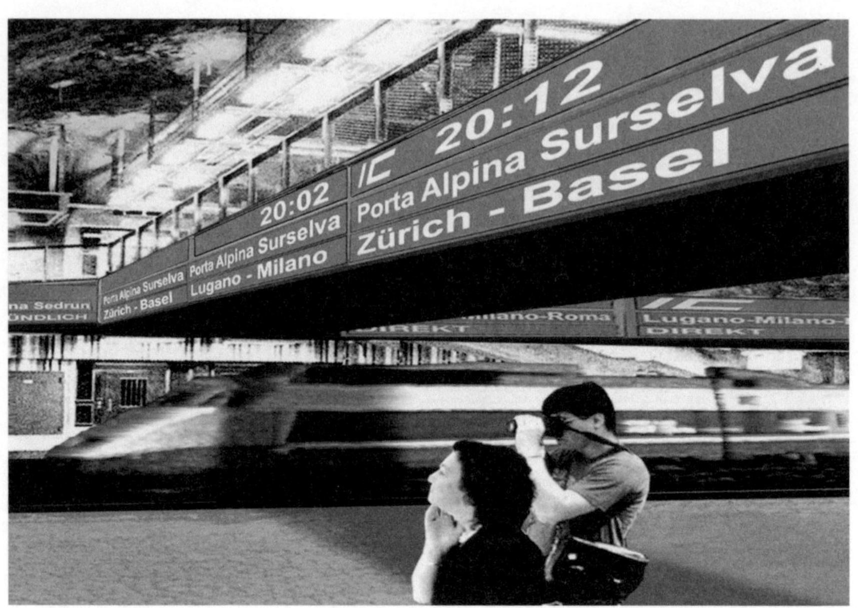

Porta Alpina (unrealized)

Arthur Loretz

Porta Alpina

Porta Alpina was – unfortunately I have to emphasize the world "was" – a project that stirred up hope in Switzerland, and especially in the canton of Graubünden. It was therefore a great disappointment when the project was stopped for political reasons this year. Nevertheless, let me look back on the visionary plan we had.

Our project started in 2001 and had been related to the transit route from Zurich to Milan. This is one of the most important Alpine crossings, and the Gotthard Base Tunnel is under construction along this route right now. It consists of two single-track tubes that will connect two lowland areas north and south of the Alps despite the different altitudes of the mountains. Frankly speaking, they are digging a hole 500 metres below ground to connect two areas, but by doing so, the Alps basically disappear, and do not come into view again. So our initial concern was the prospect of having a kind of a Suez Canal hidden somewhere below ground.

The tunnel will indeed connect the two urban areas of Zurich and Milan. But what will happen with the regions in between, where there are in fact hardly any cities? Wouldn't it be better to have an exit leading to an Alpine region? Some people call such an area an "Alpine Brache" – a piece of fallow land in the Alps – where you can find pure nature, protected, unspoiled land, and culture that is thousands of years old, as for example the monastery in Disentis. At the same time, you can find places with large skiing areas, and a tourist infrastructure. Our intention was to bring people up to this rather isolated region and to give them the opportunity to see the beautiful landscape. For this reason, Porta Alpina was a project that wanted to render the Alps visible again. It was meant as an exit leading to the region, or an entrance into it, so to speak. Our idea was to profit from the shafts that will be built for the construction of the tunnel. A double shaft 800 metres high has already been built in the middle of the Gotthard Base Tunnel, and we wanted to use this shaft, or better still, convert it into a lift. At the foot of it there would have been a railway station. By using what is so far the highest lift in the world, people would have been able to access the Alps. Imagine how visionary it would have been to construct the deepest railway station in the world by using the world's highest lift inside the world's longest tunnel.

The railway station could indeed have become a tourist attraction by itself. In this regard, we should not forget that railways have always been linked to the experience of landscape. Rail travel is not only about being transported from A to B, but also about seeing a landscape, experiencing it and enjoying beautiful views. Furthermore, we intended to show that with the underground station, the "Alpine Brache" could become economically viable despite indications to the contrary: research conducted by the ETH Studio Basel came to the conclusion that the area actually had no economical future at all – to put it bluntly. Nevertheless, our vision was initially received positively and stood a good chance of being realized. The Swiss parliament approved start-up funding in 2005, and by the end of 2006, first blasting operations took place in order to create the waiting halls. The aim of the government was, of course, to create a station that would help to revitalize the "Alpine Brache" and develop the region economically. From the project would have benefited not only the village near the exit to the lift but the entire area. After further studies, however, the Swiss parliament, fearing that the project might prove unprofitable, decided to put the project on indefinite hold. From my point of view, this decision, this political suicide, was a mistake and the whole region is now very depressed: a vision has been turned into an illusion.

Arthur Loretz (b. 1969 in Sedrun/Switzerland) studied philosophy at the University of Zurich and architecture at the Swiss Federal Institute of Technology (ETH), Zurich. From 2001 to 2004, he worked as a partner at the Büro 3 office of architects in Zurich, and later as an independent architect in Zurich and Sedrun. He is now at ZSB Architekten in Zurich. As president of the Visiun Porta Alpina, Loretz campaigned for the conversion of an emergency stop in the Gotthard Base Tunnel into the permanent Porta Alpina railway station.

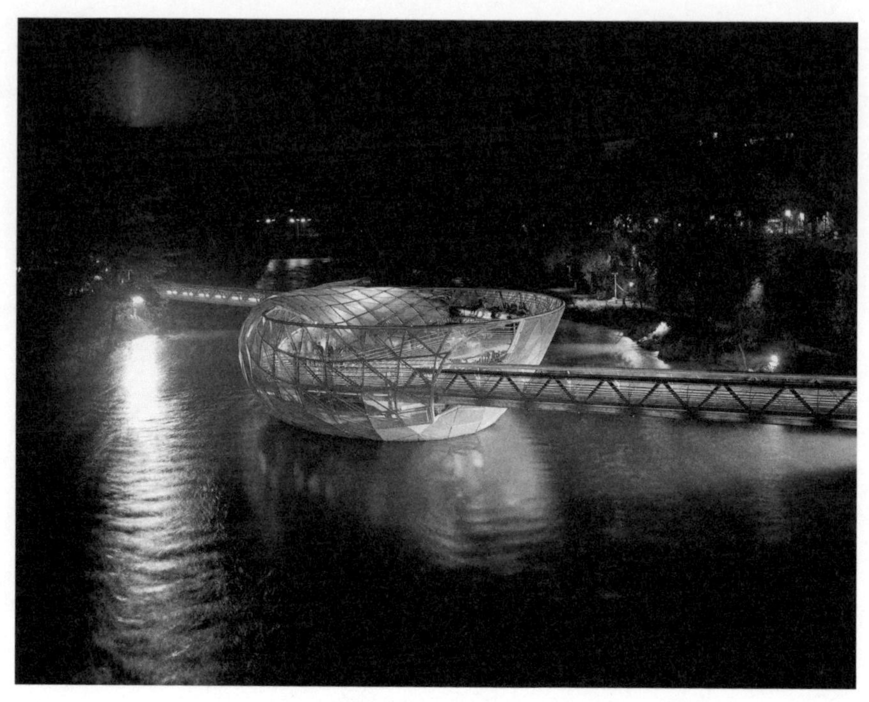

Murinsel (2003)
Artificial floating platform in Graz,
Austria

Vito Acconci

The Alps as Model for Clouds, Particles & Pixels

When I was asked to give a title for my talk, which was only about ten days ago, I didn't realize that the talks would have to have something to do with the Alps. So I gave it a kind of hang-on title. Since we are going to be in the Alps anyway, maybe the Alps can be used as a model for thick air, for breaking up things into particles, into pixels. I've been obsessed with that lately, thinking about whether we really need surfaces? Perhaps things should be floating in air so that they constantly reform. But that didn't come out of nowhere. So what I want to do is to try to give a quick survey. I'm going to talk about architecture, but some of that might be about clothing and some of it about furniture. I don't think I have done anything that should be called art since the end of the 1980s. And it is important that I do these projects as part of a group of people because I really want architecture to change. I want people to be able to change architecture, because as long as they cannot do so, they are being subservient to architecture. And I want at least to retain the hope that architecture can make people freer and not less free. It may not be so easy to do this but I think it's the only ultimate goal, and with the introduction, recently, of virtual space, maybe a mix of virtual space and physical space can do something like that. It was important to work with a group of people because I wanted architecture not to come from one person. I hated the idea of a master architect to whom other people, possibly people working at the studio, have to be subservient. I wanted architecture to come from a group of people thinking together and this should probably mean arguing together, colliding together. Ideas probably come more often from a collision of ideas than from agreement.

The way we think of architecture can obviously start anywhere. Maybe because of earlier works of mine, it seemed to be important to start architecture with the body, with things that belong to the body, that the body can use. Most of these projects are somewhere in the mid-2000s to now. For example, we were asked by a small New York art magazine to design an umbrella. They pointed out that the umbrella hasn't been redesigned in the way it's used, so we wanted to try our hand at a new type of umbrella. And I admit that it's better if someone asks us to do something because that can take us in a direction we would not reach by ourselves. It was important that whatever we came up with should fold, to make it even more portable than an umbrella. We very quickly thought in terms of folds or ruffles in clothing, and immediately thought about combining ruffles and an umbrella to make what we called an *umbruffla*. It's made of mirrored Mylar, so that when you're wearing it, you can see outside but people can't see in – they just see reflections of buildings, reflections of themselves. It has some possible advantages over a conventional umbrella. You can tie one end to your waist and one end to your wrist so your hands are free. It can act more like clothing, more like a kind of shawl that you wrap around yourself, making it easy to bring another person in with you under this umbrella.

The next step from the body, after clothing, is things you use with your hands: tools, utensils or products. A few years ago, Alessi asked a number of people to create a coffee and tea set, so we designed a set in which the cup grows as the drink is poured into it and shrinks as the liquid is drunk. The next step out from the body is almost a little house for the body. In 2001, we designed and built a piece of furniture based on a Möbius strip. Just as a Möbius strip, by twisting, seems to have first one side and then another, so the back of our bench twists to become the seat of the bench, and then twists again to become the bottom of the bench.

So a person can constantly go from one side to the other.

The next step out from the body is interiors. We did a clothing store in Tokyo in 2003. It was for a group of young designers working in New York, called United Bamboo. The outer surface of the building in which they opened their first store is usually used for homes in Japan. So the United Bamboo people thought that it would never look like a store. Our first step was to change the outer surface and to give the exterior of the building a second skin by covering it with a screen of steel mesh. The glass walls broke through the screen and sometimes bulged into the building to provide a way in, and sometimes bulged out to make a window. We wanted to do a clothing store that was as soft as clothing, as soft as skin. So we used a soft material, somewhat stretchy, and started on the ceiling, worked it down to the wall and out again to make a counter. We attached the material to the inner surface of the wall, then pulled it as far as possible to make shelves. The whole construction is built on a kind of push-and-pull system. The lighting is located within this material for reasons of space – the store is barely five metres wide and about 15 metres long, and we needed to grab all the extra space we could possibly get. All the non-structural walls of the house were removed and curving glass alcoves pushed out to provide extra room for clothes. The ground floor is the clothing store, and the upper floor the office. The upper floor with its bulging glass wall is where we installed a video screen to enable customers to view themselves while trying on clothes. If they like what they see, they can press a button on the mirror and become the model for United Bamboo clothes.

The next step out is the notion of building. In the 1990s, we were asked if we could use an elevated highway as a place for housing in São Paulo (*Highway House & Garden*). The reason was that when these elevated highways were built, they made a lot of people homeless, so people were starting to wonder what they could do. We tried to use the underside of the highway as a place not so much for a house to live in but for a house that could grab on to the underside of the highway and then extend outwards to make a kind of garden. That was the starting point. So you walked up a number of steps into the garden, where there would be other places – not so much a house to live in, but a place where people could see movies, eat food, and so on.

Then the next step is from buildings to streets. Streets have lights, and a few years ago, New York held a competition for a new lighting system. The competition suggested that there had to be many different kinds of lights, many different kinds of signs, which meant that the lamp-posts would have to be very big. We thought that was maybe a misguided message because they might not need all the lights, all the signs on every occasion. So we tried to do the opposite. Instead of designing the thickest post, we tried to create the thinnest. Each post would have one kind of light, one kind of sign. So the more you needed, the more you braided these lamp-posts together.

Away from the streets and plazas of a city are maybe what we can call the outlands of a city – if a river runs through the city, for example. There was a project we did in Graz in 2003, when the city was named Cultural Capital of Europe. We were asked to use the River Mur that runs through the city as a place for a theatre, a café and a playground. Our decision was to put a floating platform into the river. We started with a conventional idea for a theatre – a bowl-shaped form – and asked ourselves: What if we twist the bowl? What if we turn it upside down? It then turns into a dome. So we decided to create a construction made of merging forms. There is a dome where the café is located that twists into a bowl where the open-air theatre is located. The space between the theatre and the café is a playground. We arranged the theatre seats in waves, so that they can be seat people face to face when the theatre is not being used. It can be something like a plaza with person-to-person seating. The dome functions as a café, and the entrance canopy twists down to make lounge seats around the dome. There is also movable seating: stackable seats and tables that people can move where they want. The construction is lit at night: light streams up from beneath the long wooden benches, or bleachers. There is also light in the bowl, and from the roof structure.

The next step from outlands is to movables. It could be a car or it could be a rowing boat, which is what we did in the early 1990s. We were asked to do a piece for a park in Holland and we used two aluminium rowing boats. We sank one rowboat into the dirt and grass and had a tree growing out of the front of it. It therefore acts as a kind of park bench from which you can look out across the water. The second rowing boat is attached to a circle of grass, which is movable. So if you go out into that rowing boat, you can move not only the boat, but also the island to wherever you want. I'm convinced that the architecture of the future will move. Maybe there aren't going to be national boundaries anymore, maybe everything is going to be portable, maybe you can constantly go from country to country. At one point we thought that we could carry this idea further, with a car based on a science or maybe a pseudo-science called cymatics, where the surface of a plate is vibrated by sound. Such plates can start to bounce and can cause movement. For a while we were working with an MIT physicist who called us and said, "I've proven that your car can go 15 miles per hour." So we thought, maybe this is the wrong track, and thought that maybe a car of the future should be a soft car. We also thought that maybe in the future not that many people will want to drive anymore, and designed soft cars that could be joined together.

We were asked to do a piece, a kind of public project in the courtyard of the Buildings Department Administration Building in Munich (2000). When we went to see the site we were really struck by the fact that there was a tower in the corner and a low courtyard. We immediately thought we wanted to do something on the tower that could affect the courtyard. We installed a windwheel, a wind turbine, on top of the tower. Inside the courtyard, we cut a ring out of the grass and pavement. Under this ring is a mechanism powered by the wind turbine that keeps the ring in the courtyard in constant motion. But it moves so slowly that you hardly notice it. You can be looking out of the window and see a tree there, and some time later, when you look again, you notice that the tree is elsewhere.

These examples show that the notion of movement is amazingly important to us. Again, movement itself doesn't mean people are doing something, but it does at least perhaps represent the first step. I must also admit that most of our projects have not been realized. I think we have built possibly ten to 15 per cent of our projects. However, we suggest things we believe are capable of being realized. We regard them as feasible, and then all we have to do is to convince other people.

Vito Acconci (b. 1940 in the Bronx/NY) studied literature and poetry. In 1962, he received a BA from Holy Cross College Worcester, Massachusetts, and in 1964 an MFA from the University of Iowa. After working as a poet and teacher, he moved to the visual arts in the late 1960s and worked with photography, text, film, video, sound and performance. In 1988, he founded Acconci Studio, where he develops projects in architecture, furniture and urban spaces. He lives in Brooklyn, New York.

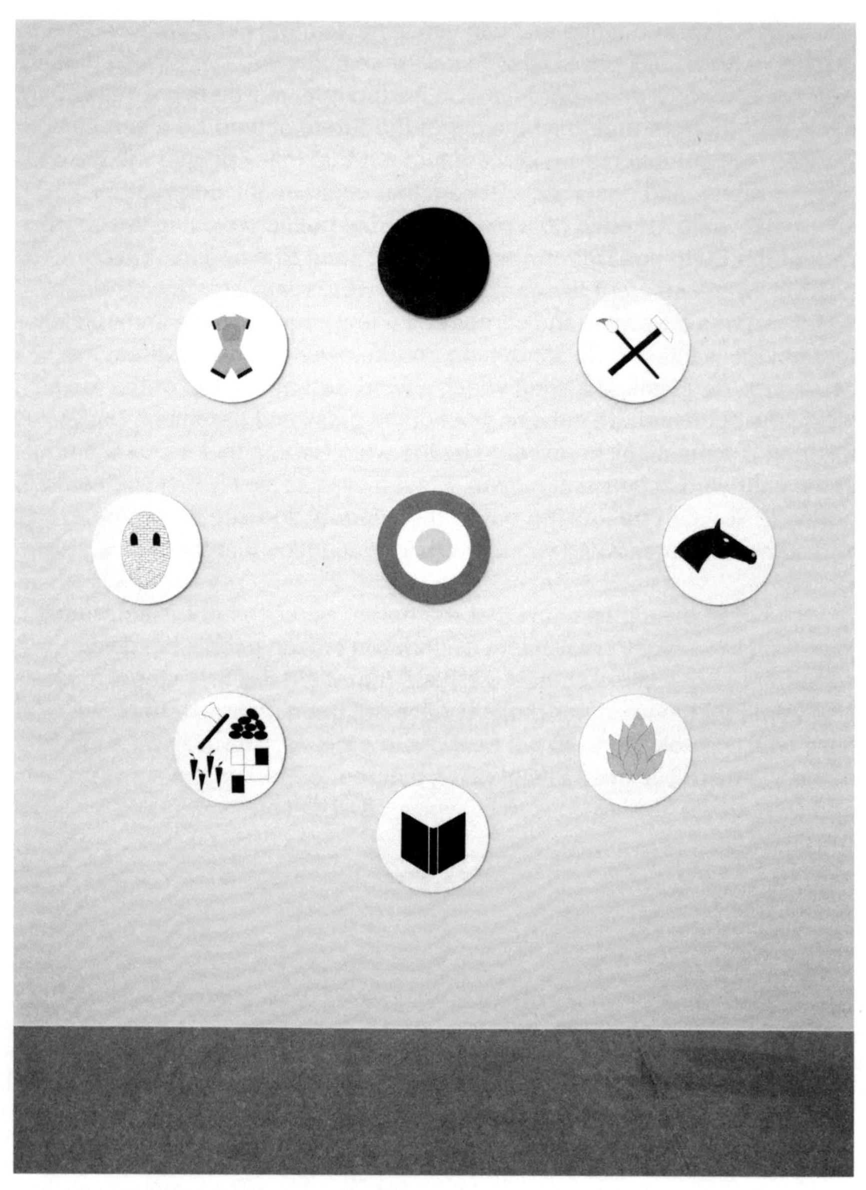

Mai-Thu Perret, *Perpetual Time Clock* (2004)
Acrylic paint on wood, 240 × 240 cm,
Ricola Collection, Laufen

Mai-Thu Perret

Utopian Projects

I am going to talk about my work and maybe mention some works that have to do with mountains as well. Actually, I have always been more afraid of mountains than in love with them. This claustrophobic quality that mountains have can be quite repulsive. During the May 1968 events in France you heard people calling out "Sous les pavés, la plage" (Under the paving stones, the beach) and in 1980, the Swiss youth movement was shouting "Nieder mit den Alpen! Freie Sicht aufs Mittelmeer!" (Down with the Alps, for a direct view of the Mediterranean!). So we have had a kind of reverent take on mountains up to now and there is also the notion that the mountains are a "Réduit national". The mountains are part of a slightly claustrophobic Swiss identity and it has taken me a long time to get to like them. Actually I like them better now than I did before. I have always dreamed of much more open spaces, like seas or especially deserts, because one thing we definitely do not have here is a desert.

When I started working as an artist – I did not actually study arts, I studied literature – I wanted to find a way to integrate a sort of narrative system or storytelling into my own work. For me, fiction and narration – especially about utopian groups or people who leave the city and who leave the modern world to create their own environment and their own society – were a very inspiring way to begin working. So my first work was to start writing a story about a commune of women in the desert in New Mexico (*The Crystal Frontier,* ongoing since 1998). It is a complete invention inspired by actual communes that have existed in lots of different places. The idea was that these women had left modern capitalist society out of frustration with jobs, labour, employment, relationships, patriarchy, and the whole deal, and had gone to New Mexico, in order to find a new way of working, to build their own space and, for instance, recreate freedom, recreate their own relationship to labour – manual labour – and then later reintegrate men within their environment. I began by writing the diary entries of the members of the commune, and then I would try to make objects that these people had made. The narrative was a way of generating artworks, such as a hammock. I was doing all this arts and crafts kind of thing. I really started with more utilitarian objects than these people had designed and which very often involved textile or ceramics or materials associated with, let's say, feminine craft. It is also often a quite ironic take on feminist art. For example, the hammock bears the inscription *Llano del Rio 1915,* which refers to a commune in the Mojave Desert in California that was founded by Job Harriman, who ran for the vice-presidency of the United States in 1900. As a socialist, he obviously was not going to win in America, and when his candidacy failed, he decided to found this commune near Los Angeles. The commune built a school, had a farming section, a printing press and its own sort of propaganda organ, and at some point even had a small film studio. All these kinds of stories are really inspiring to me. Unfortunately, this particular commune was very short-lived: because some property developers in the Mojave Desert wanted to get rid of the colonists in order to build sectional homes, they switched off the commune's water supply. Once it was switched off the commune had to leave and go somewhere else. But in the few years they were there, they developed all kinds of interesting ideas about how to live communally, such as sharing the education of their children. Llano del Rio was designed by the architect Alice Constance Austin, who was hired in the early 1910s by Harriman. She was one of the first people to develop a system of underground tunnels for laundry, to plan kitchenless houses, communal day-care areas, etc. – so as to liberate the women from the pressure of domestic work. It is quite fascinating, and I constantly embedded these stories inside my own work.

For an exhibition in the Kunsthaus Glarus, which is located in the mountains in Switzerland, I designed a rabbit hutch called *Pyramid of Love* (2003). The women in this commune have to raise animals in order to survive. They are engaged in agriculture, they build objects that they sell in order to make money and they raise rabbits, so I created a rabbit hutch composed of interlocking triangular boxes. Then I got deeply involved not only with making the utilitarian objects that these women would make, but also with portraying their self-expression or their artistic drives and tendencies. So I started working with ceramics and clay. That is something I have continued doing, and actually it is now taking on an autonomous life of its own. An early project with ceramics is called *25 Sculptures of Pure Self-Expression* (2003), which basically consists of a number of ceramic objects I imagined as originating from the self-expression of these fictional people. For me, the commune and the group have always been about trying to unburden myself of the pressure of being an individual who takes decisions and has an artistic ego. So inventing fictional people and doing their work is a way of freeing oneself of a burden. That has always been the idea, although it does not always work.

The women in the commune not only want to change their relation to labour, but they also want to change their relation to time. One of the things that they are against is this mechanical cutting up of time by clocks and machines. They are against the fact that we now have machines that tell the time, and that every second is equivalent to any other second and that you can measure it. So experienced time is broken down by machine-measured time. I designed the *Perpetual Time Clock* (2004) that the women of the commune would have made. It does not have hands. It has only pictograms that indicate the different activities that you are supposed to do in one day in order to have a fulfilled day: on top is sleep, and going down clockwise is labour and artistic labour, taking care of animals, yoga and meditation, reading and studying, agriculture and food supply, psychoanalysis and, finally, sport. Sport is represented by the emblem of the sports costumes that Varvara Stepanova designed in Russia in the 1920s. I did another piece about Stepanova, and these early utopian projects and the arts of the Russian Revolution have become a recurrent obsession of mine.

The women of the commune also survived by doing business – this is something that I have read and seen in many communes, including ones that still exist. Even people like the Shakers (The United Society of Believers in Christ's Second Appearing) in America in the 19th century had businesses in order to survive. The Shakers, for example, manufactured their famous furniture, which became so important for modernist design, in the belief that it encompassed the harmony and the purity of shape that their religion believed in. They sold the furniture outside the commune, which brought money into the commune. So my fictional commune was based on this model and I imagined, for example, the women of the commune going to market and selling the things that they had made. This was also quite convenient, because it could then fall back on the real-life situation of being an artist and of working with galleries and working with art fairs and stuff like that. In effect, I go to market giving things to galleries, but at the same time, it also replicates the sort of fictional things that happen in my stories in the universe of *The Crystal Frontier*. So the women of the commune make clothes as part of their interest in utopian design, but also as things to sell. The clothes were made in collaboration with the fashion designer Ligia Dias, with whom I have done quite a lot of other things, like a dance piece, a choreography project. Ligia and I share an interest in the shapes and ideas of Russian fashion design, but also of Jugendstil and the whole clothing reform idea. She designed all the clothes for this project, which was shown in the Statements section at the art fair in Basel (*A Uniform Sampler,* 2006). I decided to show the clothes of the commune and also some ceramics and pottery that they make. The clothes are shown on mannequins made out of papier-mâché. They also reproduce the display that you would have in a department store where clothes are shown on life-size mannequins. But since, of course, the commune of *The Crystal Frontier* does not use manufactured objects, its members had to think of a way to recreate the display elements for their clothing out of poor materials. So that is why these papier-mâché mannequins were made. Then Ligia designed the clothes, which are all based on geometric shapes and motifs: the jacket is a circle with holes in it, the white poncho is a square with a spiral, and so on and so forth. And there is also a beige outfit, which is actually a copy of the Stepanova sports costume that was displayed on the clock I mentioned before.

For a few years I really focused on the story of the commune. And then it sort of got a little bit out of hand and I ended up making objects that became more and more detached from the actual narrative of the commune and had more and more their own dynamics, such as the dancing mannequins of neon called *Apocalypse Ballet* (2006). The dance is, I guess, part of another interest in utopian and communal movement. It is the idea of dance as a liberated space for the body. The mannequins, for example, dance with neon circles and that was my first take on the dancing theme. In this regard, I want to speak about Monte Verità, because that was one of the main influences on making these works. There was the Monte Verità commune, which existed in Ascona in Switzerland in the 1910s – I guess you can call them proto-hippies. The commune consisted of young people who were tired of the restrictions and the life of the bourgeoisie of the post-Biedermeier, post-Victorian era, and who decided to experiment with "alternative" life in the open sun of Ascona. They danced and bathed naked, exposing their bodies to the sun. This is a very interesting moment of odd Swiss history, when all these people who became important for Expressionist dance, such as Isadora Duncan, Rudolf von Laban, and Mary Wigman, spent time in Monte Verità and got involved in what appears to be this completely hedonistic and playful choreography outdoors in the natural space of Ticino. All these moments were fundamentally inspiring to my work.

Coming back to my interest in narrations about utopian groups or people who create their own environment, the communal movement of Monte Verità was a visionary approach to a new way of life roughly 100 years ago. There are other examples of such secessionist groups and of people trying to live in utopian scenarios at that time. But whenever I look at the pictures of Monte Verità, there is this strange sense of innocence to them. I think it would probably be quite different right now. It would be much more political today or maybe the people participating would be more self-aware than those you see in these period pictures.

Mai-Thu Perret (b. 1976 in Geneva/Switzerland) lives and works in Geneva. In 1997, she received a degree in English literature at Cambridge University, and she participated in the Whitney Independent Study Program, Whitney Museum of American Art, New York (2002–03). After a longer stay in the USA (1997–99), she began with her artistic work. Perret's art comprises sculptures, installations, paintings, videos and literature, and it relates to a wide range of references, such as avant-garde movements of the 20th century and utopian concepts of life.

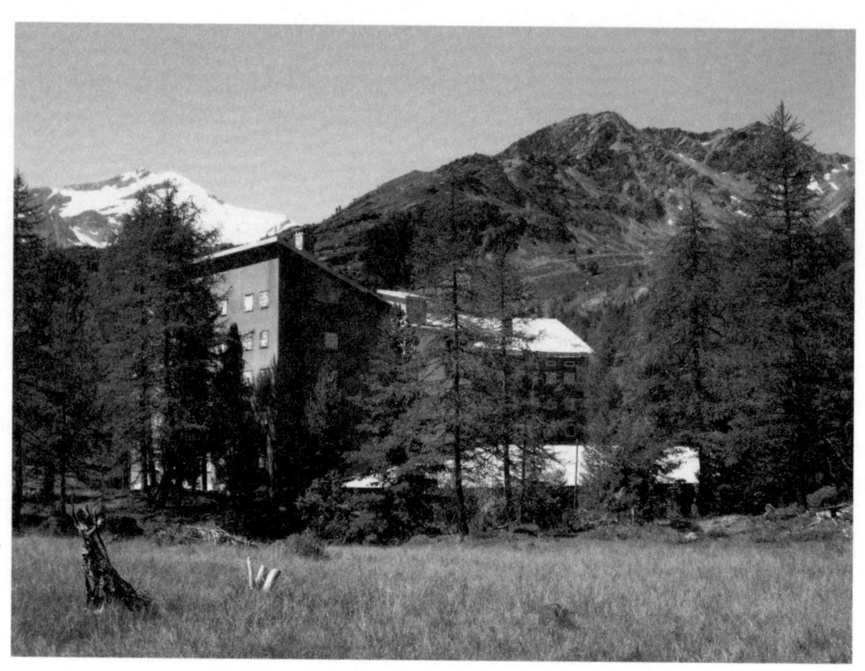

Tobias Rehberger, *Paradies* (2009)

Tobias Rehberger

Paradiso del Cevedale

Today, I am not going to speak about my own work, but about somebody else's, with which I have created a kind of secondary work: it is the small book *Paradies*, which consists of a couple of images and was published by Onestar Press in 2009. Even though this year's topic for the Engadin Art Talks is "Visions for the Alps", I would like to start with something that appears to be almost the opposite of a vision. Let me very briefly talk about ruins and a theory of ruins, because the moment something becomes a theory – even if it is ruins – it also turns into a vision.

The first person to actually write profoundly about a theory of ruins was the Austrian Alois Riegl, whose comprehensive and pioneering essay *Der moderne Denkmalkultus: Sein Wesen und seine Entstehung*, published in 1903, is still well known today. He was the first art historian who always related architecture to its context. According to Riegl, a building can have a designated use or meaning at a certain time, yet develop another use or meaning later on. A second groundbreaking field for Riegl – especially in Germany – was "Denkmalschutz" (the protection of historic buildings and monuments), in which he appraised the value of aging and thus considered its traces – the ruins – to be important. Other people would later also take up this approach to ruins. One of the best-known is Albert Speer, who created the word "Ruinenwerttheorie" (Theory of Ruin Value). In his autobiography (*Erinnerungen*), published in 1969, he claimed that he had invented the Theory of Ruin Value in relation to Nazi architecture. Speer stated that his intention had been to erect Nazi buildings whose ruins – 1,000 years from now – would convey the greatness of the Third Reich, comparable to the Roman ruins that are today regarded as an echo of that great civilization. Speer was convinced that one could erect buildings in a way that included their calculated collapse, allowing them to become so-called beautiful ruins. His approach was based entirely on Rome's vision of "Weltherrschaft", or world domination – a perception that has changed considerably since then. However, theoreticians today postulate that Speer was probably not already engaged on his Theory of Ruin Value when he was constructing Nazi buildings. Some of those buildings were indeed not very well built, but this had more to do with material shortages at the time than with his idea of ruins.

Nevertheless, the idea of ruins was again used a couple of times during postmodernism. A typical example is James Stirling's Neue Staatsgalerie in Stuttgart (1977–84), where a part of the museum was conceived as a ruin from the beginning. Robert Smithson also referred to this idea in his *Hotel Palenque*, one of my favourite works. During a trip to the south of Mexico in 1969, he had photographed a hotel called Hotel Palenque, which was half decayed, half unused. His work consists of the slides he used in a lecture given to architecture students at the University of Utah in 1972 and of his recorded voice. It is a fantastic piece because you hear him describing the building, part of which is in a serious state of disrepair, and you hear him describing it as though it had been planned to look like that from the start.

Finally, I would like to speak about Giò Ponti, the famous architect and designer from Milan. On the initiative of the Tourist Ministry of South Tyrol, he started to plan a huge – or rather megalomaniac – project to open up the Dolomites in the early 1930s. The plan called for the construction of 18 hotels linked by a 160-kilometre-long network of cable railways. Ponti made studies and drawings and, between 1933 and 1935, was finally able to realize one of the hotels. The project was supported by a company run by Colonel Emilio Penatti, a member of the Fascist Party. The hotel, called Albergo Sportivo Valmartello al Paradiso del Cevedale, was a unique project: the building site was located 2,160 metres above sea level at the very end of Val Martello, a small valley near Merano known mostly for its berries. What made the hotel quite exceptional was that it was one of the first hotels to offer a stay far from any semblance of civilization yet with all the modern conveniences of a city hotel: there was a butcher's, a telegraph and a post office, a confectioner, a hairdresser, a masseur, a ski instructor, a sauna and 250 beds – all of which was quite unique at that time. The hotel was divided into two parts according to the social groups it was accommodating. Whereas one part, for well-off guests, was lavishly decorated and equipped with every comfort of a luxury hotel, the other part was kept relatively simple – for example sleeping rooms and a restaurant – since the hotel also wanted to attract sportsmen and hikers. The Albergo opened in 1935, but had to close down again at the outbreak of World War II. It was occupied for two years by the German Wehrmacht, which used it as a school for its intelligence service and also as a base from which to control the nearby glacier, over which some deserters tried to flee. The hotel was reopened after the war, but went bankrupt a year later. In 1952, it was bought by a Venetian shipowner, Mr. Benati, who enlarged the building, had a number of annexes built to it and painted the once green hotel a Venetian red – but he never reopened it. Since the late 1960s, the hotel has belonged to the owners of Frost, the biggest brewery in South Tyrol.

The hotel is, by the way, not very far from the Engadin: to reach the valley, just drive over the Ofenpass and continue for another 90 minutes. When I heard about the abandoned hotel, I decided to visit it. I drove up to the very end of Val Martello, parked my car and walked for about half an hour up the beautiful valley, until – suddenly – the hotel came into view. It has not been used or renovated since the 1950s and is now a ruin. Although it is a Ponti building – the only hotel he ever built in the mountains – and although it is a beautiful house located on a fantastic spot, it is in a derelict state. On the one hand it has been completely destroyed, but on the other hand it is quite amazing to see how intact it still is. There is still the bar inside, there is still the library, the kitchen, the chimney, and there is still the tiling. There are also some stripes that look almost like typical eighties' style, but I found out that it was also part of Ponti's design to have them painted.

I was so fascinated by the building that I decided to start a small series of books about ruins. Besides this one, called *Paradies*, I am working on two other books: one about Krampnitz, the former Nazi and Russian military base in the south of Potsdam/Berlin, which was used by the German army from 1937 to 1945, and was then taken over by the Russians, who abandoned it in 1992. This huge area is still relatively intact. You can recognize the sports hall with its wooden floor, the officers' mess and the kindergarten, and there is Russian graffiti in the attic. Of course, it has a lot of beautiful ruin qualities. The other project I am working on is also a site near Berlin, an abandoned Luna Park built in the late 1990s. I am fascinated by the fact that funfairs, which once enabled people to have fun, are now dying, melancholy places.

While I was at Ponti's hotel, I started to think about what would have been better: a realized utopia with 18 hotels and 160 km of cable railway, or a lovely ruin waiting to be discovered 50 years later. If I had to decide, I would save the hotel in the state it is in. People are no longer permitted to enter the building for fear of falling debris. I would therefore renovate the hotel only insofar as to make the ruin safe for visitors. And then it would undoubtedly be a very beautiful ruin.

From 1987 to 1992, Tobias Rehberger (b. 1966 in Esslingen/Germany) studied at the Städelschule in Frankfurt with Thomas Bayrle and Martin Kippenberger. He was appointed a professor there in 2001. The artist, who lives in Frankfurt and Berlin, is internationally known for working with methods of architecture, design, sculpture and film. He undermines artistic ideals such as genius and authenticity, and questions forms of presentation, functionality and perception. In 2009, he was awarded the Golden Lion at the 53rd Venice Biennale.

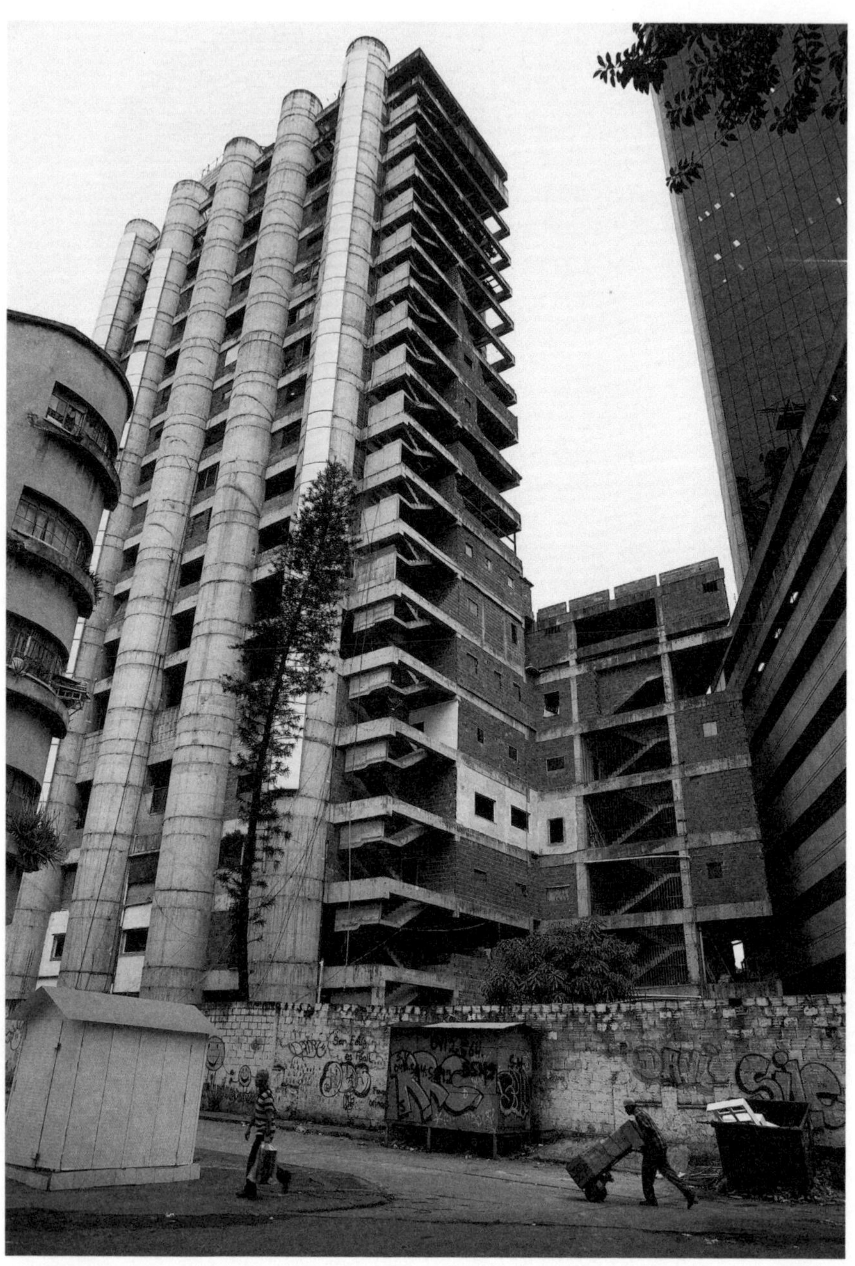

Torre David, Caracas (2012)

Urban-Think Tank /
Alfredo Brillembourg &
Hubert Klumpner

Urban Mountain Utopia: Torre David

Torre David, a 45-storey office tower (formerly known as the Centro Financiero Confinanzas) stands in the heart of Caracas's former central business district. It is unlikely that the building will ever be finished – at least not in a conventional sense. Designed by the distinguished Venezuelan architect Enrique Gómez, it had almost been completed when it was abandoned following the death of its developer, David Brillembourg, in 1993 and the collapse of the Venezuelan economy a year later. Today, it is the improvised home of a community of more than 750 families, living in an extra-legal and tenuous occupation that some have called a vertical slum. The residents have turned a ruin into a home, although they are only temporarily tolerated.

For the last ten years, we have had Torre David in mind as a laboratory for a different kind of informal settlement, but it was only in 2011 that we were able, along with our research and design teams at Urban-Think Tank and the Swiss Federal Institute of Technology (ETH), Zurich, to spend a year studying the physical and social organization of this ruin-turned-home. Since 2007, the people living in the Torre have began to modify and adapt the structure to their needs, using recovered brick and other found materials. Currently, there are around 3,000 residents in the complex, which consists of five distinct volumes. Most of them live in the 45-storey tower itself, where many of the services are also to be found. There are shops, coffee shops and car workshops, a football pitch, a basketball court and a church within the premises. People living there have to follow some written rules, drawn up by a community that operates as a cooperative (Asociación Cooperativa de Vivienda "Caciques de Venezuela" R.L.). For security reasons and because there is no lift, residency is not allowed from the 29th floor all the way up to the rooftop helipad.

Where some see only a failed development project, we have conceived Torre David as a laboratory for the study of the informal. With the support of the Schindler Group, we also explored innovative design solutions to address new modes of vertical mobility. We argue that the future of urban development lies in collaboration among architects, private enterprise, and the global population of slum dwellers. We see in the informal settlements of the world a potential for innovation and experimentation, and intend to design in the service of a more equitable and sustainable future.

Alfredo Brillembourg (b. 1961 in New York) founded Urban-Think Tank (U-TT) in Caracas in 1993, and was joined by Hubert Klumpner (b. 1965 in Salzburg) as co-director in 1998. The philosophy of U-TT is to deliver innovative yet practical solutions through the combined skills of architects, civil engineers, environmental planners, landscape architects and communication specialists. Since 2007, Brillembourg and Klumpner have taught at Columbia University, where they founded the Sustainable Living Urban Model Laboratory (S.L.U.M. Lab), and since July 2010, they have held the Chair for Architecture and Urban Design at the Swiss Federal Institute of Technology (ETH), Zurich. In 2012, Urban-Think Tank was awarded the Golden Lion at the Venice Architecture Biennale.

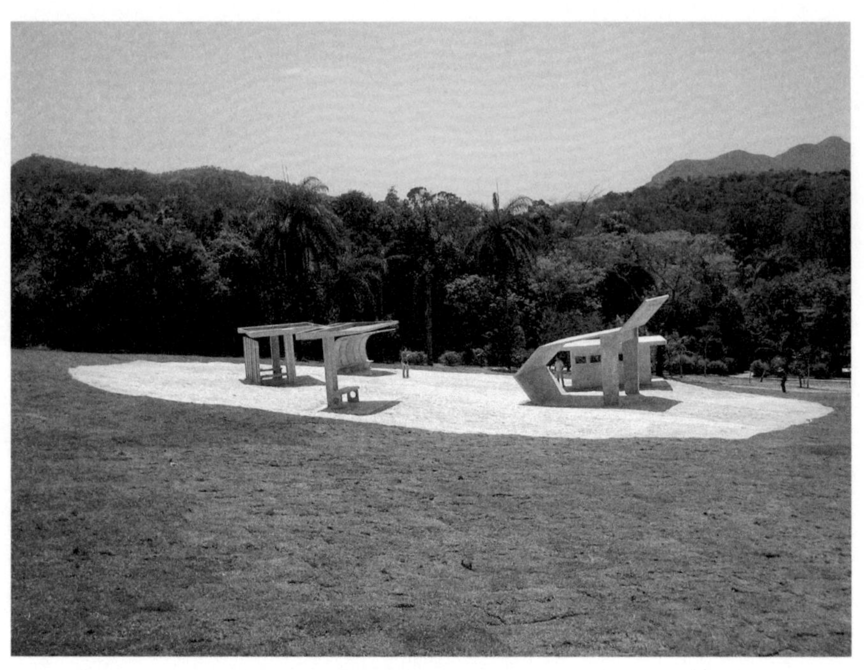

Dominique Gonzalez-Foerster, *Desert Park* (2010)

Dominique Gonzalez-Foerster

Stay or Go?

It is strange that we are in an empty swimming pool, because this is a rendering for a project for Ballard. I have been planning a kind of homage to the writer James Graham Ballard consisting of a garden that I imagined after the day of his death in 2009. I was invited to plan something for the International Arts Campus deSingel in Antwerp. They have several theatres and did a lot of great architecture exhibitions with the curator Moritz Küng. He wanted me to imagine something for a weird triangle that used to be a kind of a concrete and water garden. I wanted to do a homage to Ballard, since my visit was strongly connected to his death and since he is for me one of the most inspiring writers. But he is also someone who has completely redefined what beauty, aesthetics and landscape can be. The homage is planned to consist of an empty swimming pool in which you can walk around, and the area around the pool, which is filled with water. There are concrete volumes: some have already been there forming part of the existing garden, and some will be added by me – my plan is to make it look like a drowned city. It relates quite precisely to two books by Ballard: on the one hand to *The Drowned World* (1962), where the world is tropical and flooded, and on the other hand to *The Drought* (1965), where the water is – in opposition to the first book – completely missing. So far, the project is still in the making, and it might stay in a kind of unfinished zone.

Parallel to this garden project, there was another invitation, a project in an entirely different context: the Inhotim Collection near Belo Horizonte in Brazil. This is an amazing art collection situated in a green cube – as opposed to the white or black cube – and where the tropical forest is a possible environment for artworks. It mixes huge outdoor pieces with pavilions that are made specifically to house very large environments. I find it very important that there are collections that are able to collect and house not only small works, but also large ones, such as the great ensemble by Cildo Meireles. So parallel to Antwerp, I started to work on this project *(Desert Park,* 2010), which also refers to Ballard and his main issue, or main question. Very often, the question crops up with his characters, when they find themselves in exceptionally intense environments – either in a very dry one, in a forest turning into crystals, in a tower becoming crazy, on a highway that is about to end, or in some other extreme landscapes. The question arises through the very few dialogues. In fact, I think Ballard's literature concentrates not so much on dialogues as it does on how people feel in a specific environment, how it affects them. At the end, the main question is always whether they want to leave or to stay, and they hesitate over how to decide between the two possibilities. For me, this is also a very important question in any exhibition context, where there is – in contrast to cinema or theatre – no given time for an experience.
With Inhotim, too, the question arises of how long and to what degree I am willing to accept being affected by an environment, by an art piece or by an extreme cultural situation. Should I stay or leave immediately? I think there are really some similarities between the questions raised through Ballard's figures and those raised by visitors to an exhibition.

In the tropical context of Inhotim, I have chosen a place belonging to an unorganized part of the forest. There is also a park, an early part of which was designed by Burle Marx, but on the edges there are some areas that are much wilder. I thought it could be strong to implement a completely desert-like moment into this edge of wild landscape. And so I put white sand and a collection of real-size concrete bus stops on it – replicas of local bus stops that are very common in the different states of Brazil. Maybe one or two are in fact from Brasilia, but most of them are just replicas, or even ready-made Brazilian bus stops, which form a kind of small history of this local modern architecture. The point is also to bring into one extreme environment another even more extreme environment, which might be either a possible future for that forest or a fictional idea. At the bus stops, there are also books by Ballard and other people. During the rainy season, the whole installation gets a bit destroyed, the sand flows away, partly because the site is located on a hillside. Nevertheless, it has been there for two years now and somehow it stays.

I was reading a lot of Edgar Allan Poe last week, especially *The Narrative of Arthur Gordon Pym of Nantucket* (1838), which I have never read before, but which I highly recommend. This book is a collection of radical moments, from being stuck in a small room on a boat to visiting many other extraordinary spaces. Suddenly, I was sure that, in literature, there was a whole path of intense and radical narrative environments. From Edgar Allan Poe, whose work was translated into French by Charles Baudelaire – and which is how I read it – to Baudelaire himself, who is another specialist in creating extreme environments. Then I discovered Jules Verne's *Twenty Thousand Leagues Under the Sea* (1869). Whereas Poe explored some landscapes and radical moments connected to the sea, the forest and the city, Verne goes into the mountain and into the earth. I found out that Verne wrote a sequel to Poe's *The Narrative of Arthur Gordon Pym of Nantucket* in 1897. It is an incredible sequel (*An Antarctic Mystery*) in which he continues the story and finds some of the characters again. He really establishes this fascination for moments and environments that are beyond the normal. Jean Ricardou wrote about the Nouveau Roman, and now that I have been deeper into Edgar Allan Poe I believe that the Nouveau Roman owes a lot to him – because he was so much into literature that combined big knowledge and science but also explored specific situations. He created narratives in a completely different way, which I find very similar to how some exhibitions or some environments or installations are planned now. It is a specific way of collecting information, locating them in a zone, and creating an intense moment, or a moment in which information is connected in a completely different way. Coming back to Ricardou, he said that when Arthur reaches the South Pole in the *The Narrative of Arthur Gordon Pym of Nantucket,* Poe went to the limit of the written page, the possibilities of writing and the possibility of a text. And in fact the text ends very abruptly. After having read Verne, I suddenly realized that Ballard was completely into this dream of turning landscapes, moments and climates into characters that sometimes are even more important than human beings. Or, in which the dialogue between environments, sights and humans are at least as important as dialogues between humans. I think that is mainly what brought me here today.

A few days ago, I was in Bayreuth and Salzburg and was fascinated by the capacity to create a cultural site connected to a landscape. In Bayreuth it is this hill, in Salzburg it is this very dramatic connection between the opera houses and the mountain, to the point that even one of the theatres combines the stage with the back of the mountain. I was thinking about how amazing it would be to have a whole city that functions in relation to stages and narratives. And I was trying to think of similar situations maybe in the mountains. But suddenly, I had a completely opposite thought, which is maybe in a way linked to the national parks that were invented a hundred years ago in the USA to protect or to even to create a certain kind of landscape. And I had this very strange thought that – as interesting as it is to bring art everywhere – it could also be great to have some kind of art-free zones and to keep certain landscape isolated from art contamination.

Dominique Gonzalez-Foerster (b. 1965 in Strasbourg) is a French artist and film-maker who lives in Paris and Rio de Janeiro. She is particularly interested in establishing a meaningful relationship between place, object and the potential user. Since the early 1990s, she has built her oeuvre around "space", beginning with the intimacy of "Chambres" and working through films and environments to her extreme urban situations and landscapes. In 2002, she won the Marcel Duchamp Prize.

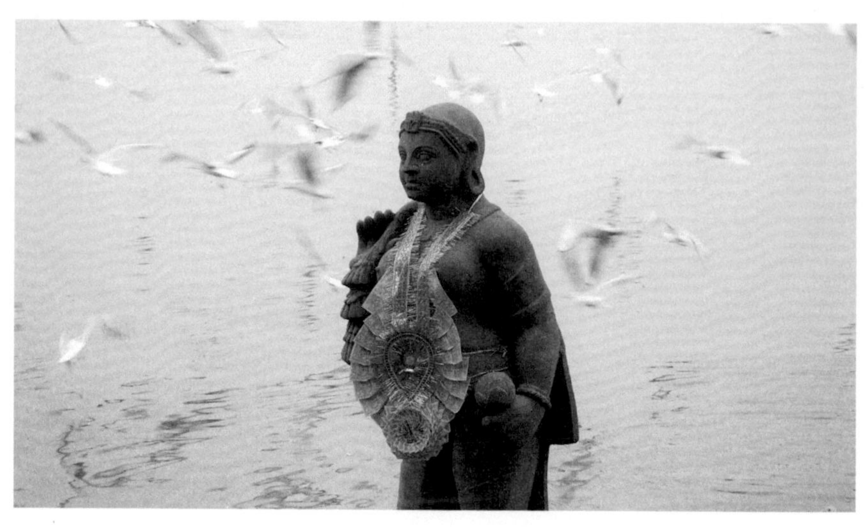

Raqs Media Collective, *Sleepwalkers' Caravan* (2008)
Film still

Raqs Media Collective

The Third Man

Monica Narula

Sometimes, when the air is thin, and when oxygen supplies plummet, our minds begin to play tricks. Mountaineers know what this means: the higher you go, the greater the likelihood that you will hallucinate. Mountains, like all wild places, have their spirit guardians. In our part of the world we have yakshas, guardians of mountain passes, river valleys and forests. The modernist sculptor Ram Kinkar Baij – who was especially active in India in the 1950s – created a yaksha and a yakshini. Both of these figures stand guard outside the gates of the Reserve Bank of India, the country's central bank, on Parliament Street in New Delhi. They are enormous, maybe 20 feet high, but their monumental presence is the secret of their invisibility. On our part, we set them free to lurk by rivers and mountain passes again.

Yakshas are clever, dangerous, fickle, wise, capricious, generous and given to lying in wait at mountain passes, in forests and on river banks for unsuspecting travellers, who invariably face an ordeal of demanding questions. Failure to answer the yakshi's questions usually results in a terrible curse or horrible death. Success may reveal the path to a hidden treasure.

Universally, mountaineers experience seeing what has come to be known as a "third man" – neither the mountaineer nor his or her climbing companion, but a third other. Someone who appears vividly real a few steps ahead, stopping when the climber stops, walking when he begins walking again. Is the yaksha, the mountain spirit, this "third man"?

Shuddhabrata Sengupta Could the "third man" be an aspect of the self and its experience of itself, projected outwards? Does it mark a disruption of the nervous system's ability to synthesize a coherent unitary sense of self, under conditions of hypoxia or oxygen deprivation, (which happens at high altitude). It can also be a life-saver. More often than not, the "third man" is a means of survival. If you read mountaineering stories or narratives, there is often of this "third man" who appears on a difficult ascent or climb. He prevents the climber from falling into a kind of solipsistic despair by eliciting responses, by providing a form of companionship or partnership that keeps the climber focused on the proximity of the goal rather than on the fatigue of the climb. His synchronicity with the climber – the echoing of the rhythm of rest and movement, breathing and breathlessness – suggests that the climber hears something along the lines of: "If I can do it, you can, too", and then says to himself/herself: "If he can do it, I can do it, too". Let us consider this "third man", at a remove, sometimes vivid, sometimes fuzzy, a step or two ahead, yet close enough to make possible a meaningful albeit silent, questioning camaraderie between life and art. Let us think of the splitting of ourselves, with the non-artist as the climber and the artist as the "third man", goading us on to new promontories.

MN A yaksha crosses us on a mountain top and asks this question: "Why are you three people here? And what are you doing on the mountains?" We reply: "It is said that all accounts of the world can be simplified into a three-step operation. Three makes a triangle. A triangle is a mountain. Here lie the beginnings of mathematics, mountaineering, philosophy, performance, literature and of every attempt to speculate about the world."

There is me, one, there is you, two, and then there are many, three. Three marks the beginning of plenitude. The escape from the prison of

"I and you", "self and other", into the world. With the number three – the first wild card, the first odd prime, our account of the world takes us out of the interlocked prison of the dyad of either opposition or reflection or echo. "Three" is the key move as well as the option out of the treadmill of the dialectic. With "three" we begin to understand plurality and plenitude. To ascend the steep slope of the calculus. It is with "three" that we begin to glimpse infinity, to become the necessary "third man" or "woman".

SS He who glimpses infinity has a taste of eternity. Eternity is a sum mit in time, a mountain of moments. The geological signature of mountains gives us an approximation of eternity. The Alps, for instance, began to form 300 million years ago. In the Sanskrit canon, we know of seven immortals, one of whom was Krishna Dwaipayana Vyasa, the creator of the epic *Mahabharata*. In *The KD Vyas Correspondence Vol. 1* (2006), a work by us with eighteen screens that invoke eighteen letters, an exchange between us and a notionally immortal KD Vyas corresponding to the eighteen canons of the epic, we find ourselves face to face with the idea of declining time; with the realization that we may be living after, not before an apocalypse.

We collaborated with Nikolaus Hirsch and Michel Müller on a mountain, a cultural laboratory called *Cybermohalla Hub* (first prototype: 2008), which is a hybrid architectural structure between school, community centre and gallery. It is an evolving structure that will never be finished, but will grow along with its production of texts, videos and objects. We wanted to create an armature that could appear to float as if it had no beginning or end, in which every moment, every instance could appear connected to every other moment. The structure had to suggest a certain temporal altitude, a height in time from which the passing of empires, the rise and fall of powers, the careers of utopias that shine, stain and then become ruined can all find their place in an undulating topology of time. How does one make sure of not losing one's way while ascending from one time to other times? How do you know yourself as the "third man"?

MN Three photographs, printed large: one of a donkey crossing an empty road; a man standing on an empty highway with a surveying instrument covering his face; and a camera on a tripod on a sand dune in the desert, accompanied by a man's shadow or a person's shadow, apparently left behind in a hurry by an absent photographer. The donkey, the surveying man, the camera and the photographer's detached shadow seem to be caught in an eternally deferred time, waiting for something to lend meaning to the emptiness of the stretch.

SS Take the solitude of the donkey: it could be an image of what it means to be forever crossing the road to yourself.

MN Take the camera and the shadow of the absent photographer: it could be an image of understanding what it means to glimpse the shadow of the mind of a body that is not available to ask because it is not our own.

SS Take the man surveying the world and it could be just that: an image of what it means to survey the worl d, to see the world and to take its measure with reference to the self.

MN Each is the "third man" to the other two.

SS Each the yaksha to the other.

MN The yaksha asks again: Why climb a mountain?

SS Because it is there. And again: Why make art?

MN Because it is not there. The presence of a mountain is the motivation of the mountaineer. The absence of a work of art and its anticipation is the reason for the work of an artist. When the terrain is rough, it pays to be closer to the ascending surface. Sometimes you have to get down on your hands and knees. This means that the mountaineer has to get close to the surface of the mountain and that the artist may have to come face to face with what is not art in order to negotiate its rough terrain. Those who take Alpine-style climbing seriously climb without oxygen cylinders. They make do with the oxygen they can harvest from the air. In such circumstances they have to carry with them the apparatus of their artistic life and make it lightweight. Nothing is taught more than the history of failed attempts. Pay attention, while you climb, to storms and crevices, debris and sudden avalanches.

Jeebesh Bagchi Last week, we opened the exhibition *Sarai Reader 09* in New Delhi, where the above-mentioned architectural structure *Cybermohalla Hub* by Nikolaus Hirsch and Michel Müller was included, too. It is a nine-month exhibition that began with empty rooms.

There has been nothing in the exhibition halls, and the opening consisted of inviting people to an empty gallery. The idea is that over nine months, a lot of people – about 100 artists and non-artists – will work in the exhibition space to produce art works. These works can be timed for specific durations, so over nine months, the exhibition space will keep transforming, and at the end, we will have 100 works in it. The starting point is our proposition, a series of empty rooms and proposals by 27 artists, explaining what they expect to make there. This is the beginning of a process we call the "third man process".

SS So, the boundaries between what constitutes culture and what constitutes the domain outside culture is constantly tested and broken. The "third man" hypothesis is at work. Bacteria, lichen moths, ferns, crabs, tropical fruit trees and mountain pines convert light into breath. We know that artists – not just us – but all artists can stare hard at a blank beach or canvas or silence or darkness or an empty space and imagine life and form. The emptiness comes as a proposition to us. And we come as propositions to the empty page. This is how artists stumble into shaping the future. This is how we climb the high mountain of the absence of cultural infrastructure. The proliferation of forms of life on its slopes throughout its elevation is the only guarantee for life on a summit. Climbing without oxygen is essentially about placing one's trust in the oxygen-generating powers of the planet.

MN The relationship between breathing and photosynthesis, between likelihood and the unattainable, between possibility and failure and also between hope and the permeation of danger is essentially irrational. A percentage: the mental operations we perform on the basis of our understanding of the idea of percentage are the triggers that catalyze most of our crucial decisions with regard to the future. We are forever calculating the arts. As the intensifying economic crisis begins to affect the global cultural infrastructure – we know them all: diminishing budgets, crashing institutions and meagre grants – it produces a new scenario. The art scene needs a new institutional ecology, a new combination of how even a sparse institutional infrastructure can provide the scaffolding for high-intensity, but agile and lightweight forms of artistic activity. We need epiphytic relationships and partnerships between museums, collections, institutions, galleries, artist-run spaces and initiatives, research and training programmes, social initiatives, publications and crucially ephemeral and transient processes and a host of artistic energies.

SS The highest mountain in the world is actually not Mount Everest, but Mauna Kea, a massive volcanic bulge – part submerged seamount, part dormant volcano – that ascends from the sea floor of the Pacific Ocean to form part of the landmass of Hawaii. If you measure how high it ascends from the sea floor to its top, it is higher than Everest. Seamounts are engines of life. Strong convection currents that hit against their slopes produce eddies that contain immense ecologies – entire life-systems. Most of the breathable oxygen in the world is formed by the biomass in the oceans. This includes algae, cyanobacteria and large colonies of microscopic and minute plant life, along with marine continents of seaweed and floating sargasso that change light into oxygen through photosynthesis. The plants on land also contribute to this but to a lesser extent than the plants of the sea. The higher we ascend, the more we depend on the oxygen produced on land and in the sea. To breath oxygenated air in the North Col of Everest or here or anywhere else at any location, you need to have not just a patchy bit of moss that might grow there. And there is a kind of moss that grows beyond the snowline on Everest. You know, a peculiarly extreme form of life that actually grows where nothing else can grow. But we also require the immense algae colonies and plant life on a pacific seamount and all the photosynthesis done by life on earth ever since the rise of cyanobacteria 2.7 billion years ago. Translate that analogy into thinking about art and you realize that the higher you grow, the higher you go in the world of art, the more you require the oxygen of the entire history of cultural production.

MN A conversation takes place in the Archipelago Sea, a branch of the Baltic Sea above the south-west coast of Finland. A marine biologist begins talking to us about the impact of global warming on a precarious and unique ecosystem generated by the eccentric salinity of the Baltic Sea. Climatologists and oceanographers have expressed their concern that global warming may increase the salinity of the Baltic Sea and by doing so cause irreversible damage to the unique ecosystem of this environment. Or a change in conditions, including excess rain and fresh water leaching from the ground, may also lead to a sharp decrease in the salinity of the sea and thus endanger this fragile ecosystem.

Seen from a distance, the work *More salt in your tears,* which we did last year, appears as a reflecting interruption on the water whose shapes also resolve into letters and words. When the sun strikes the surface of the letters and the water in the right angle, the work can look as if it were a sign written in letters of fire. The letters form a set of polished surfaces gleaming like mirrors as they emerge above the water and across the surface. The forms mirror the horizon reflecting the changing sunlight, the sea and aspects of anything that sails or swims past. The clear surface changes colour as the sea and the sunlight themselves and the sky and the sunlight themselves vary over the course of the day. In this way, the work acts as an index of the living, changing surface of the sea, the seasons and time itself. Art, like the sea, helps the world to breathe.

SS Vision, like all other bodily faculties, relies in oxygen. The cornea is a massive consumer of oxygen. Perhaps second only to the brain and the heart. Diminished intake of oxygen or hypoxia affects the cornea. The lens of the eye finds it difficult to focus, leading to a phenomenon called brown-outs or grey-outs, where everything appears grey or brown to the eyes. The visual field becomes monotonous, vision becomes blurred, outlines become fuzzy and nothing is seen distinctly. And this is typically the condition in which mountaineers begin seeing the "third man". Strange things happen to vision at higher altitudes: as we ascend, the horizon recedes. The world spreads itself up before our eyes. We see further be-cause we are given more to see. And if we rotate on a summit on a clearer day, it is possible to imagine that our eyes are taking in all that is visible. Eventually, we see visions as we see less. High-altitude cerebral oedema, another consequence of hypoxia, leads to hallucinations. We see things that are not visible. People often have revelations high up. Prophets, adventurers, fugitives, shepherds, madmen and artists climb mountains. Not everyone makes it to the top. Not everyone who has made it to the top returns, but that does not stop anyone from climbing.

Hans Ulrich Obrist Thank you very much for your amazing presentation, and I would like to ask the first question. You have been collaborating with Nikolaus Hirsch for a long time. He has, for the most part, moved his architectural office to Delhi and you are working there on projects. But since Nikolaus also spends a lot of time in the Engadin, I was wondering if you have any – unrealized – projects for mount-ains?

SS We could return the sea to the mountains … which would be inter-esting to think about. I believe that one of the ways in which the chronology of the earth was established was by the amazing discovery of marine fossils in the Alps. It was the discovery of ammonites on slopes, as was the case nearby in the Engadin mountains, that made it possible for geologists to speculate that this was once the sea floor. And if this had once been the sea floor, how long would it have taken for the sea floor to rise this high? It might be interesting to actually think of a marine park on the Alps. That would be an interesting, although unrealizable project.

JB Bear in mind that yakshas appear not only on mountains but also by rivers. So it is interesting to remember that all the rivers actually come from mountains and go to the ocean. Rivers are, in a sense, what connect the sea floor with the mountain. And yakshas always appear either on mountains or riverbanks.

HUO Let me come back to the question of unrealized projects. What projects has Raqs not been able to build yet, which ones have been too big, or too small, to realize? Do you have dreams, utopias …?

MN For the artist, the project or artwork is only a rendering at that particular moment, and the moment gets rendered at that point, and beyond that it does not really matter. If you think that you want to change the world in a fundamental way, then you have to keep changing the world. It is sometimes realized in some small way and sometimes it does not work out in any precise formation, but the project is principally always the same. The forms of artistic realization are just steps along a longer mountain climb.

JB Actually, we have invested more in failed projects than in realized ones, or rather: in projects that may be regarded as having failed, but may actually not have lost all of their potential. In the history of sport there have been athletes who, in a manner of speaking, failed, but who were actually trying out a different way of being, and perhaps it was other people who made them fail at that specific moment. We may need to rethink and reinterpret words like “failed” or “unfulfilled” or “unrealized”.

MN Coming back to a project we are realizing now, I would like to mention the exhibition *Sarai Reader 09* in New Delhi, which began with the idea of architecture and an empty space. The emptiness is not about four walls but about creating space. One has to think about making space, conceptually, figuratively and literally – and also with light, sound and ideas. For the exhibition, there are proposals and books, but crucially, in this instance, there is an open call, because it is important for the call to remain open to the public. This does not mean that every proposal is accepted. We have conversations with the people proposing their work, and discuss ideas and various factors: where we could put their work within the space; what they think about cohabiting with other works; how one work will grow on top of another that has yet to be created; how to keep in mind future companions that don't yet exist but will at some stage enter the space ... There are three episodes, three rounds of proposals. The idea is to keep everything open. Therefore, the curatorial aspect is not only a question of selection, but also an attitude that says let us think about what constitutes artistic life as opposed to the artistic object. In a way, it is also a process of inviting people in Delhi to be companions on a longer journey, which has never happened before.

JB A lot of the exhibition should in some way look like the cities of the south, where – like in a palimpsest – there are life forms on life forms on life forms, and you are not able to figure out exactly where you are navigating.

HUO Why, then, is there an end? If you think about the palimpsest or the mountains – these are very long irrational processes – or if you think about Fernand Braudel in relation to the mountains. This curatorial approach is very interesting because then perhaps an exhibition, which has that self-organization inscribed into its DNA, could actually last for 50 or 100 years.

SS In 2009, we wrote a text called *Earthworms Dancing: Notes for a Biennial in Slow Motion*. It was a kind of oblique homage to Charles Darwin's affection for earthworms, because Darwin really loved earthworms. He said that the entire process of agriculture and earth had been prepared for millions of years by active earthworms turning the soil. I think that in contemporary art we tend to have a very restricted temporal horizon. We tend to think in terms of the opening and closing dates of exhibitions whereas we could also be seeing the activity that all of us do as somewhat akin to the earthworm that turns the soil. In some ways, we are also creating the conditions for a culture 100 years from now, or 500 from now, or 1,000 years from now. A thousand years from now, people will look back on what we are doing. Whether we like it or not, and whatever fragile evidence future generations have of what we are doing, the contemporary art of today will constitute the art history of the future. This means also thinking about unleashing processes in our activities that will anticipate the long temporal footprint or shadow that recursively integrate even their own obsolescence and think about what will come after them. They can also produce expectations of the future. As a general comment: think about how one creates a kind of temporal signature of a work that is of the present but extends into the future.

HUO I saw Danny Hillis the other day, the computer guru or inventor of the fastest computer who said he was developing an eternal clock, the *Clock of the Long Now* (project start: 1986; first prototype: 1999). He said that if you were thinking of doing a very long-duration project you would have to do it high up, because everything else will be flooded. I met Eugène Ionesco a long time ago and he said that it was possible to do something with time, which acquired qualities almost comparable to marble. He was telling me that his piece *La Cantatrice Chauve* (*The Bald Prima Donna*, 1950) has been performed since 1957, which is astonishing. He is dead now, but his play is still performed every night in Paris. Ionesco said that in this way, it was actually even more present than many public artworks. If you put up a monument, it can be removed after 20, 30 years. Because you talked a lot about time in your speech, I was wondering if that was something you were interested in?

SS Time is what we – in Raqs Media Collective – eat. Time is our source of nourishment and it is also what we, I suppose, digest and excrete. And time really is this substantive bedrock of a lot of our work and thinking. We are interested in it because we live in a time in which people access very different kinds of temporal rhythms – a temporal rhythm that is almost instantaneous in terms of our communication networks. But at the same time, because of, say, computing and digital technologies, the past in the archival proposition is available to us in ways that was unprecedented before. Whether we like it or not, everybody is archiving their work and their lives, We are all constructing archives, which are fragile, but there is an archival impulse that works in all our lives. The other thing is that the intensification of production processes also assumes that people can work at faster and faster rhythms. This affects our bodies and our minds in a way we are not yet entirely conscious or aware of. And finally, we now live longer. The average life span of human beings is almost double what it was at the beginning of the last century. So people have opportunities to reinvent their personalities and their careers at least once if not twice in their lifetime. In the future, it is quite possible that there will be artists who used to be insurance agents before their retirement and that suddenly, 65-year-old artists will be considered young. These are conditions related to work, leisure, productivity and memory where we face a new temporal landscape. It is interesting for us, at least as artists, to constantly think about this and process it in our work.

The Raqs Media Collective was founded in 1992 Jeebesh Bagchi (b. 1965), Monica Narula (b. 1969) and Shuddhabrata Sengupta (b. 1968). Raqs is based in New Delhi, where all three members were born, and is still closely associated with the Sarai programme of the Centre for the Study of Developing Societies, an initiative they cofounded in 2000. The members of Raqs play a number of roles, appearing as artists, curators, researchers and editors. They make contemporary art, have made films, curated exhibitions, edited books, staged events, have collaborated with architects, computer programmers, writers and theatre directors and have founded processes that have left a deep impact on contemporary culture in India. Their work engages not only with urban spaces and global circuits, but also with myths and histories of diverse provenances. The word "raqs" describes the state that dervishes enter into when they whirl. For the Raqs collective, it also signifies a kinetic contemplation of the world.

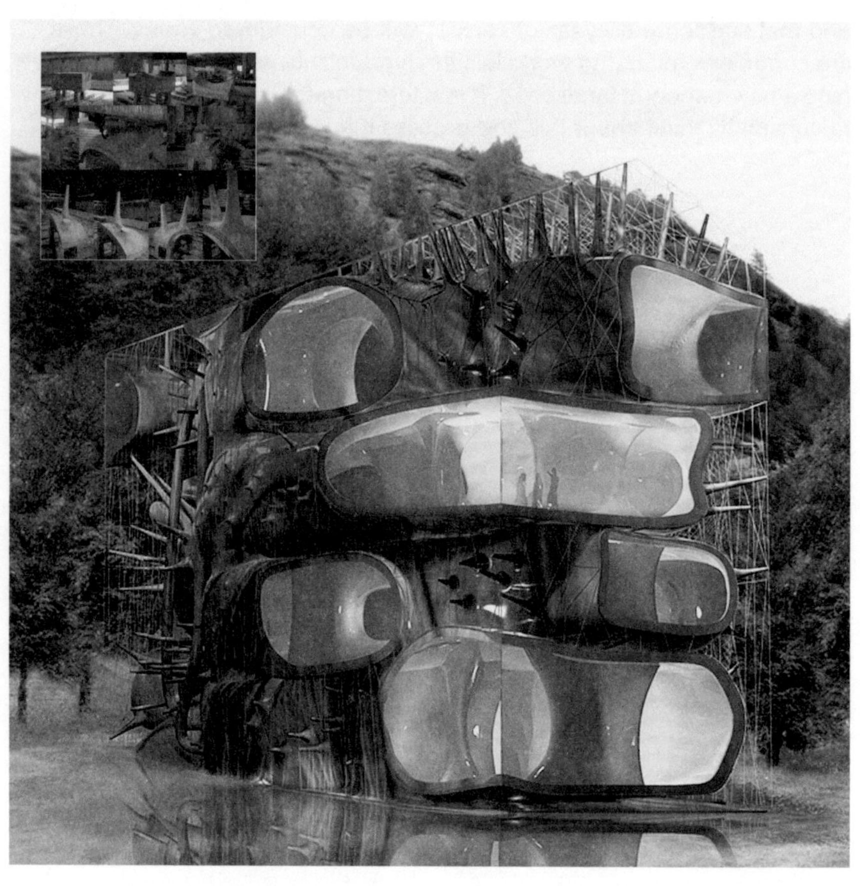

New-Territories/R&Sie(n), *waterFlux*
(Evolène/CH, 2005–15)

François Roche

gre(Y)en

(a history of local operative criticism including an ALP mountain trajectory)

… that seems to pretend to be a history of stuttering position between Green and Grey, between chlorophyll addiction, dream of an ideal biotope, re-primitivized, re-artificialized, in the pursuit of the lost paradise, of the lost Eden Park, as a story for little boys and girls, for sleeping their fears and … the Grey, the deep grey, which never appears in the visible spectrum ("The greatest *trick* the *devil* ever played was convincing the world that he did not *exist.*",[1] said Baudelaire) as an antagonism stealth forces, an embedded demon: mixture of contradictory human desires emerging from the mud, from permanent, unpredictable and irreducible conflicts, factor of domination and servitude, destruction and emergences, which are fireworking an unlimited source of arrogance and illusion, where the notion of success and failure are depending on a kind of absurd Pendulum[2] of life and death, caressing the boundaries of the both, as an infinite unstable movement, polymerizing ugliness and beauty, obstacle and possibilities, of waste materials and efflorescence, of threats and protection, of technological phantasm and revenge of nature, in a knot, in the process of becoming, a never-ending movement ... where we glide into this silky, strange sensation that scares you and caresses you ... That scares you and caresses you ...

We are at the crossroads, where, faced with the autistic, blind, deaf and mute violence of our mechanisms of technological, industrial, mercantile and human servo-mechanism, nature reacts … with violence and without warning, in a faltering of the original chaos … in mutiny against the organization of men … Gaïa seems to take revenge (Katrina, El Niño,Cyclone Jeanne, Tomas and Nargis, the Xynthia storm, Ewiniar typhoon, Indonesian and Japanese earthquakes, collateral Tsunamis all the way to Fukujima … chain of devastating incertitude, unpredictable in spite of our seismographic sciences). The elements rage and the gods, so quick to pardon our folly, seem powerless to appease the rebellion, armed with infernal force …

Nature is not an ideological "green washing" for backyard politics, nor the millenarian, eschatological dream of Eden Park, from which we have very fortunately escaped, freeing ourselves from the gatherer-hedonist blindness, to negotiate consciousness with the hostile dark forces that get stuck, in the depths of the forest …

But these forces have come out of their hiding places, their biotopes, they are invading the spaces that Man had thought he could take without giving anything in exchange, without transaction … the war has been declared … nature's revenge is not a bedtime story for innocent brains … our bellicose enemy operates openly … in the light of day … ultimate arrogance …

How could we reveal the conflict between the strategies of "knowledge and domination" of the first and the monstrous wild beauty of destruction of the other … as the field of an unpredictable battle, disconnected, cleared of all the greenish moralism jumble and its post-capitalism lure …

To help to feel this ambivalence, this permanent disequilibrium, where contingencies are the main factor of emergences, let us navigate in this history of *gre(Y)en.*

... From a physiological early simple dualism *shadow & light* in 1990, where Neuschwanstein[3] Grotto is f®ictionally adjusted to Play-Time[4] mirror refection, weakly connecting a cavernous, dark, humid, sensorially primitive atmosphere with its schizophrenical antagonist twin brother, crystalline, cold, luminous, dry, technologically blind as the recognition of an impossible stuttered dialogue, to …. a *Growing up* for a chlorophyll energy and entropy in 1993 that will collapse and strangle a fragile "chicken legs" house, wrapped and dominated masochistically by the danger of its own predictable death if the maintenance is not ritualized by the owner as a permanent conflict against the destructive strength and his needs to survive … to a blur petrochemical *Filtration* in 1997, with 5,000 m^2 of plastic stripes floating in the tree, on the edge of a seasonal tidy wild river, carrying nitrate and insecticide plastic bag residues that the farmer abandoned on the bank of their field, waiting for this rising up for a depolluting natural service, in charge of erasing the trace of their chemical addiction, and paradoxically back to the visible spectrum when the river is down again, hanging from the branches. The "Filtration" layer reveals by the concentration of the plastic wasted in the canopies an aesthetic countryside planning coming directly from its human managing … to travel to the weird … *aqua alta1.0,* in 1998, sucking up the disgusting, viscous, over-polluted liquidity called the Venetian Lagoon, to use capillarity's water forces of the contaminated to infiltrate literally, the building emergences from these lagoon substances, to … *aqua alta 2.0,* the Venetian bar in 2000 at the Venice Architecture Biennale, where "conventioneers" could refresh themselves by drinking "in live" the lagoon soup, but depolluted through a military purification machine[5] to test in the condition of the Biennale; the schizophrenia between green washing rhetoric discourse and repulsive digestive paranoia on the doubt of the reliability of the cleaning engine, which people promote as efficient technologies (for the others) … to *shearing* in 2001, as a simple stealth private House, organizing a simulacrum of its own impermanency and apparent fragility, unfold in the countryside, but using for the whole envelope the authorized petrochemistry non-biodegradable fabric that is spread and disseminated in nature to preserve planted young trees from destruction by rabbits, in an agriculture industrial logic … to *Dustyrelief,* in 2002, for the contemporary Art Bangkok museum where the dust of the city and the residue of the traffic jam (Dioxide and Monoxide of Carbon) dressed her skin and her biotope, as the recognition of public transportation failure in the "greynish" equatorial erotism, where this special fog of specks and particles becomes the traces of hypertrophic human convulsing activity, as a second adaptive nature, through a bottom-up unpredictable unmastering unplanning city aesthetic. Without delegating the power to autocratic and aseptic technocratic experts at the place of the chaotic emergences of the multitudes, the aleatory rhizomes, the arborescent growth are at the same time a factor of her transformation and her operational mode. The non-hygienic intoxicating urban chaos is the sign of its human vitalism, as a permanent vibe between Eros and Tanatos … the invisible but breathable substances are bred, attracted by an electrostatism machine to "skin" the hairy freak, exacerbating a schizo climate between indoor (white cube and labyrinth in Euclidian geometry) and outdoor (dust relief on topologic geometry) … and … and in a second step collecting the particle substances, dropped down in the monsoon period, through drainage systems … to create on the side the tea pavilion extension directly coming from the compacted particles brick produced "by" the failure and the beauty of the city … to the … *mosquitosbottleneck* scenario, in Trinidad, 2002, trying to negotiate with the infestation of the Nile Virus carried by Mosquitoes, for the recognition of this disease as an objective paranoia triggering strategies for safety, in a week-end residential house. The fragile net, through a Klein bottle apparatus, preserves, protects, but also disjoins the living of the first in resonance with the death of the other. And the sound of their agony, buzzing in the double trapped membrane, becomes the proof of the efficiency of the system, preserving human against nature, against its offensive non-inoffensive biotope, protected and surrounded by the theatre of its own barbaria … to the buffalo Machismo no-tech Machinism in *HybridMuscle* in 2003, Thailand, as a local mammal muscling power station, lifting with gears of a two-ton steel counterweight, transformed in a battery house, transformed first in electricity plugs and connections and secondly in pneumatic rubber muscles movement of leaves in elastomer membrane to wind the suffocatingly hot sweaty climate… as an endogenous-exogenous story telling … to the *greengorgon,* in 2005, as a phasmid morphologies, embedded in a wood, which feeds the confusion between artificial and domesticated nature, where all the outdoor surfaces are dedicated to vertical wet swamp recycling the inert grey water ... as a purification plan infrastructure, rejecting only clean liquidities in the Leman lake ... to the *Mipi,* in 2006, a PI Bar in the temple of cognitive science, the MIT-Cambridge, as an extension of the Media Lab, to experiment through a urine therapy absorption, the immunotherapy of the individual human production, including a schizoid balance between disgusting and healthy effect ... to a stochastic machine that vitrifies the city, in *Olzweg,* 2006, starting the contamination from a radical architecture museum in the pursuit of Frederick Kiesler endlessnesslessness. This smearing is done through the industrial glass recycling (mainly French wine bottles), swallowed and vomited through a process of staggering, scattering and stacking by a 12-metre-high machine. The random aggregation is a part of this unpredictable transformation, as a fuzzy logic of the vanishing point. The machine works to extend the museum and collect "voluntary prisoners" wrapped in the permanent entropy of the graft, testing the glass maze through its multiple uncertain trajectories, to lose themselves and rediscover this heterotopian non-panoptical sensation of their youngness, using if necessary PDA on RFID to rediscover their positioning ... at the opposite of an architecture that petrifies, historicizes, panopticalizes ... to the *waterFlux*[6] in 2007, for a scenario scooping out hollows in a full wood volume by a 5-axis drilling machine with 1,000 trees (2,000 m^3) coming directly from the maintenance of the forest around the location of extracting-manufacturing-transformation, as an anthroposophic logic, where technologies and machine are territorialized from the site, endemic to a situation and its mutation, reactivating accessorily local forest economy ... to the *gardenofearthlydelights,* in 2008, a toxic garden in a new green house in Croatia, on the right place of the initial middle-age Apotiker Franciscan monks medical plantation, protected behind a restricted area, but able to be tasted and tested through a distillation deconcentration machinism processes, and bar ... only by voluntary desire, in a similar way to the Japanese "Fugu" physiological and psychological effects ... with an "at your own risk" protocol, and where ecosophy is considered a global interaction, porous to human body, as Gaïa[7] exchanges, a chain of interaction and dependences ... articulating life and death and its knitting paranoia ... to *Heshotmedown*, in 2008, for a tracked biomass machine penetrating into the (de)Military Zone, the DMZ, between North and South Korea, collecting the rotten substances, the superficial coating of the forest in decomposition, and bringing back this material to plug all the external surfaces of the ballistic-like building, for a natural eco-insulation, through the fermentation of the grass and the heat coming from its chemistry transformation. Full of land mines, the DMZ is a restricted zone, where North and South never stop to play the Cold War. The machine collects the ingredients of this pathological period and recycles them for productive use, from a highly dangerous no man's land abandoned since the end of the war (more than half a century ago), which come back to its natural wildness, with the reappearing of elves, wizards, witches and harpies, and some new vegetal species. Legends and fairy tales are transported out of the deepness of the forest, as in a "Stalker"[8] experiment to touch the unknown ... to *I'mlostinParis,* in 2008, as a laboratory for bacterial culture, called the "Rhizobium" agent cultivated in 200 beakers, for its potential to increase the Nitrogenize per cent without chemical manure of the substract of each plant, after the re-injection of these substances in the individual nutritional aeroponic system ... for a "Rear windows"[9] minimum distance to the conservatism and "petite bourgeoisie" of Parisian neighbourhoods, on the opposite views on closed courtyards ... this Devil's Rock[10] emergence is constituted by 2000 ferns coming from the Devonian period and technologically domesticated to survive in the actual "regressive monarchic French period"... to a paranoiac system, the *TbWnD (the building which never dies)* in 2011, as an alert detection or a marker of our past/future symptoms: a Zumtobel laboratory on "dark adaptation" and on solar radiation intensity detection, covered by phosphorescent components *("Isobiot®opic" oxide pigment made from raw uranium)* working as a UV sensor and detector to indicate and analyze the intensity of the UV rays that touched the area by day (including on humans and all other species). 5,000 glass components reveal the depletion of the ozone concentration in the stratosphere and simultaneously the origin of this phenomenon, the sun's radiation. This Lab articulates the risk coming from the Ozone weakness (industrial pollution / CO2) combined with the paranoia coming from the last Century of scientific ignorance or criminality, developed by the exploitation of the characteristic of some natural element[11]... to several escaping, coming first through a utopian protocol the *_an architecture des humeurs_* , in 2011, with a self-organized urbanism conditioned by a bottom-up system in which the multitudes[12] are able to drive the entropy of their own system of construction, their own system of "*vivre ensemble*", Based on the potential offered by contemporary bio-science, the rereading of human corporalities in terms of physiology and chemical balance, to make palpable and perceptible the emotional transactions of the "animal body", the headless body, the body's chemistry, and inform about individuals' adaptation, sympathy, empathy and conflict, when confronted with a particular situation and environment ... to adapt the "malentendus"[13] of this result to an endless process of construction through "machinism" undeterminism and unpredictable behaviour with the development of a secretive and weaving machine that can generate a vertical structure by means of extrusion and sintering (full-size 3D printing) using a hybrid raw material (a bio-plastic-cement) that chemically agglomerates to physically constitute the computational trajectories. This structural calligraphy works like a machinism stereotomy comprised of successive geometrics according to a strategy of permanent production of anomalies … with no standardization, no repetition, except for the procedures and protocols, at the base of these technoïd slum emergences … and … at last but not least for the last experiment, the *hypnosisroom* in 2006 (Paris) and 2012 (Japan) … using hypnosis cession for the stargate effect, in the pursuit of the Somnambulist feminine political movement, from the first half of the 19th century, using hypnosis (called magnetism at this period) for an attempt to develop spaces of freedom, egalitarian unracial, unsexist social contract, which could not be perceived and explored without travelling through this layer … at the opposite of the impossibility (or difficulties) to modify the mechanisms of the real, tangible, political state of the world … this prefeminist movement strove, on the contrary, to create this suggestive, immersive and distanced layer of another social contract ... Although diabolized and treated as charlatanism, nevertheless all of premodern reformist thought drew on this movement … and …

End of the first chapter …

waterFlux

Evolène, Switzerland, 2005–15
Architect: New-Territories / R&Sie(n) ...
Creative team: François Roche, Stéphanie Lavaux, Jean Navarro
Engineer: Guscetti & Tournier, Geneva
Interior design; R&Sie(n)
Museum apparatus; Gorka Arrizabalaga
Key dimensions: 1,000 m^2
Client: Maison des Alpes, Public Foundation
Cost: 13 million Swiss francs
Design of a building for an art museum/Alpine ice research station
Scenario:

1 Digitization of the envelope of a traditional habitat
2 Scooping out hollows within this volume as if it were an ice cavity, but in full wood by a 5-axis drilling machine
3 Water's state and the way it flows vary according to the seasons: the ice flows and freezes; the ice façades freeze and melt, forming a pond in front of the building.
4 Exacerbation of the winter climate by artificial snow (500 m^3)
5 Construction by CNC machine processing, 5 axes, in full wood (2,000 m^3–1,000 trees) and reassembling the manufactured 180 pieces on site
6 Reactivation of local economy

1 "Mes chers frères, n'oubliez jamais, quand vous entendrez vanter le progrès des lumières, que la plus belle des ruses du diable est de vous persuader qu'il n'existe pas." Charles Baudelaire, *Le spleen de Paris* (1869).

2 Edgar Allen Poe, *The Pit and the Pendulum* (1842) as the first scenario of Bachelor Machines.

3 Neuschwanstein Castle (1886). The palace, with its romantic artificial grotto, was commissioned by Ludwig II of Bavaria as a retreat and as an homage to Richard Wagner.

4 *Playtime* (1967), a film by Jacques Tati, with its glass-cold-deterriolised futuristic urbanism.

5 A machine using both ozone and a ceramic system to create drinkable water without giving the Italian authorities the right to call it "Natural Venice Water".

6 We could spend more time on this project / This scenario in Switzerland is located in La Fauchère near Evolène *(waterFlux)*. We won a competition ten years ago for a centre for glaciology and geology (Le Cairn), initiated by the foundation *La Maison des Alpes*. You need sometimes ten or 20 years in Switzerland to complete a project, so it is still running. We did the entire studies for the construction, and now we are in fund-raising phase – the budget

is 13 mio Swiss francs. The building will be erected at around 1,500 metres above sea level in a mountainous area where – 20 years ago – the location was covered by a glacier. It will look somewhat like a cocoon and be made entirely of wood. A five-axis drilling machine will scoop out hollows within the wooden volume as if it were an ice cavity. So you could say that one natural element, the glacier, will be substituted by another natural element, the pine. We want to understand how we can cut the material and how we can shape the architecture by extracting, by cutting out through a sophisticated technological process of transformation that uses the material directly from the situation. The building is monstrous in a way, like a Rabelaisian building – talking about this chimera or this kind of stuttering between existing nature, primitive nature and how the technology could transform them both. So we intend to log trees from the nearby forest with a machine and bring the wood to a village at the bottom of the mountain. For this project, we are not designing a special machine, but are using a tremendous computer-driven CNC machine. So we will come back with roughly 180 elements, each of them unique, and will reassemble them on site, as a topological Lego, with branches outside to maintain the illusion of the snow in a warming environment period to a topological shape similar to the melting ice cavern, indoors, as the dilemma of the glacier disappearing, as a schizophrenia. The Val d'Hérens, the valley where Evolène is located, is a region with potential seismic activity, with earthquake risk, so we are also trying to invent a way to project this dangerousness onto the building: but in fact we reinforce in appearance the fragility of the multiple stacking elements in equilibrium. The wood we are using is absorbing through the variation of its thickness, depending on its location in the building, the structures, the insulation, the waterproofing. Some of the indoor spaces are frozen at -10 °C, like an attempt to keep the frozen fragments of a lost paradise, "what was the Alpine mountain" before the changing of climate, as a sanctuary. As usual in Swiss projects, the architect has to convince the people to avoid a petition against it. So last year I was in front of 1,500 people, and the mayor predicted to me that it will be my last day in the village. But I came with a mask, this kind of pagan mask that local people traditionally wear at the "Mardi Gras" (Fat Tuesday) carnival, to historically exorcise the winter period and welcome in the vitality of spring. They wear masks, they scream, they even beat each other up in the street, in a multitude of Bibendum Michelins, filled by grass in a hessian fat suit, running through the streets, as a ritual, as a ceremony of grotesque medieval behaviour. So before the voting, I justified the building insofar as it could exorcise global warming, testing a line of illogical and subjectivities to argue and articulate the monstrous design. And surprisingly, people, all from this mountain, reacted strangely positively and collectively adopted this interpretation as a plausible one, confusing the mask, the exorcising, and the design … with a high degree of logic and lack of logic. I was in this case the ideal architect speaking about science but in a pataphysical way, articulating the true and the false, the reason and the madness and mainly the forbidden, where ghosts, witches, wizards, and yetis of the mountains were part of the common sharing of knowledge.

7 Gaïa hypothesis is a biogeochemical scientific possibility that the earth should be a dynamic physiological system, including the biosphere, designed to maintain, for the past 3 billion years, the planet in harmony with life.

8 *Stalker* (1979), a film by Andrei Tarkovsky with a kind of post-war interzone.

9 *Rear Window* (1954), by Alfred Hitchcock, about voyeurism, relationships within a neighbourhood location, phantasms and realities …

10 Devil's Rock, in the USA, was used by Steven Spielberg as the location platform for an alien gathering point, in his film *Close Encounters of the Third Kind* (1977). It was reproduced by Richard Dreyfus in the movie, in his own living room.

11 From the discovery of the property of radium by Pierre and Marie Curie to the Plutonium day after-effect of the Little Boy bomb.
12 In Spinoza's and Antonio Negri's sense.
13 A French word that navigates between mishearing and misunderstanding.

François Roche (b. 1961 in Paris) was originally trained as a scientist, but graduated from the School of Architecture of Versailles in 1987. Two years later, he set up R&Sie(n) architecture studio along with Stephanie Lavaux and Jean Navarro. The office changes its name every few years and has recently expanded to Bangkok (studio [elf/b^t/c]). Roche – who is also a visiting professor at the Columbia University in New York – follows an investigative approach to architecture, and seeks to articulate its contradictions. He has variously participated at the Venice Biennale. He lives in Paris and Bangkok.

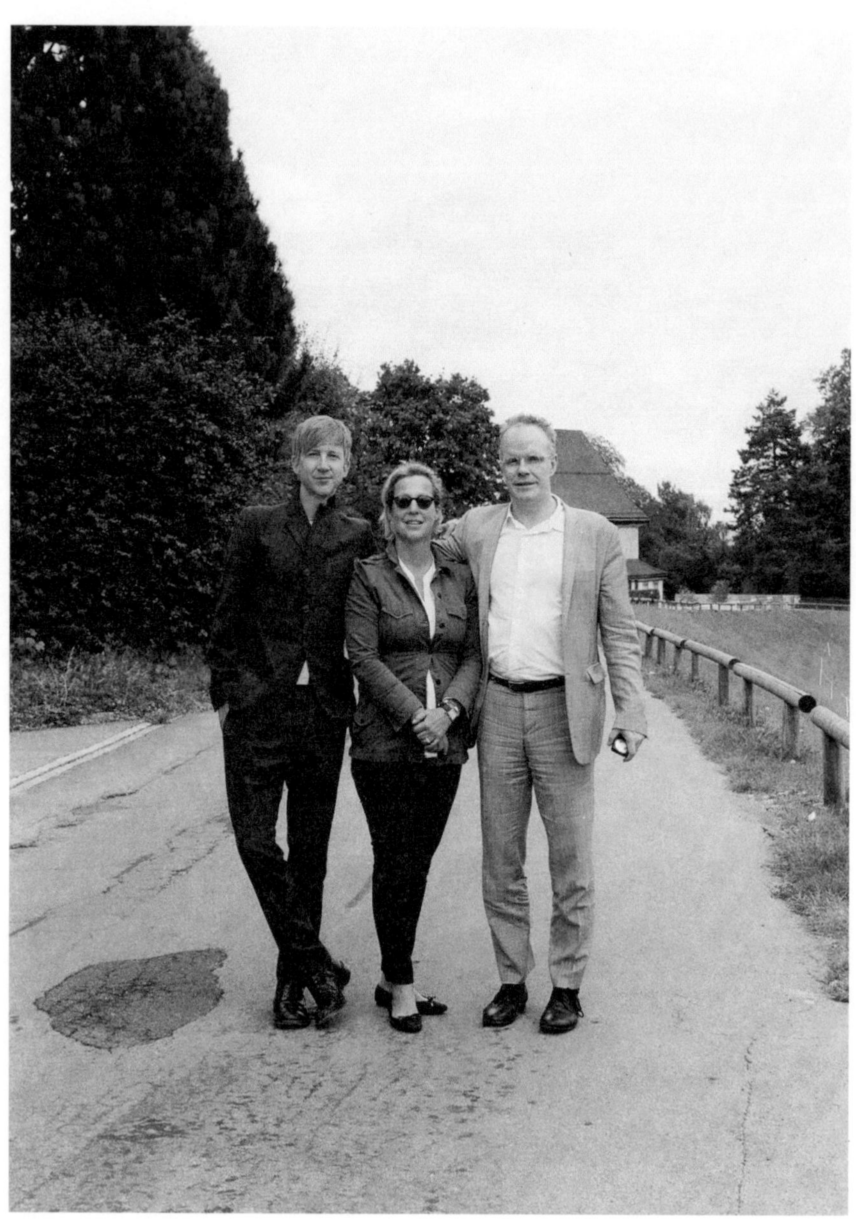

Jefferson Hack, Cristina Bechtler and Hans Ulrich Obrist on the *Robert Walser Sprint*

Jefferson Hack

Slowness vs Speed:

The Robert Walser Sprint

Robert Walser – a post-Engadin Art Talks literary action. A year ago, after the last Engadin Art Talks, Hans Ulrich Obrist, Cristina Bechtler, photographer Matthieu Lavanchy and I embarked on a one-day, literary pilgrimage. So, the idea was initially conceived as an attempt at slowness. Hans Ulrich, this we know, is one of the fastest speakers, thinkers and multitaskers on the planet. And I was fascinated to discover a couple of years ago that one of his favourite writers was Robert Walser, a specialist in slowing down the pace of his life to a walk and reducing his texts to smaller and smaller microscripts until they became illegible. Walser was a Swiss modernist writer and essayist. He wrote four novels and many hundreds of stories and had a huge influence on writers such as Franz Kafka and Hermann Hesse, and continues to have a powerful influence on artists today. Walser's extraordinary personal life has inspired a mythology cult around his persona. He had a complete disregard for material possessions. It was said that he had neither a house nor a fixed abode, and owned not a single piece of furniture. He rarely even had the paper to write on. As far as clothes were concerned, he most likely owned only the suit he was wearing. The one thing that Walser prized more than anything else were his long walks, which he undertook almost daily. As with Nietzsche, the walk was an essential attendant to the Walserian world-view. It was on the walk that the thinking was done. "Remain seated as little as possible" was a Nietzschean refrain and Walser said that he did just that. Walser was found dead on Christmas day in 1956, stretched out in the snow on his final walk.

Hans Ulrich and I had always dreamed of taking a long Walserian walk to our grandparents' home town of Buchs in St. Gallen, of which we had fond childhood memories. We wanted to stop along the way to visit various Walserian landmarks. However, this utopian walk in Walser's footsteps was doomed by all our joined schedules – Cristina's, Hans's and mine. The journey of discovery, the window into the world of Walser became a conceptual walk as it involved very little walking whatsoever, and was actually conducted at incredibly high speed. We set off one morning from the home of Werner Morlang. It was in Zurich. It was Monday, the 29th of August. It was the day after the Engadin Art Talks. We arrive at his home. He is Walser's scholar, the former director of the Walser archive, and the man who cracked the code of Walser's microscripts. One of the most telling myths surrounding Walser were his microscopically handwritten scripts, which remained illegible until the 1990s, when Morlang decoded them. An interview was conducted between Hans Ulrich, myself and Morlang and I am going to read a short extract from it:

"It was absolutely necessary", says Morlang, "that what Walser wrote had an aesthetically pleasing appearance. And so, when he could not do this anymore, because of writer's cramp, which he developed, he started to have problems. The first microscripts we have are dated from 1924, and from then on the handwriting gets smaller and smaller and smaller." – "Why do you think this is?" asks Hans Ulrich. – "First of all, there was his predilection for everything that is small, and then he had the opportunity to practise the three genres he was writing – short prose, poetry and dramatic scenes – on one small sheet of paper. He also liked to end a text at the end of the sheet. And when there was free space, this was inspiration enough for him to fill it with a short poem. Also, for his novels, he did not number the sheets. And to be certain of the sheet order, he made sure he finished the chapter at the end of a page with a couple of extra lines, linking it to the next one." – Hans Ulrich replies: "So, he was very visual then?" – "Indeed, he was very visual. Not only was he visual in the way that he wrote with his pencil in the microscripts, but he was also incredibly visual in the way that he commissioned the typography and the illustrations of his books. Karl Walser was Robert's older brother, and was well known as an artist and book illustrator. And when Robert decided to move to Berlin, his brother, who already lived there, introduced him to Bruno Cassirer, who would later be the publisher of Robert's first books." – Walter shows us some first editions with examples of Karl's illustrations and also the beautiful typesetting and printing techniques that Walser commissioned.

Hans Ulrich wanted to make sure that we did not leave Morlang without a set of "Fluxus"-like instructions for our journey. And they were given to us: Visit the Museum in Herisau to see the manuscripts, visit the grave and take the final walk that Walser took. Hans Ulrich then wanted to add one more of his own instructions into the mix: Walser lived in Berlin for many years and, for a time, in Zurich, in Berne, and later in life he travelled. He suffered from hallucinations and anxieties and moved to a mental home in Waldau near Berne. And finally, against his will, he was moved to Herisau, to the sanatorium there. And that is where he stopped writing, saying to his friend and legal guardian, Carl Seelig: "I am here to be crazy, not to write."

In May 1992, Hans Ulrich founded the Robert Walser Museum as a museum on the move, with its starting point at the Hotel Krone in Gais, in the canton of Appenzell, not far from Herisau. And this migratory museum, as Hans Ulrich always pointed out, is a migrant figure in the form of a movable vitrine. As he once described, the idea was to establish a non-monumental, modest and very discreet museum, in the spirit of Walser.

So we drive with Cristina to Gais. We take several wrong turns on the motorway. Without the photographer's I-phone and Google maps, we would never have made it to the Hotel Krone. When we arrive at the hotel, it is closed. Hans Ulrich, Cristina and myself stand outside for a commemorative art-tourist snapshot. With the aid of Lavanchy's GPS I-phone, we then drive to the town of Herisau, where Walser ended his life in the mental institute. And we are here to visit the museum of Herisau, the home of the manuscripts, the microscripts. As it is a Monday, the museum is sadly closed. Lavanchy's GPS had not been able to warn us about that. Also, his GPS was unable to direct us to the graveyard. We drive through the town, with Cristina leaning out the driver's window to ask locals for directions. It takes four failed attempts before a fifth person can direct us to the grave of Robert Walser. Even in his own commemorative town he is an outsider figure. Night is beginning to fall and we are certain that the graveyard will be closed or closing, so we park and run in the direction of the graves. There are no signs that point to Walser's final resting place. It is not like looking for James Morrison at Père Lachaise – we split and take different directions: Hans Ulrich, Cristina, myself and the photographer. Time is running out. The second direction on Morlang's "Fluxus" list could surely not be a failure, too. It was Hans Ulrich who stumbled upon the modest grave. The inscription reads, and this is a translation from the German: "I make my way, it goes on a bit, towards home, then without a sound, without a word I put aside." On the way back to the car, we pass by a sign marked: Philosopher's Path. And then we realize that the sprint from the "Friedhof" from where we had parked the car was the route of Walser's final walk – the beginning of that route, the Philosopher's Path. So we took our final group photograph, our final commemorative art-tourist picture to fulfil complete Morlang's set of instructions.

Really, I tell you that story because it was a little personal journey that we made, but what came out of it was the inspiration to make a literary supplement for the magazine that I am the editor of. In the new issue, which will come out in a month's time, we have a literary section called "AnOther Document". And this research trip, with its successes and its failures, was the inspiration behind the commission of this document, a production of reality, as Hans Ulrich would call it. It is commissioned around the theme of walking, with Walser as the central protagonist, but not the only one connected to odd stories. There is a series of beautiful black and white images, illustrating the writing, which were shot by the artist Jack Webb. Inside, we reprinted Walser's short story *The Walk*, a philosophical stroll through a small Alpine town. A transcript of the interview between Hans Ulrich, myself and Werner Morlang is in there. There are contributions from Will Self, Geoff Nicholson, the poet John Denton and Bruce Chatwin, as well as works by Susan Sontag and Ray Bradbury and a revealing story about an incognito walk with Greta Garbo through New York by Raymond Daum. So, it is my great pleasure to be able to have produced this reality from my last visit to Engadin and to be here to share it with you before it is even published.

Jefferson Hack (b. 1971 in Montevideo, Uruguay) studied at the London College of Printing, and lives now in London. He founded *Dazed & Confused* magazine with photographer Rankin Waddell in the early 1990s, covering British music, art, fashion and film. Since then, their publishing group has widely expanded and includes – among others – the luxury biannuals *AnOther Magazine* and *AnOther Man*, Dazed Digital (an online ideas-sharing network), and AnOthermag.com (an interactive, luxury-focused platform).

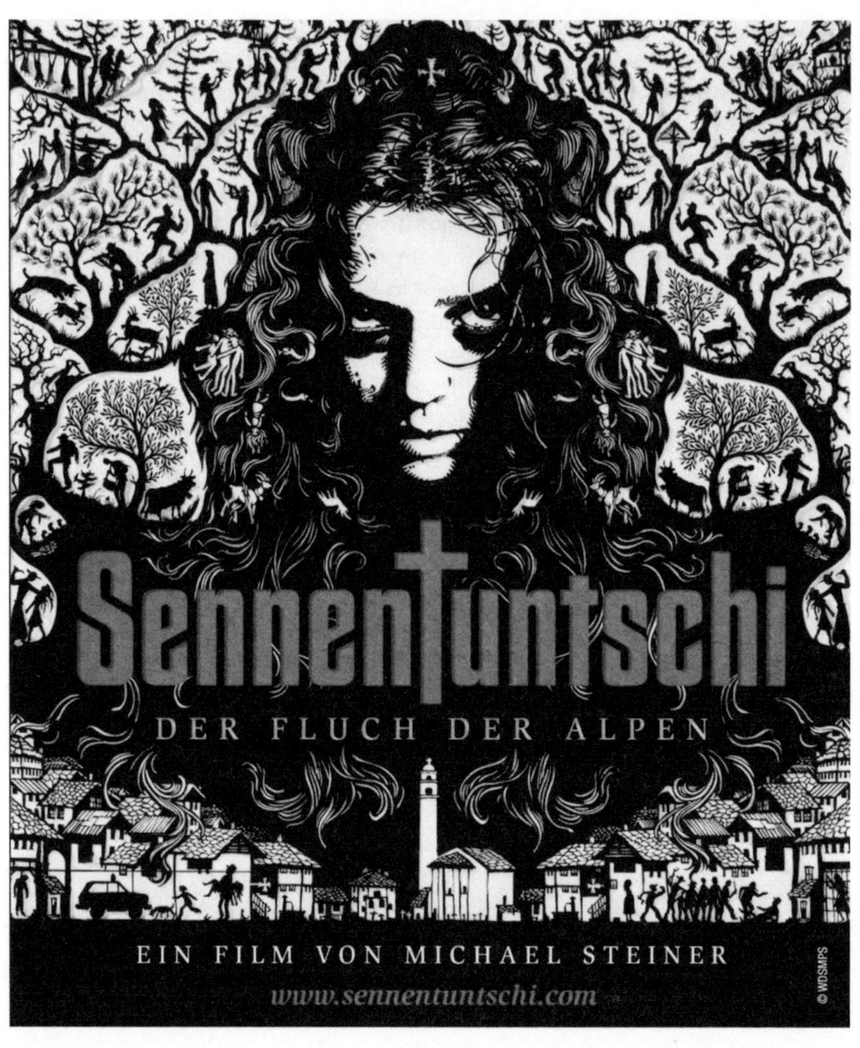

Sennentuntschi. Der Fluch der Alpen (2010)
Film poster

This Brunner

and

Michael Steiner

in Conversation

Michael Steiner In 2010, there was the first screening of the movie *Sennentuntschi*, which I had directed. The story is based on one of the many mythologies of Switzerland, which very often take place in remote mountain regions. I grew up in the mountains myself, and when I was a child, farmers used to tell me many ghost stories. Since then, I have been fascinated by Swiss myths and legends, and one of these myths is *Sennentuntschi.* It is about three herdsmen who take their cattle up to the "alp" – a seasonal mountain pasture – in the summer, leaving their family and friends back in the village. On the alp, they produce cheese, but spend most of the time drinking and dreaming about women. They have no female companion and feel lonely, and therefore decide to create a woman out of a broom and to baptize the doll. Suddenly, like the story of Frankenstein, the doll comes to life. The woman is regarded as soulless. She is simply an object that is heavily misused for domestic work and for the satisfaction of sexual desire. When the Alpine herdsmen return to their wives in the village in autumn, they want to leave their living doll behind on the alp for the winter. According to the myth, she is so attached to the men that she does not want to let them go and kills them. I wanted to adopt this myth but was aware that I could not, today, tell a classical Frankenstein story with a linear narrative; I had to find alternatives. So I decided to make a postmodern movie, which is why I brought the village life into the narrative and interlocked the myth with real life, so to speak. Furthermore, I merged different time axes, and left it ambiguous whether the *Sennentuntschi* was a real person or a ghost.

But let me now speak about the locations I chose for the movie. The main action was shot on above tree level a mountain pasture, where the landscape is still archaic. In my opinion, areas below tree level are usually man-made nowadays. There are just two small regions in Switzerland – one is the Muotathal and the other the National Park in the Engadin – where landscape is left to itself, but otherwise it is cultivated land. In the movie, I wanted to show the impact of archaic male violence in a harsh surrounding, where you get this feeling of an empty, dull and even sad landscape. The only colours you see in areas like this are the green of the grass, the grey of the rocks and the light grey of the fog. In fact, I did most of the shooting in fog. This was rather difficult because there were stones tumbling down the mountain slopes, which the crew was unable to see in such weather conditions. Therefore, we decided to deploy "listeners" among the rocks. Every time they heard stones tumbling down, they would yell "rocks" and everybody had to run and hide behind a bigger rock.

This Brunner Something similar also happened to Georg Wilhelm Pabst and Arnold Fanck, who directed the film *The White Hell of Piz Palu* (Die weisse Hölle vom Piz Palü, 1929). The actress Leni Riefenstahl had to perform on a spot situated high up in the mountains. Since they wanted to show how she ran off an avalanche, they would set off the avalanche on purpose, and would calculate the time she needed to get away without being hit. They had to deal with the weather conditions in winter, with avalanches and ice, and you had problems as well, but in summer with tumbling rocks.

MS Unfortunately, the rocks in the mountains usually tumble when it is rainy and foggy, not when it is sunny, so you cannot see them falling. Apart from that, we had the problem that the technicians got very tired, because we were shooting 2,000 metres above sea level, where the air is thin. And finally, our gear bogged down. I love to shoot with a lot of weight, which was not ideal considering the soft ground.

TB You could have told your team that for the movie *The White Hell of Piz Palu* they would have had to carry cameras weighing hundreds of kilos up to 4,000 metres above sea level. In comparison to the conditions 70 years ago, it was much easier thanks to the new technical equipment and the lower level on which you were shooting your movie.

MS Besides, they had the possibility to drive the lorry to a place 500 metres away from the set. But still it was hard because when you are shooting 2,000 metres up, you are far away from cities and you do not have the whole technology at hand, like the tracks of the dollies, for example. I love to shoot with cranes, but they are heavy and can easily sink into the soil. Unfortunately, after several days of shooting, it started to snow. The cranes and tracks were bogged down in the soil and even the filming spot had changed completely: my alp was not green anymore, but white. That can happen when you shoot in the mountains because you are exposed to the open countryside. Basically, the shooting came to a complete standstill for two days. The whole crew went down to the valley – there were just two people from the alp who remained on site – and waited until it had stopped snowing. When it had melted, the grass was brown, so we tried to make the grass look green again as fast as possible by spraying it with green colour. When you start shooting with a crew of 60 people in the mountains, you don't anticipate such hard weather conditions. Nevertheless, I prefer filming in a genuine surroundings to filming in a mock-up. And of course, for me as a Swiss film-maker, the mountains are my best motifs. They are exceptionally beautiful and impressive.

TB It comes as a surprise that there are very few films shot in the Engadin even though it is in one of the most beautiful surroundings of the world. Several James Bond sequences were made there, as well as a number of films by the famous German directors Pabst and Fanck I mentioned earlier, but in general, the beauty of the landscape is rarely used in the movies compared with other regions.

MS I am afraid that nowadays it is not so easy to shoot a film in the Engadin. It has become a scary sort of place. Wherever you set up the camera, whatever angle you choose, you always have ugly buildings and ski slopes or cable railways within view. It might have looked wonderful 100 years ago, but now it is spoilt and no longer a place for film-making. There is no doubt that I love the Engadin – the air and the light are still exceptional – and I love to be here for holidays, but to shoot a movie has become very difficult. For this reason, I chose to shoot in a village in the Val Bregaglia called Soglio. It is a beautiful little hamlet situated on a very sunny spot that is still unspoilt and looks wonderful.

TB Thirty years ago, Daniel Schmid shot in Soglio as well and made his *Violanta* (1977). He worked without any mock-ups, but used the houses of the village, such as the famous Palazzo von Salis. In contrast, I have seen the incredible mock-ups you built for *Sennentuntschi* two years ago. Did you finally use them on the location or did you work with what you found in Soglio?

MS I shot only in the village itself. At the beginning of the movie, Sennentuntschi comes down to the village and begins to shatter the precarious idyll of the hamlet. Thus, it becomes the place where the villagers look for her. Everybody is immediately convinced that she is a witch because the priest tells everybody how dangerous and demonic the woman is. At the end of the movie, she turns out to be his illegitimate daughter. Soglio was the site for the village scenes, but for the "alp" scenes, I shot in the canton of Uri, close to the Gotthard. for the simple reason that I found there a wonderful and much rougher landscape than in the Val Bregaglia. It is so rough that even Swiss people would not spend their summer holidays in that region. It looks very hostile and that is exactly what I wanted for that kind of movie – the rough landscape should mirror human abysses such as religious fanaticism, hypocrisy, incest and murder.

Michael Steiner (b. 1969 in Hergiswil/Switzerland) is currently one of the most successful Swiss directors. His movies *Mein Name ist Eugen*, *Grounding* and *Sennentuntschi* were blockbusters in Switzerland, attracting more than 1.1 million cinema-goers. *Mein Name ist Eugen* won the Swiss Film Prize for best movie in 2006, and *Grounding* and *Sennentuntschi* were nominated at several international festivals. Michael Steiner has shot more than 60 commercials and is a specialist for show events. He lives in Zurich and in Makati, Philippines.

This Brunner (b. 1945 in Zurich) began his career as an advertising consultant but soon became known for his engagement in arthouse movies. He has been a member of different programme committees at the Locarno Film Festival, and has acted as a consultant for several film festivals in Switzerland and abroad. For 35 years, he directed the Arthouse Commercio Movies in Zurich. Since 2002, he has been the curator of Art Basel's film sector, and since 2002, film curator for Art Basel Miami Beach. He has won several prizes for his work, among them the Zurich Film Prize, the Europa Cinemas prize for best European curator of arthouse movies, and the French government's award Officier des Arts et des Lettres.

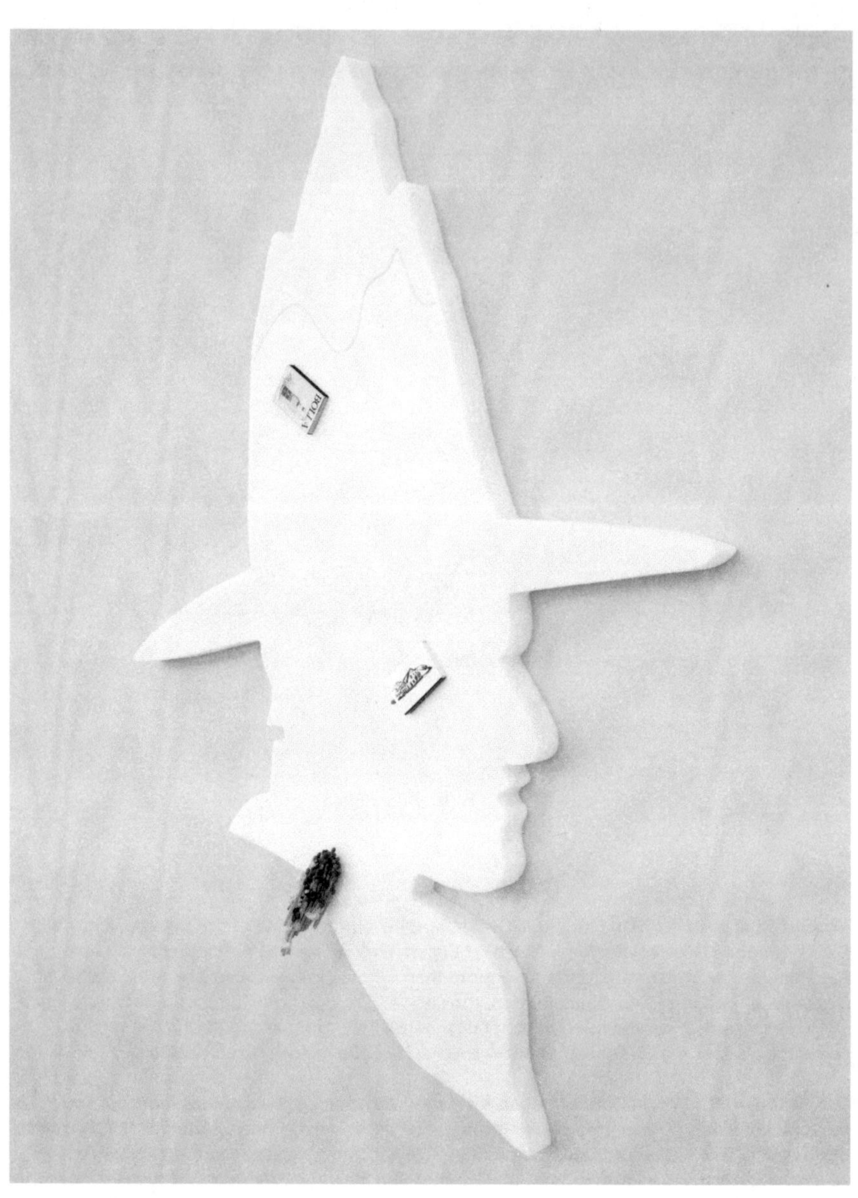

Helen Marten, *Hot Frost (line ice)* (2012)

Helen Marten

Hot Frost

Beginning with this idea of the mountains, I would like to speak about three heads I recently made. Entitled *Hot Frost (Blueberry/Lime Ice/ Glacier Ice)* (2012), these works play with the paradox of "hot frost" but also with the label "hot", of being "hip", of the collision in temperatures between making and consuming. The material has a phenomenal weight – so it is classical in the sense of marble – and it is cold. The series consists of three male profile silhouettes made of Corian, a calcareous, heavy and fashionable material conventionally employed in the production of kitchen worktops. Coloured in the slightly frosty colours of pale blue, pastel lime and cold white, one head has a hat, another glasses and the third a beard. Caricatures, their foreheads morph into the outlines of mountains and become snow-covered peaks, while the oversized heads, whose materiality evokes associations with snow or ice, are made to falter under threat of melting from the heat of the matches blobbily bundled onto their surface. The images on the matchboxes depict bottles of alcohol and Alpine retreats, motifs referring to an idea of complete relaxation or regress into slowness. Furthermore, the drinking of the alcohol alludes to a kind of cathartic emotional behaviour, but also to the deadening of material spirit. Like all socially murky substances, alcohol is both a great emancipator and psychological enslaver. The glorious wonkiness it asserts on human behaviour is phantasmagoric because of the games it plays on our understanding of time. There is something erotic in this absurd elongation of the heads into engorged peaks, a pictographic suggestion of desire, of a bodily swell in a statically slapstick action of melting and freezing, pooling in and out of legible shape.

I think mountains can be regarded as substances with a strange psychological density: they are sublime *things,* built from rubble, but they are ecological constructions with an eventual aspect of dust. So inevitably, there is a geological weightlessness to them, something uncanny and somehow removed. And at the same time, they contain a sort of puffy comedy, a melancholy or a barren weightlessness. Although their size is so extravagant and the forces are huge, there is certainly a kind of cartoonish behaviour about them.

Helen Marten (b. 1985 in Macclesfield/United Kingdom) attended The Ruskin School of Drawing & Fine Art, University of Oxford, from 2005 to 2008. In her installations and videos, Marten entwines real surfaces with implied linguistic scenarios, poking fun at issues related to ownership and dishonesty in materials, and to the relationship of object to artefact and of package to product. In 2012, she won the LUMA award, and participated in the Venice Biennale in 2013. The artist lives and works in London.

CREDITS

p. 22	© Josiah McElheny
p. 30	Courtesy of 303 Gallery, New York, © Doug Aitken
pp. 34, 36	all photos © Filippo Simonetti, Brunate (Italy)
p. 42	photo © Sergio Gómez
p. 52	Evaporated Rooms: photo © Nicolas Pauly/Taichung: © Philippe Rahm architects, Mosbach paysagistes, Ricky Liu & Associates
p. 60	© Studio Mumbai
p. 64	photo © Sally Stein
p. 68	Shoulder-Objekt: photo © Paolo Buggiani/Landscape: photo © Gian Battista von Tscharner
p. 74	photo © Ali Janka, Courtesy White Cube
p. 80	© White Crane Films
p. 84	© ETH-Studio Monte Rosa/Tonatiuh Ambrosetti (2009)
p. 92	© John Baldessari, Lawrence Weiner, Ink-Tree, Küsnacht & Mai 36 Galerie, Zurich
p. 100	© Gianni Pettena
p. 114	photo © Jürg Düblin
p. 128	photo © vonsalis.ch
p. 140	© Nairy Baghramian
p. 146	photo © Norbert Miguletz
p. 154	© Sarah Morris
p. 162	© Ron Arad Architects
p. 166	© Rolf & Maryam Sachs
p. 170	photo: Katherine Wetzel © Virginia Museum of Fine Arts, Richmond
p. 176	© Hans Danuser
p. 182	© Visiun Porta Alpina
p. 186	Courtesy of Graz Tourismus, © Graz Tourismus and Harry Schiffer
p. 192	photo © Annik Wetter, Geneva
p. 200	© Tobias Rehberger
p. 206	© Daniel Schwartz/U-TT & ETH Zurich
p. 210	Courtesy of the artist and Esther Schipper, Berlin; photo © Dominique Gonzalez-Foerster
p. 216	© Raqs Media Collective
p. 228	© New-Territories/R &Sie(n)...
p. 240	photo © Matthieu Lavanchy
p. 246	© WDSMPS
p. 252	Courtesy of the artist, Sadie Coles HQ, London, Johann König Galerie, Berlin, T293, Rome and Greene Naftali, NYC; photo © Annik Wetter, Geneva

EDITORS' ACKNOWLEDGMENTS

We would like to thank all the participants for making the E.A.T. symposiums the very special events they became:

Vito Acconci, Doug Aitken, Nina von Albertini, Ron Arad, Nairy Baghramian, Jan von Brevern, This Brunner & Michael Steiner, Hans Danuser, Andrea Deplazes, Cerith Wyn Evans, Simone Forti, Hamish Fulton, Christophe Girot, Dominique Gonzalez-Foerster, Jefferson Hack, Nikolaus Hirsch, Bijoy Jain, Arthur Loretz, Helen Marten, Josiah McElheny, Sarah Morris, Paulo Sergio Niemeyer, Mai-Thu Perret, Gianni Pettena, Walid Raad, Philippe Rahm, Raqs Media Collective (Monica Narula, Shuddhabrata Sengupta, Jeebesh Bagchi), Tobias Rehberger, Camilo Restrepo Ochoa, François Roche, Hans-Jörg Ruch, Rolf Sachs, Ritu Sarin & Tenzing Sonam, Kai Schlenther, Urban Think Tank (Alfredo Brillembourg & Hubert Klumpner), Lawrence Weiner, Annalisa & Peter Zumthor & Philip Ursprung

We are also thankful to all those who helped to realize this project, in particular: Linda Schädler and Katharina Pilz; Lionel Bovier, Nicolas Eigenheer, Rémi Brandon and Vera Kaspar (JRP|Ringier).

IMPRINT

This book was published on the occasion of the Symposium *Engadin Art Talks / E.A.T.* in August 2010, 2011, 2012 in Zuoz (CH).

SYMPOSIUM

TEAM
Cristina Bechtler, Founding Director E.A.T.
Michael Hiltbrunner, Project Manager (2010)
Katharina Pilz, Project Manager (2011, 2012)

ADDRESS
Quellenstrasse 27
8005 Zurich
Switzerland

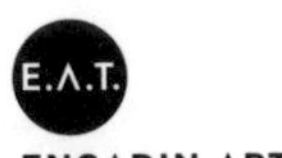

The publication has received generous support from
G+B Schwyzer Stiftung
Kulturförerdung Graubünden

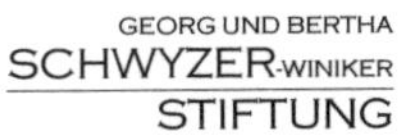

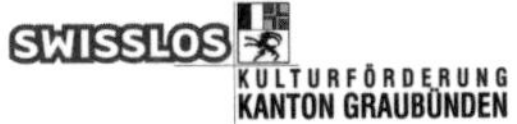

PUBLICATION

EDITORS
Christina Bechtler, Hans Ulrich Obrist, Beatrix Ruf

EDITORIAL COORDINATION
Linda Schädler, Katharina Pilz

EDITING
Linda Schädler

DESIGN
Rémi Brandon for JRP|Ringier

TYPEFACE
Theinhardt (www.optimo.ch)

PRODUCTION
Musumeci S.p.A, Quart (Aosta)

All rights reserved.

© 2013, the authors, the artists, the photographers,
and JRP|Ringier Kunstverlag AG

Printed in Europe

PUBLISHED BY
JRP|Ringier
Limmatstrasse 270
CH–8005 Zurich
T +41 (0) 43 311 27 50
F +41 (0) 43 311 27 51
E info@jrp-ringier.com
www.jrp-ringier.com

ISBN 978-3-03764-350-1

DISTRIBUTION

JRP|Ringier books are available internationally at selected bookstores and from the following distribution partners:

SWITZERLAND
AVA Verlagsauslieferung AG, Centralweg 16,
CH–8910 Affoltern a.A., verlagsservice@ava.ch, www.ava.ch

FRANCE
Les presses du réel, 35 rue Colson, F–21000 Dijon,
info@lespressesdureel.com, www.lespressesdureel.com

GERMANY AND AUSTRIA
Vice Versa Distribution GmbH, Immanuelkirchstrasse 12,
D–10405 Berlin, info@vice-versa-vertrieb.de,
www.vice-versa-distribution.com

UK AND OTHER EUROPEAN COUNTRIES
Cornerhouse Publications, 70 Oxford Street,
UK–Manchester M1 5NH, publications@cornerhouse.org,
www.cornerhouse.org/books

USA, CANADA, ASIA, AND AUSTRALIA
ARTBOOK | D.A.P., 155 Sixth Avenue, 2nd Floor,
USA–New York, NY 10013, dap@dapinc.com,
www.artbook.com

For a list of our partner bookshops or for any general questions, please contact JRP|Ringier directly at info@jrp-ringier.com, or visit our homepage www.jrp-ringier.com for further information about our programme.